The Global Deception

How a String of Lies Reshaped Our World

Walter Hensley

While every precaution has been taken in the preparation of this book, the publisher assumes no responsibility for errors or omissions, or for damages resulting from the use of the information contained herein.

THE GLOBAL DECEPTION

First edition. March 30, 2024.

Copyright © 2024 Walter Hensley.

ISBN: 979-8224617463

Written by Walter Hensley.

Table of Contents

A world of lies

Webster's dictionary defines *deception* as *"the act of causing someone to accept as true or valid what is false or invalid"*. In today's world, many of us have recognized that this is a tool frequently used by oppressive governments, multinational corporations and oligarchs in order to gain more power, wealth and control over the average people. However, there is also a less well known, but increasingly prominent use for it; namely to aid pseudoscientists when they need to make their activities, which could otherwise in no way be called scientific, in fact appear scientifically credible to the public. This is generally done in such a way that only those with the utmost discernment can even hope to see through it, and yet, it affects all of our everyday lives on a fundamental level.

Many may be familiar with this quote - increasingly used nowadays - from the period between the two world wars: *"If you tell a big enough lie and keep repeating it, people will eventually believe it"*. Indeed, the small lies tend to get caught sooner or later, while the truly great ones often become the new "undisputed truth". The one who had written those words must have known quite well what he was talking about when he used them to describe the propaganda methods of his enemy at the time. Of course, not much has changed even to this day - both in regards of the methods and the enemy itself. It is said, and is quite well observable, that lies spread just as fast as actual knowledge, but lies are more pervasive than truth. Therefore, the greatest liars always aim to lie so much and so shamelessly that eventually even the truth appears to people to be a lie, simply because they can no longer distinguish between fact and fiction.

This is especially true in our modern world, whether it comes to history, certain branches of science or even entertainment. With the rapid advances in technology over the last century, it is indeed becoming increasingly difficult to discern whether some of the things we see or hear are in fact real or only exist virtually.

Such tools of mass manipulation were already being perfected during the First World War. The President of the United States at the time, Woodrow Wilson, asked his chief propagandist Edward Bernays - a nephew of Dr. Sigmund Freud -, also known as "the father of mass manipulation", to persuade his populace to support and assist him in intervening in the war. Since the majority of the American citizens did not see the need to participate, he thought that it would be necessary to convince them to obey the government's will - even at the cost of spreading lies and deceit among them. So the lie-factory was set in motion, with posters flooding American cities depicting the whole of the so-called "enemy forces" as bloodthirsty beasts and inhuman war criminals. Although these wild claims had little to do with reality - as was later admitted even by largely biased pro-American sources - the method worked brilliantly and soon had its effect; American men rushed to the draft offices with increasing enthusiasm to travel across half the world and fight the thought to be "wicked, evil-minded" foes they have only ever "met" through propaganda posters. Bernays wrote about mass manipulation in his book *Propaganda* as follows (p. 9.):

"The conscious and intelligent manipulation of the organized habits and opinions of the masses is an important element in democratic society. Those who manipulate this unseen mechanism of society constitute an invisible government which is the true ruling power of our country. (...) We are governed, our minds are molded, our tastes formed, our ideas suggested, largely by men we have never heard of. This is a logical result of the way in which our democratic society is organized.

THE GLOBAL DECEPTION

Vast numbers of human beings must cooperate in this manner if they are to live together as a smoothly functioning society. (...) In almost every act of our daily lives, whether in the sphere of politics or business, in our social conduct or our ethical thinking, we are dominated by the relatively small number of persons...who understand the mental processes and social patterns of the masses. It is they who pull the wires which control the public mind."

Then, referring to the war propaganda, Bernays later said the following in an interview:

"When I came back to the United States, I decided that if you could use propaganda for war, you could certainly use it for peace. And "propaganda" got to be a bad word because of the Germans using it, so what I did was to try and find some other words so we found the word "counselor of public relations."

And if that were still not enough to illustrate our vulnerability to one power or another, here are the words of the newly installed director of the insidious mass manipulation organization known as the CIA in 1981, William J. Casey, at his first staff meeting:

„We'll know our disinformation program is complete when everything the American public believes is false."

This is in line with what another organisation with a similar function, the then Director of the FBI, J. Edgar Hoover, said in 1956:

„The individual comes face-to-face with a conspiracy so monstrous he cannot believe it exists. The American mind has not come to a realisation of the evil which has been introduced into our midst. It rejects even the assumption that human creatures could espouse a philosophy which must ultimately destroy all that is good and decent."

This claim points in the same direction as do the words of John Fitzgerald Kennedy, who was - presumably because of his "overly sincere" nature - assassinated about two years after these lines were said in front of the American Newspaper Publishers Association in April 1961:

„The very word "secrecy" is repugnant in a free and open society, and we are as a people inherently and historically opposed to secret societies, to secret oaths and to secret proceedings. We decided long ago that the dangers of excessive and unwarranted concealment of pertinent facts far outweighed the dangers which are cited to justify it. (...) And there is very grave danger that an announced need for increased security will be seized upon by those anxious to expand its meaning to the very limits of official censorship and concealment. That I do not intend to permit to the extent that it is in my control."

However, journalism itself, as the only written means of mass communication in the old days, has for centuries not been primarily about providing credible information at the top levels, but rather about spouting political narratives and in many cases outright demagoguery. Thomas Jefferson, the third President of the United States, wrote the following about this rather worrying phenomenon in a letter to John Norvell in 1807:

"The man who never looks into a newspaper is better informed than he who reads them, inasmuch as he who knows nothing is nearer to truth than he whose mind is filled with falsehoods and errors. He who reads nothing will still learn the great facts, and the details are all false."

And for those who might still have doubts about the reason for these statements, these words from William Blum, former U.S. State Department worker and journalist's book *Rogue State: A Guide to the World's Only Superpower*, which are known as the *"Watergate laws of American politics"*, are surely worth considering as well (p. 22.):

THE GLOBAL DECEPTION

"No matter how paranoid or conspiracy-minded you are, what the government is actually doing is worse than you imagine." As well as: *"Don't believe anything until it's been officially denied."*

Similarly important words of wisdom have been also written by him in his book *America's Deadliest Export* as follows (p. 33.):

"Propaganda is to a democracy what violence is to a dictatorship."

But before we were to think that all the misinformation is exclusive to the United States or even the Western world, we should remember that in most cases we can see exactly the same kinds of programmes and news on television, hear them on the radio and read them in the newspapers and websites as they do just about everywhere in the world - even if perhaps not always at the same intensity. However, it is quite obvious that - as the only superpower in the present time - it is primarily the government of the United States that determines the direction in which the whole of the West, and more increasingly also the rest of the world is heading. This is, of course, also true in the case of the information to which the average person anywhere has access as well, unless having done extensive research by deliberately looking up unofficial sources to unveil what's actually true of the official narrative. Unfortunately, most people nowadays seem to be either too busy, lazy or possibly lethargic to do such research and would rather just reluctantly believe and accept what the authorities tell them, even when they do have at least a faint suspicion that it might be wrong. I offer this book, therefore, not to tell the reader what to think, but rather how to do so in a way that can prevent them from ever falling for otherwise transparent deceptions again. In this book, one will find no conspiracy-theories whatsoever, only provable facts. Furthermore, all of the quotes that appear in it can be looked up on the Internet by anyone within seconds – certainly at the time of writing, at least. However, my goal with this book is not to simply share information that anyone can find online even by accident, but instead to reveal certain important but less known facts and use them to actually connect such dots that otherwise would remain invisible. This will allow the reader to see a much bigger picture of how the world truly functions than most could ever hope to see throughout their entire lives. Another important thing I aim to teach all readers is a new way of thinking; one without any dogma. That is why I urge everyone not to simply accept anything written by others - or even myself -, but instead think it all through logically. And, if doubt should ever arise, I want them to feel free to cross-examine the information received with any number of different sources and thus make sure that it indeed corresponds to observable reality – for one cannot afford to trust blindly in others when it comes to truth.

They teach it in schools so it must be true?

In today's world, most people seems to think that the answer to this question is obviously yes. When sitting in the classroom, especially as a child, we tend to think that whatever the teacher tells us, we can rest assured it's nothing but the truth. It is rare that the layman would ever dare to question the knowledge or credibility of any teacher who jumped through all the hoops in order to become an educator in a school. It also seems reasonable to most to assume that whatever is included in the curriculum has already been through the steps necessary to validate all the information transferred to us through them and that only the most accurate and unmistakably correct data can be put into our textbooks and exercise books. The majority may also deem it fair to assume that, within their own subject of expertise, pedagogues know considerably more about a given topic than the average layman.

However, this comfortable position of simply assuming the best of any figure of authority that was placed above us has not always been the case everywhere. For example, just think of the period before the fall of communism in the eastern half of Europe, where it was common knowledge that the official curriculum contained a significant amount of propaganda of interest to the powers that be, as well as the distortion of facts deemed necessary to maintain their power. Therefore, it is clear that, at the very least, history lessons often become the victims of those in power, and especially the victorious superpowers of the world that wish to write - and often times rewrite - history. What much fewer people know is that this distortion of the truth was in fact never exclusive to the content of history textbooks, granted that those are probably the easiest to find and reveal even as a layman.

Over the past decades, the curriculum has essentially become the same all over the Western world and even large parts of the East. If you ask the average "civilized" person how they think man "came into being", you are almost guaranteed to get some form of evolutionary theory as an explanation, just as you are likely to get an industrially produced answer to the question of how the world came into being in the form of the Big Bang theory. At best, when these concepts are mentioned, they will know that they are merely theories - and not in the scientific sense -, while at worst they will boldly declare that "the theory of evolution and Big Bang now stand as proven facts". However, it is interesting to see that even in the latter case, after a few sentences of questioning, granted that we are sufficiently well-informed, we often get the confession: "it's all just a *theory* anyway". During my research, I have also learned that many people asked their primary school biology or "science" teacher what is the evidence that man or the universe came into being in this way, and in many cases they were simply told *"I don't really believe it either, but I have to teach it"*.

So it would be fair to say that often even our educators themselves don't believe integral parts of what they teach us, yet students are always expected to learn and accept it as fact - preferably without a question. However, what's even more worrying is the fact that if, let's say, the knowledge of another teacher who has taught that one is inherently wrong, the same faulty knowledge will be passed on for generations upon generations with everyone thinking it's all correct. This is precisely how it's possible that in most parts of the world, entire generations have now gone through an education system in which certain dogmatic subjects are not even allowed to be questioned or reviewed.

The British writer Dresden James once summarized this phenomenon as follows:

THE GLOBAL DECEPTION

"When a well-packaged web of lies has been sold gradually to the masses over generations, the truth will seem utterly preposterous and its speaker a raving lunatic."

Unfortunately, all this means that we come out of the classroom with half-truths, incomplete fragments of knowledge and misconceptions, just as our teachers did, since they learned from books written from the same sources. Therefore, there is no such thing as an all-knowing, infallible pedagogue whose every word can be trusted without any doubt - even if we would like to think so when we go to school or send our children there.

I personally consider myself one of the lucky ones, since my high school history teacher regularly, regretfully remarked in class: "If I could one day truly tell you everything, you guys wouldn't believe the things I'd have to say..." All this happened in a relatively developed and supposedly free Central-European country, almost two decades after the regime change and the fall of Communism in the region. Although it may have been boring and somewhat disappointing to hear her say this all the time, it was probably thanks to these musings of her that I was able to embark on the bumpy road of developing and applying critical thinking and searching for the truth above all else from a young age.

Dogma versus critical thinking

Currently, the goal of public schooling in most parts of the world is simply to drum as much knowledge as possible - whether real or invalid - into the heads of students who are generally completely at the mercy of the educators and don't know any better than to unconditionally trust their words. This method of schooling is supposedly a heritage of the Prussians who may well have considered rigour and obedience to authority some of the greatest virtues. However, this way of educating young minds can - and in most cases does - lead to the creation of a population with a follower's mindset that is completely at the mercy of it's leaders and therefore easy to control, manipulate and even enslave. This deficiency of individual freedom is the almost inevitable result of continuously withholding real information and feeding propaganda to the public.

Therefore, if we are to build a truly free and self-reliant society, it's crucially important that the public school system is either completely overhauled or entirely replaced with better alternatives. In addition to providing only scientifically validated information, teaching what basic human rights are and preparing students for their actual life as an adult, it would be just as vital to teach encourage critical thinking as opposed to the unquestioning, robotic memorization of data. If there is anything that one can currently learn excellently while sitting in a school these days, regardless of the curriculum, it is to always obey the authorities and the powers that be, to always trust them to the utmost and believe that every word and action of their loyal servants is also in society's very best interest. The public education system in the overwhelming majority of the world can only give the students subjected to its torture a few basic skills - and usually not enough of that either - in terms of knowledge that can be considered useful, which could all be easily acquired within merely a few months through alternative methods of education anyway. This, of course, also means that in the additional more than a decade of primary and secondary schooling, we are unlikely to learn anything that will be of real use to us for the rest of our lives, therefore it ends up being nothing more than a huge waste of time.

Not to mention the fact that, if someone is forced to study a subject for years that is not only useless to them but also not interesting at any level, that will only make them resent it for a lifetime. Unfortunately, however, all the signs are that this is exactly what most schools are intended to do. This fact is probably most striking in the teaching of mathematics (at least in the case of countries where the education system is considered "strong"), a subject which, in upper primary and secondary schools, is gradually becoming more and more difficult, quickly becoming extremely complex and a great challenge for most to understand and thus very demanding, and requiring a great deal of practice over many years. Overcoming all this and mastering the expected knowledge naturally takes up a considerable amount of energy even for the most talented students.

Not to mention the bitter struggles of those pupils who have no inherent affinity for the subject and can thus find it very difficult to even achieve a passing grade in it. As a result, these unfortunate children often suffer lifelong psychological trauma, which even decades later, in adulthood, causes them to experience frequently recurring, exceptionally realistic and therefore very unsettling nightmares. All of which then goes on for years or even decades, as their minds make them continuously relive the crushing stress and hardship of their former classes in a feeble attempt to process them. Such a level of psychological trauma will usually have a negative impact on these people's daily lives, well-being and even physical health as they lose sleep night after night, indefinitely. Of course, this can also be the case for any other complex subject, or even just one where the teacher is especially strict and demands perfection. All this hassle is done in order to make the students acquire unnecessarily complex, exhausting knowledge which, of course, the vast majority of them will never, ever need after getting graded on it by way of a test. So a question arises, and it is one that all parents and teachers concerned should probably reflect on: is it worth causing potentially permanent psychological damage to someone just for a chance to perhaps make them believe that they have not wasted their childhood? The answer would seem obvious, but alas, not in today's society.

A further problem is that in public education, the knowledge to be imparted is broken down into small segments through the subjects, so that the student will never see the bigger picture of the world, which, if delivered in a complete yet concise and to the point way, would contain an infinitely exciting, interesting and extremely useful body of knowledge. Currently in most public schools, even in the event that students are given information in which they even show a degree of interest, a loudly ringing bell interrupts their scant three-quarters of an hour's train of thought as a Pavlovian reflex, signalling that a completely different lesson is about to begin, to which they will have to tune in after a short break. Intellectual interest and the ability to think for oneself are thus curbed, so as to produce more docile, robotic, easily programmable personalities. Rather than rewarding clever questions and ideas, the only value perceived is to be able to repeat as accurately as possible what one has heard, even if one is not even able to interpret it.

So, instead of developing good logic, broadening the intellect, nurturing creativity, and teaching a healthy way of thinking, only one's memory is being developed, just as it would be for a robot. This is not surprising, however, when one considers that the governments overseeing these institutions in many cases work in close collaboration with a number of multinational corporations. Which, in some places, have even taken control of the school canteen, giving them the opportunity to freely promote their own brands and thus create lifelong brand loyalty among the unsuspecting and defenceless students. Clearly, it is hardly in the interests of these corporations to have the most intelligent and resourceful individuals come out of the classroom, as they would obviously have no desire to find competition among them. And certainly not seeing any of them raise his knowledge so much that he may be the creator of a revolutionary innovation or invention that could make their existence obsolete and run them out of business.

An excellent example of this kind of brainwashing can be found in an article that was written by Ethan Siegel on the website of the prestigious Forbes magazine on July 30, 2020, under the title *"You Must Not 'Do Your Own Research' When It Comes To Science"*. The essence of this rather lengthy article is probably best captured in the following paragraph:

„(...) Even those of us with excellent critical thinking skills and lots of experience trying to dig up the truth behind a variety of claims are lacking one important asset: the scientific expertise necessary to understand any finds or claims in the context of the full state of knowledge of your field. It's part of why scientific consensus is so remarkably valuable: it only exists when the overwhelming majority of qualified professionals all hold the same consistent professional opinion. It truly is one of the most important and valuable types of expertise that humanity has ever developed."

Despite the fact that the author of the article is clearly trying to stand up for the glaringly obvious logical fallacy that underpins it *(Appeal to consensus),* there could be some truth in some of what he says, since experts can often actually know more about their field than lay people. However, if we look a little deeper into the issue, we'll find that the following problems arise:

- Experts are just as human as anyone else, which means that they can also make mistakes and be wrong about things.

- Just like the average layperson, they live off money, which means they can be corruptible, not to mention that the scientific studies they conduct must also be supported financially by one or more people with what often seems to be a questionable agenda. Whether it is the state, a company, a private individual or even a so-called "charitable foundation", they will often have certain expectations regarding the results achieved by the researchers in return for their funding. Unfortunately, in many cases this results in a situation where only ostensibly-scientific work is being done in these institutions and the results are to be used as a tool to advance a political narrative.

- There can be many standpoints among a group of experts, but the vast majority of the mass media typically present only one of them and expect the consumer to accept it as the only absolute truth. It is often the case that the same experts are regularly heard to speak on certain issues, but if their opinion on another issue, also within their field, no longer fits a certain expected narrative, they will present someone else's position instead, immediately depriving the uninformed individual of a significant amount of available information, which may be critical to forming an educated opinion.

- Even in the case of supposed experts who are mostly an integral part of the consensus manufactured by the powers that be, they may often contradict each other, or even their own former words after a certain period of time, which generally indicates that their claims in question were most likely not at all based on scientific studies, but were simply part of commissioned propaganda and demagoguery.

With all this in mind, we can conclude that it is actually very much worthwhile to question the official position in all cases and to do the necessary research on any subject ourselves as thoroughly as possible.

However, we have to realize that the powers that be around the world are often willing to do almost anything to prevent this and even try to convince their own people that knowing more is not in their best interest, but trusting strangers blindly is. It is a sad fact, but one of the main aims of public education institutions today is clearly to separate children from their parents and, thanks to age segregation, also from their siblings, for as long as it's physically possible. Then there is the homework, which in most cases serves only to repeat what students have already heard at school and to prevent them from spending the rest of the day doing something that would prove to be more beneficial to them – which wouldn't be hard to do. Not to mention that it can also often be a source of conflict within the family, as students who are overworked and worn down at school are forced to carry on at home this way, which can create a lot of tension, especially in the higher grades, where, tragically, it is not uncommon for them to escape to suicide as they break under the overwhelming pressure of increasingly unreasonable expectations. In view of all this, it is perhaps not surprising that, in the absence of appropriate external stimuli, most of them become little more than submissive sheep or well-trained parrots, partially or totally alienated from their families once the public school system has finished indoctrinating them. Thus, it will only be those students who have resisted this evil system at least to some extent that may be able to retain some capacity for independent and critical thinking – in spite of popular belief.

Of course, all this was not made the way it is by coincidence. Nor is it a coincidence that the political elites who create it typically send their own children not to institutions with the structures they have created, but to ones where they can learn real problem-solving, to see the historical context and thus anticipate future events, and, by learning to be resourceful and innovative, become confident in an ever-changing world. So they are, of course, taught different things in different ways. State power never needs citizens capable of thinking for themselves and questioning orders, but only obedient tax slaves who exist as easily controlled biomasses. The current system of public education throughout the world serves this purpose perfectly well, and there is also a great deal of political propaganda, especially in the West, by which governments unilaterally and biasedly try to impose their views on the masses of vulnerable students. Then the more tyrannical ones will also make sure that anyone who protests is immediately branded with a pejorative epithet, often one that's considered so bad that it holds the threat of ostracism from society.

However, since in most cases we would not even think of assuming that we are being taught incorrect knowledge in these institutions, we do not typically ask questions, let alone do extra research in a particular subject to verify the veracity of what we hear. And if this is the case, what guarantee is there that we have received only the correct information when we sit at the school desk? I would ask this question with particular trepidation in the case of teaching materials that contain data which, for one reason or another, not only the average student but also a much more able adult would not be able to verify. This category includes all data that would require either considerable financial resources – amounts that typically only governmental institutions (and in many cases not even them) possess - or an investigation of the world long gone. Of course, the average citizen would not even think of undertaking such a task, since he trusts the opinion of "specialised scientists" and knows full well that it would be virtually impossible for him to do anyway.

In order to truly understand the extent of our vulnerability, it is worth considering the views of Nikola Tesla on this issue, possibly the greatest scientist of the 20th century, who, in 1934's July's issue of the magazine *Modern Mechanics and Inventions*, wrote the following about the pseudoscientific community that was already rampant at the time:

"The scientists from Franklin to Morse were clear thinkers and did not produce erroneous theories. The scientists of today think deeply instead of clearly. One must be sane to think clearly, but one can think deeply and be quite insane. Today's scientists have substituted mathematics for experiments, and they wander off through equation after equation, and eventually build a structure which has no relation to reality.

Unfortunately, the situation in this area has only gotten worse since then, and extremely so. Although mathematics can be a useful tool to help science, it cannot, by its abstract nature, explain or prove causal relationships by itself, so it is important to treat it as such and never base a scientific theory solely on mathematical equations. Sadly enough, this important rule is increasingly being broken, which is why the situation in much of the world is now so tragic that young people who have been deceived and duped by schools, deprived of a genuine childhood, will only be able to think healthily and see the world around them with sufficient clarity if they manage to forget enough of their indoctrination. The aforementioned scientifically unverifiable disciplines are by definition pseudoscientific, and their number seems to be growing. It is therefore crucial for us to understand what exactly is meant by science and pseudoscience. So let us now see how they can be described in the most authentic and logical way possible.

- **Science:** a practical and intellectual activity involving the systematic study of the structure and functioning of the physical and natural world through observation and experimentation. To be called scientifically valid, a claim must necessarily meet the requirements of the scientific method in every case. It is of the utmost importance to note that the creator of a truly scientific theory is not opposed to doubt, but instead welcomes the fact that as many people as possible try to challenge and refute it, since only in this way can his discovery become publicly validated and gain greater credibility.

- **Pseudoscience:** beliefs or practices that are claimed to be scientific but are not actually based on the scientific method. It is typically aimed at promoting an ideological view for one's own benefit. Most often, pseudoscientists make claims that seem like they could be taken as credible when it is in fact impossible to actually validate them scientifically. They often rely on inductive inference, which is not part of the scientific method because it only provides a probability rather than empirical conviction, and is therefore not much better than guesswork. In contrast to real science, claims based on mere pseudoscience are typically dogmatic and the person making them usually treats any counter-argument or challenge as a malicious attack, while those who express doubts about them are often seen getting discredited, silenced or even ruined.

Although many of us were lucky enough to have learned about the scientific method in our school years, and some of us may even remember it in broad outline, the pseudoscientific speculations that are drummed into us in the next lessons that come right afterwards.

Unfortunately, this can quickly obscure this rather fundamental knowledge in the minds of students, who are then completely vulnerable to the torrent of lies coming their way. It is therefore important for all of us to recall how real science is actually done in practice.

The scientific method: a procedure designed to systematically prove a hypothesis that was made for investigating and explaining cause and effect relationships in nature. The most important steps of the method can be divided into four main points, which cannot be changed in any particular order:

1. Observing a natural phenomenon: we look around in nature to find a natural phenomenon for which we do not know the cause. It is important to note that if the observed phenomenon can only be observed within a man-made structure (e.g. inside of a vacuum chamber or a gyroscope), it is not considered a natural phenomenon and therefore not scientifically acceptable.

2. Creating a hypothesis: a hypothesis is a well-grounded educated guess, in which we come up with a possible explanation for an observed phenomenon in a way that is consistent with our experience. It is not a question, but a testable statement that must be based on prior research. The most important requirement for a hypothesis is that it should be able to make predictions that we have not yet observed. A hypothesis that cannot do this is scientifically useless. In addition, it must be scientifically falsifiable, i.e. it must be able to conditionally be proven wrong when new evidence in a different direction is found. It must also be clearly defined, i.e. it must not be a matter of personal interpretation. If the prediction is unclear, the person testing it will in fact only be testing the reinterpretability of his own flawed theory. Each experiment requires two hypotheses which are mutually exclusive, therefore one must always turn out proven wrong:

Null hypothesis: the default assumption that changing the independent variable will have no effect on the dependent variable. If the alternative hypothesis is not sufficiently proven, this should be accepted as the correct one.

Alternative hypothesis: the assumption that our experiment will result in a certain observable effect. The aim of the experiment is to prove this hypothesis.

3. Testing the hypothesis: gathering empirical evidence through experimentation, which is then compared with our prediction to test for causality. Experimentation is the reason why our hypothesis must be falsifiable. If it is not, the experiment is meaningless, as we will not be able to draw any new conclusions from it. The information extracted from our experiment may disprove our original hypothesis, which we can then reformulate accordingly. It is important to note that mathematics, although it can help as a tool in an experiment, can never in itself produce evidence; being an abstract discipline it can only describe something, but cannot explain it. A scientific experiment consists of the following three elements:

Dependent variable: this is one and the same with our observed natural phenomenon. If measurements are required in addition to observations, they should be repeated frequently to improve the accuracy of the data.

Independent variable: this is the hypothesised cause of the observed natural phenomenon. The experimenter modifies this in order to find out what effect it has on the dependent variable. It's important to note that, since we cannot manipulate dimensions, distance and time, and they do not cause anything just on their own, we cannot use them as a hypothetical cause of any effect. Each experiment can have only one independent variable, because only then can we deduce what exactly is causing the observed change. Although it is probably (hopefully) obvious to most of us, it's important to note that we can only hypothesise something to be a cause if we know that it actually exists. This, of course, means that conceptual things that exist only on a theoretical plane (e.g. invisible gnomes, unicorns or the bending of "spacetime") are not acceptable independent variables.

Controlled variables: quantities or factors that are left unchanged during the experiment. They must remain constant so that they do not affect the dependent variable. Monitoring and controlling them allows us to determine how our hypothesized cause affects the observed phenomenon.

4. Sharing, replication: if our hypothesis has stood the test of experimentation, it becomes a valid scientific theory. We then have to share the result with others, who can then re-check its accuracy by repeating the experiment, further ensuring and confirming its validity or possibly finding flaws in our process of testing.

The easiest way therefore to determine whether a supposedly "scientific" theory is indeed scientific is to test it against the four simple aspects of the methodology: ***observability, testability, repeatability*** and ***falsifiability***. If any given theory fails even just a single one of these criteria, it can and must be classified as pseudoscientific without further ado.

Applying this method, it is clear - even at first glance - that the following three disciplines all meet the first criterion at best, i.e. they are based solely on observations followed by arbitrary statements - and are therefore without doubt pseudoscience: *astrophysics, astronomy* and *cosmology.*

And the following seven related disciplines mostly cannot even meet the criterion of observability, and therefore possibly have even less value as far as pseudosciences go: *theoretical physics, evolutionary biology, geology, archaeology, cosmogony, evolutionary anthropology* and *paleontology.*

For example, in the case of theoretical physics, even Michio Kaku, co-author of the – inexplicably - famous string field theory and professor of theoretical physics at New York City College, seems to confirm this in the following quote from an interview he gave on *BookTV* in 2010:

"In science, we always say that you make observations, you have a theory, you go make more observations and it's a very, very tedious process. Wrong. Nobody that I know in my field uses the so called scientific method. In our field it's by the seat of your pants, it's leaps of logic, it's guesswork."

Well, isn't that just enticing? Apparently, we don't even need to do any of those tedious experimentations or even make any observations, we can just make things up instead – at least according to the highly esteemed professor. So, while Mr. Kaku doesn't really seem to understand the point and the purpose of the scientific method, nor does he seem to know all of it's constituent steps, he is clearly well aware that whatever he and his fellow "scientists" are doing has nothing to do with it. Their world is one where guesswork, speculation, fantasy and theories based solely on assumptions can become official, state-recognised, supported, propagated and funded "science".

Another quite shocking statement from a subject matter expert confirms very well just how baseless the discipline of astronomy is, too. What's especially astonishing about these lengthy but important lines is that they were written (supposedly by Andreas Osiander, although it's highly debatable if we consider the official story regarding its process) into the preface of none other than Nicolaus Copernicus' last and arguably most "important" book, *On the Revolutions*, published in 1543:

"There have already been widespread reports about the novel hypotheses of this work, which declares that the earth moves whereas the sun is at rest in the center of the universe hence certain scholars, I have no doubt, are deeply offended and believe that the liberal arts, which were established long ago on a sound basis, should not be thrown into confusion. But if these men are willing to examine the matter closely, they will find that the author of this work has done nothing blameworthy. For it is the duty of an astronomer to compose the history of the celestial motions through careful and expert study. Then he must conceive and devise the causes of these motions or hypotheses about them. Since he cannot in any way attain to the true causes, he will adopt whatever suppositions enable the motions to be computed correctly from the principles of geometry for the future as well as for the past. The present author has performed both these duties excellently. For these hypotheses need not be true nor even probable. On the contrary, if they provide a calculus consistent with the observations, that alone is enough. (...) For this art, it is quite clear, is completely and absolutely ignorant of the causes of the apparent nonuniform motions. And if any causes are devised by the imagination, as indeed very many are, they are not put forward to convince anyone that are true, but merely

to provide a reliable basis for computation. However, since different hypotheses are sometimes offered for one and the same motion (for example, eccentricity and an epicycle for the sun's motion), the astronomer will take as his first choice that hypothesis which is the easiest to grasp. The philosopher will perhaps rather seek the semblance of the truth. But neither of them will understand or state anything certain, unless it has been divinely revealed to him. (...) So far as hypotheses are concerned, let no one expect anything certain from astronomy, which cannot furnish it, lest he accept as the truth ideas conceived for another purpose, and depart from this study a greater fool than when he entered it."

So, to summerize the author's words: the previously established, geocentric worldview was working just fine, but let us appreciate this new one anyway, despite it providing no explanations for any causalities, there being absolutely no way to prove that it's correct or truthful and only really being able to reinforce a certain paradigm by way of arbitrary mathematical equations - based on numbers that were acquired with the help of that very same paradigm in the first place. It truly is a fitting preface for the book that perhaps marks the pinnacle of modern astronomy and the birth of the heliocentric view of the world...

However, as if contrasting just how much more coherent and clear thoughts could be heard even from someone partially involved in pseudoscience, let us now read the much wiser words of the famous American theoretical physicist, Richard P. Feynman - who was apparently not afraid to contradict even the basic principles of his own field -, as heard in one of his old lectures in a school when teaching a class about the "key to science":

THE GLOBAL DECEPTION

„It doesn't make a difference how beautiful your guess is, it doesn't make a difference how smart you are, who made the guess or what his name is, if it disagrees with experiment, it is wrong. That's all there is to it."

So this is what we should be sticking to if we are really interested in finding the – sometimes uncomfortable – truth, as opposed to some more comforting (and possibly lucrative) lies.

The aforementioned ten branches of pseudoscience are all helping to perpetuate carefully prepared systems of belief, and the pseudoscientists who practice them are responsible - among other things - for the birth of such so-called "scientific", but highly destructive, ill-founded theories as that of the "Big Bang", Darwinist evolution and the concept of the spherical, heliocentric model of the Earth - as well as the propagation of these ideas.

It is safe to say that essentially these three pseudoscientific theories, sold to us all as science, and those created to cover up their errors, constitute the global deception that gives this book its title. Each of these is dependent on the others, since they are built on top of each other and one is used as glue to hold the others together. What's worse is that, in the absence of empirical evidence, they are in fact mostly just referring to each other, their propagators using them as tools to argue in a circular fashion to "prove" their otherwise unfounded claims. Moreover, several of the above-mentioned disciplines have been created in the first place only in order to institutionalise and integrate the unprovable pseudoscience they entail into the public consciousness, now as real science. This – to the layman's eyes - barely perceptible manoeuvre has made possible the seemingly inconceivable fact that even the most basic knowledge - which we can often acquire simply through our own senses - is misinterpreted and distorted by people of perceived authority. However, for the victims to even take notice of this, they will have to scrutinize each of them, one by one, to discover their origins, their assumptions and their evidence. Of course, since it never occurs to most people that they are in fact being fooled by what they thing is science in it's purest form, very few do. Of course, even if we discover that we may have been deceived somehow, we still have the seemingly impossible task of untangling and unravelling the endlessly intricate web of lies, which are, of course, sometimes even interspersed with half-truths or even, in some rarer cases, obvious facts, to make them even harder to see through.

Since most of humanity has grown up with these dogmas, as adults they cannot even imagine a reality where none of it is true. At first glance, these three pseudoscientific theories may seem plausible enough to them, not to mention they're all that most people in the western world hear around them today. Thanks to the fact that, thanks to a virtually monopolized mass media industry, we are largely only one-sidedly informed, few people have any doubts about them. And those who might have them, and who would like to voice them, will find that it's almost impossible to reach large masses with their message, simply because the owners of all the major media platforms, which have been built up with the necessary large sums of money, typically have a political and therefore also financial interest in promoting a consensual, politically correct position rather than a consistent stand for the truth. Unfortunately, most people are - apparently - unable to see through this particular filter and therefore tend to accept without question what they have heard from a source they believe to be credible, even if they may have previously figured out that the talking heads on their screen, as well as the owners of certain large corporations, already lied to them on multiple occasions regarding a number of different topics. And if one does not have questions, he will obviously not get any answers either. With this in mind, let us see what other tools we have at our disposal to help us uncover the truth.

In cases where we want to investigate simple matters of fact rather than cause and effect, the scientific method will undoubtedly not be applicable. In such cases, we can, however, still rely on deductive logical inference in order to obtain an answer to our question. The following two basic logical theorems can help us in this:

- **Modus Ponens:** if P is true, then Q is true. P being true means that Q must be true as well.

Example: If it's a car, it has wheels. It is a car, therefore it has wheels.

- **Modus Tollens:** if P is true, then Q is true. Q not being true implies that P is not true either.

Example: If it's a car, it has wheels. It has no wheels, therefore it's not a car.

There are, however, cases where a hypothesis cannot be validated either by the scientific method or by deductive reasoning, and that's when the various razor principles can help us to find the most plausible of several possible explanations. The purpose of razor principles, as their name implies, is to "cut off" or remove the unnecessary or erroneous parts or variations of a hypothesis, so that only what's relevant and valuable remains. Such a philosophical answer may not in itself be scientific proof, but in many cases it can help us to understand how our world works and bring us one step closer to the truth. So let us have a look at the most relevant ones of these razor principles, regarding the scope of this book:

- **Ockham's razor:** the best known of all razors and probably the most widely used. William Ockham coined this philosophical principle in the fifteenth century, which states that if we have two theories explaining the same facts, we should accept the simpler one until there is clear evidence to justify the other. In each case, the simpler one is the one that requires fewer presuppositions or is better supported by what we already know. The rationale behind this principle is that there are an infinite number of theories that can be created to explain a phenomenon, therefore we should always start with the simplest possibility. This principle is also a tool to be used in the scientific method when generating a hypothesis and evaluating the results of an experiment, as it is easier to both prove and disprove simpler theories.

- **Alder's razor:** Mike Alder came up with it as an extension of Ockham's philosophy. It's basic principle is that it is not even worth discussing questions that cannot be proved by experiment. It may seem like an extremely strict way of thinking, but it's also very down-to-earth and logically strong, therefore it can easily filter out all the unsubstantiated and thus unprovable claims made by any pseudoscientist.

- **Hanlon's razor:** an aphorism by Robert J. Hanlon, according to which, one cannot attribute a false statement to the result of malice if it can be satisfactorily explained simply by the person's ignorance. It is important, however, to be aware of the limits of this philosophical principle, otherwise one can quickly fall into the trap of naivety and credulity. Therefore, it should only be applied when the circumstances have been thoroughly examined and it became evident that a proper conclusion can indeed be drawn from them by using this razor.

- **Hume's razor:** a principle established by David Hume which conveys that extraordinary claims should require extraordinary proof. This means that we must not simply accept a personal opinion or an anecdote as an explanation of something unless the falsity of the claim would be clearly more improbable than its truthfulness. Adherence to this principle, of course, makes much of pseudoscience extremely vulnerable and easy to debunk.

- **Hitchens' razor:** created by Christopher Hitchens, inspired by Hume's razor. He added to the existing principle that a frivolous claim without evidence can be simply dismissed as frivolous without the need for evidence. It can be useful primarily in debates. All one has to do is to ask his opponent, "what evidence can you provide for this claim?" If he doesn't get a satisfactory answer, he can consider the argument to be without merit, having a good chance of coming out of the debate a winner.

So whenever someone watches a spectacular, eye-catching computer-animated "documentary" film on television about, for example, the origins of the universe, he should ask himself: has the scientific method been used to establish the claims made on the show? Were there any natural phenomena that were in fact observed by someone and could actually be investigated? Could a valid hypothesis have been created to explain it? Have a number of scientific experiments been carried out to gather empirical evidence in support of this hypothesis? Would an ordinary person be able to replicate and falsify it? And if they only talk of speculations, conjectures and possibilities, are those really the most plausible explanations for some seemingly mysterious phenomenon, when examined with Ockham's razor? Are they really the ones that require the least amount of presupposition? Are the arguments used to support them really logically sound? As unpleasant as this may be, we would unfortunately have to admit that in most cases the answer is no.

The models of deception as collections of fallacies

When it comes to any of the models of deception – be that globular, heliocentric, or one for the creation or the evolution of our world -, first of all we must understand that they are officially not even claimed to represent reality. They are merely theoretical manifestations of a worldview that is just presented to us as something we should accept and submit to without thinking much about it. In fact, when someone talks about them, they are actually simply referring to results of a speculative brainstorming session spanning over the past few millennia. Ones that are based on mere assumptions and guesswork, without any scientific basis. The so-called "models" themselves are, therefore, essentially nothing more than sets of diagrams and numbers as described by the long line of historical figures who either came up with or further shaped these concepts throughout history, up until the point, of course, when they are taught in the schools of much of the known world. Unlike these particular models, one that's actually scientific would be consistent with our observations, the explanations of the phenomena we see in our environment, as well as the most likely conclusions that can be drawn from them.

It is also important to note that a scientific model is never a factual statement about our world. Even if one of them seems to correctly and accurately predict something, or almost everything, it still does not mean that we can identify it with reality. Even the best of models needs constant refinement and modification as it is being tested and the contradictions between it and the actual, observable reality emerge one after another. Of course, this is no different in the case of the models of deception, hence the fact that they basically required thousands of years of patching and updating before they could take a form that would seem coherent enough for the layman to finally have trust in it and even replace his own perception of reality with a fabricated one. Unfortunately, rejecting the empirical and therefore reliable scientific method and basing a new idea solely on such a theoretical construction can only lead one to speculative, pseudoscientific explanations and dogmas.

But if we are to really understand how we have been deceived to an almost unfathomable degree, it is essential to be in possession of at least some basic philosophical knowledge as well. In a deeper study of the extrapolations published by all the pseudoscientists who created the models of deception, which essentially define all of their operating principles, we can see that every single claim about the worldview already begins with certain presuppositions which are then supported by more and more spectacular mathematical equations. From that point on, the immediate response from anyone who has been thoroughly indoctrinated in the classroom would be, of course, defending the validity of these concepts. Why this, and by implication the other propositions of the pseudoscientists at play are logically fallacious, shall no longer be a question for anyone by the end of this chapter.

Aristotle, the ancient Greek philosopher, had the following to say about the use of fallacious logic by certain individuals, as found in the book *Aristotle's Rhetoric* (book III, chapter I):

"(...) we ought in fairness to fight our case with no help beyond the bare facts: nothing, therefore, should matter except the proof of those facts."

Unfortunately, it seems that the creators of the model did not get to hear, or chose not to heed these wise words, otherwise it would never have been created.

The wise words of Bo Bennett, author of the book *Logically Fallacious*, are also not to be ignored (as read on his website):

„Expose an irrational belief, keep a person rational for a day. Expose irrational thinking, keep a person rational for a lifetime."

With this in mind, let us now look at the logically flawed methods of argumentation most often used in constructing and defending the worldview at hand.

- **Baseless assertion:** the only way we prove the validity of our claim is by declaring that it is true.

Example: "I can say with certainty that the entire universe was originally created from a single point of infinite density."

The flaw in the logic: it would be impossible to determine the exact course of the universe's creation in hindsight, so any attempt to do so would be merely speculative and therefore baseless.

- **Circular reasoning, aka. "begging the question":** we try to present the claim to be proved as proof of itself. Since heliocentrism and a large number of other colloquial theories are fundamentally built on such an argument, virtually every claim in their defence will inherently contain this fallacious logic.

Example: "We know that the Earth is round because we know its radius, which we could only calculate by knowing that it is round."

The flaw in the logic: the presupposition of the shape of the Earth cannot be taken as evidence, nor as the basis for mathematical calculations. Since all statements that start with a similar premise are fundamentally flawed, the conclusions drawn from them will almost certainly be inherently erroneous as well.

- Affirming the consequent, aka. "converse error": we assume that one of two things causes the other just because they both seem to go or change together, ignoring all other possible explanations as the cause. It goes as follows when written in a logical formula: *"if P is true, then Q must be true as well; since Q is true, therefore P must also be true."*

Example: "If the Earth rotates, we can observe the circular pattern drawn by the celestial bodies. Since that is something we can see indeed, it follows that the Earth must be rotating."

The flaw in the logic: an apparent correlation does not in itself prove causation. Circular star trails in the night sky can just as easily be caused by celestial bodies rotating above a stationary Earth.

- Appeal to public opinion: we consider our claim to be true only because many others consider it so.

Example: "Most of humanity accepts the idea that the Earth is a sphere as undeniable truth."

The flaw in the logic: no matter how many people see the Earth as a sphere, that alone does not prove that it actually is that.

- Appeal to authority: we consider our claim to be true only because someone we hold in high esteem considers it so.

Example: "My favorite teacher at school told me that the Earth is round, so it must be."

The flaw in the logic: anyone who makes a claim, regardless of their position or reputation, has to prove it in order for it to be considered valid.

- **Appeal to motive:** we reject an argument simply because we consider the reason for the argument of the person making it to be questionable.

Example: "Those who think there is such a thing as a creative power are probably driven by religious conviction, so we can't take them seriously."

The flaw in the logic: even if someone does claim the existence of a creative power out of religious conviction, they can still be right on the issue.

- **Appeal to probability:** we base our claim on the chance that it may be or might eventually become true, rather than on evidence.

Example: "Although we don't yet know exactly what actually causes what we call gravity, we are confident that a scientific explanation will be found in the future, so the current theory may be considered sound."

The flaw in the logic: it is not at all certain that the cause of what is currently known as gravity will ever be scientifically proven, and until then the theory itself should be considered to be baseless and unfalsifiable.

- **Appeal to novelty:** we consider something new or modern to be better than its predecessor only because it is new or modern.

Example: "Scientists have come up with a new theory to explain how the world came into being, and since this is the latest version, it must be the best explanation."

The flaw in the logic: the best possible explanation for the origin of the world is the one that requires the least presuppositions, which are typically not the most recent ones.

- **Personal incredulity:** we assume that a statement cannot be true because we do not think it is possible for it to be.

THE GLOBAL DECEPTION

Example: "A geocentric worldview would not work because I would not be able to imagine the movement of the celestial bodies in it."

The flaw in the logic: the geocentric worldview can explain the phenomenon just as well, so the possibility of its reality is being rejected only because of a lack of adequate knowledge.

- **False dilemma:** we only accept two possible choices to explain or describe something.

Example: "I do not believe that the universe could have been created as described in the Bible, therefore the Big Bang theory is what I consider to be justified."

The flaw in the logic: there are several possible explanations for this event, but in this case the number of known possibilities has been reduced to two due to lack of knowledge.

- **Infinite regression:** the explanation of the origin of something is determined as the given thing itself, thus forming an infinite logical loop.

Example: "Our world was most likely created by aliens, whose world was created by other aliens, whose world was created by yet other aliens, etc."

The flaw in the logic: this theory alone cannot provide a sufficient explanation of creation, since the production of all living things and matter in the world inherently requires and implies the doing of a supernatural power, meaning it would eventually need to be inserted into every explanation as an end to the infinite loop.

- **Burden of proof:** we expect someone to prove the falsity of our claim, rather than us proving its truth. It is important to know that it is always the positive claim that needs to be supported by evidence first, not the refutation of it.

Example: "The Earth is spherical, and anyone who disagrees must prove that it is not!"

The flaw in the logic: the positive claim in this case is that the Earth is spherical, so it must be proven first, while its denial is a negative claim, so it does not carry the burden of proof.

- **Special pleading:** the principles, rules or standards in our claim are different from those that would apply in all other cases.

Example: "Since the Big Bang theory contradicts the first law of thermodynamics, we must assume that this law of nature was not yet valid at the time."

The flaw in the logic: no theory can go against natural laws just because it would help justify them. The theory must be adapted to reality, not the other way around.

- **Moving the goalposts:** we change the rules in the middle of a debate by demanding more answers after the issue we initially brought up has already been answered satisfactorily, without acknowledging or accepting our opponent's argument.

Example: "- Q: What makes receding ships disappear from the bottom up, if not the Earth's curvature?

- A: This could be due to a number of optical, atmospheric and environmental effects.

- Q: But then how do you explain that all celestial bodies look round?"

THE GLOBAL DECEPTION

The flaw in the logic: since the first issue was answered in a satisfactory manner, the questioner should have responded to what was given instead of demanding an answer for another issue.

- **Complex proof:** our claim contains a reference that is too complex or verbose to respond to in detail.

Example: "Anyone who doesn't believe that the Earth is spherical should look at all of the drawings and equations that have been used to try and prove it over the past millennia."

The flaw in the logic: one cannot be expected to do a lengthy research to find the evidence for a simple proposition. If the proof of a claim is real, it can typically be supported in a few sentences by the person making it.

- **The most unlikely hypothesis:** to explain a phenomenon, we use a less likely explanation rather than an easily defensible and more obvious one.

Example:"During daytime lunar eclipses, you can probably see both the Sun and the Moon in the sky at the same time because refraction causes one of them to project as a hologram well above the curvature of the Earth."

The flaw in the logic: there is more than one possible explanation for this phenomenon, so we must choose the one that requires the least assumptions and is therefore the most plausible, based on Ockham's razor principle. In this case, this means that the two celestial bodies can be seen up in the sky at the same time simply because the Earth is not actually spherical and the Moon is not obscured by the Earth's shadow being cast upon it by the Sun.

- **Reification:** treating an abstract construct that exists only on a theoretical plane as a real, concrete event or physical entity.

Example: "According to my globe, I shouldn't be able to see that mountain from this distance, so it must be some kind of optical illusion that's allowing me to actually see it now."

The flaw in the logic: globes and maps are just models, constructs abstracted from reality. Because we do not live in reality on a globe or map, if something we experience does not match what we see on them, we must assume that the model is the flawed one, not our experience of reality.

- Cognitive biases:

Confirmation bias: interpreting new evidence in a way that confirms one's own theory or belief.

Herd mentality: the tendency to believe something only because many people we know also happen to believe it.

Biased data collection: we collect, interpret or remember information in a way that confirms our hypothesis with certainty.

Backfire effect: we react to evidence that contradicts our own by backing our discredited claim even more firmly. It typically occurs as a result of hubris or vanity.

Status quo bias: we refrain from changing our minds and strive to only accept the one possibility we know best, even when multiple of them arise.

Experimenter effect: we hope for or a predetermined outcome in our research, so we subconsciously manipulate our experiments or misinterpret the data to get the expected result.

Cognitive dissonance: we do not accept or deny statements and their evidence that contradict our own currently possessed knowledge.

Complexity bias: when we have to choose between competing hypotheses, we choose the most complex one, which is usually the option with the most assumptions and regressions. As a result, when we need to solve a problem, we may ignore simple solutions just because they appear to us as overly facile or effortless.

- Other, unofficial cognitive biases:

Mantra effect: we believe a statement only because we hear it repeated many times. Television and radio commercials, as well as political propaganda often work on this principle.

Big lie syndrome: a form of severe gullibility where we detect only the smaller lies, but still believe the biggest ones because we simply don't think anyone would dare to lie to us so boldly. Unfortunately, most of humanity currently suffers from this condition.

General acceptance syndrome: we believe a statement only because we never or rarely hear a contrary opinion. This is usually the result of being underinformed or living in a social bubble.

Where is the Earth's curvature?

Although, according to the heliocentric model, the curvature of the Earth, or the visible edge of the supposed "sphere", would be the horizon, it is important to clarify that the horizon is not actually a physical location, but merely a horizontal line marking the limit of our current range of sight, where the surface of the Earth appears to meet the sky. While in reality we have to take into account a number of environmental and optical effects for such observations in nature, the model itself only takes into account a geometric calculation to determine the limit of the observer's range of sight. For this reason, it is clearly discredited by a significant proportion of long-range observations, as in many cases we can see significantly further than the model would allow. As more and more such observations have been made in recent years, concerns about this irresolvable contradiction have grown substantially. To "remedy" this, the creator of what is probably one of the most widely used curvature calculator application on the internet eventually posted the following on his website under the so-called "terrestrial refraction" statement for the calculations made (found on *metabunk.org/curve*):

"Note: Not accurate for observations above the water surface, very close to the horizon."

He did this, presumably knowing full well that those who want to ascertain the presence of the Earth's curvature will usually want to make their observations over a large area of water, preferably as low as possible, i.e. as close to the horizon as possible, in order to obtain clearer and more definite results.

According to the model - and most of those who try to defend it -, if anything on the surface of the Earth disappears from the bottom up as the distance increases, it can only and exclusively be caused by the curvature of the Earth in our path. In order to find the truth, it is therefore critical to test the validity of this assumption. Accordingly, we will now analyse the frequently observed optical, atmospheric, water-mechanical and weather effects and conditions that can obscure ships and other objects resting on the water surface and/or on land from below, in whole or in part.

- **Wave shoaling:** the wave seen on the surface of the water arrives at a higher part of the basin, causing it to slow down. As its energy flow remains constant, the wave height increases (the wave height of a surface wave is the distance between the crest of the wave and the adjacent trough). This phenomenon can result in a wave being significantly larger than it might appear from a distance, obscuring more of the bottom of an observed object than expected.

- **Tidal boring**: a large-scale wave caused by the concentration of tides in a shallow, long and typically narrow part of a river or bay. When an object is located in the shallower part, this phenomenon greatly affects the visibility of the lower part or the whole of the object.

- **Vanishing point:** the point on the horizon where, as seen from the observer's perspective, parallel lines appear to converge and disappear. This optical effect is the most common reason ships on the surface of the water disappear into the distance. The reason this happens from the bottom up is because the only physical barrier nearby - towards which they appear to converge when they reach the vanishing point - is the water surface visible below them.

- **Resolution limit:** the smallest distance between two point objects at which they are still represented as separate pixels. Two separate point objects are resolved when the maximum diffraction point of one coincides with the first minimum diffraction point of the other *(aka. Rayleigh-Criterion)*. Therefore, the further apart the two pixels are, the more likely they are to be resolved. This causes, for example, that the two headlights of a car still at a distance are seen as only one point of light for

a while, and then both light sources gradually become more distinct as they approach us. This is why a ship that is no longer resolvable by the naked eye, meaning it has left the range of vision of the human eye, can be - unless visibility is also affected by other factors - made visible again just by increasing the aperture used for the observation, for example by using binoculars, a telescope or a video camera with a strong optical zoom. Since the equation created to calculate the Earth's supposed curvature basically uses the average resolution limit of the human eye to place the visible edge of the globe, essentially inverting reality as we see it, many who make long-distant observations wrongly assume that an object has actually disappeared because of the curvature. If, however, one of the aforementioned tools can be used to bring it back into view, we can rest assured that it can't be due to a falsely presupposed physical obstacle *(see Circular Reasoning, Affirming the Consequent, Fallacy of Reification)*. Knowing all this, we can reasonably conclude that the approximate matching of the imaginary "physical horizon" and the point of the average resolution limit of the human eye is not a coincidence, but rather an integral part of a carefully planned "global" deception.

- **Foreshortening**: a larger object in the background is partially or completely obscured by a smaller object in the foreground. In the case of observations made over the surface of large bodies of water, this also means that a small wave that is closer to us can easily obscure a significant part of the bottom - or even the whole - of an object that is much further away.

- **Refraction:** when light passes from one medium to another and is incident on its surface at an angle other than 90°, it is refracted and bent by a degree depending on the difference in their density. If a medium and the object placed in it have the same refractive index, the object becomes invisible to the observer. In some cases, this may cause the optical distortion or reduced visibility of parts of an object near the surface of water.

- **Visibility conditions:** our ""atmosphere"" (an oxymoron phrase, as "atmo" means air, but gases have no shape of their own, since they simply take that of their container) contains constantly varying amounts of particulate matter, pollutants, clouds and aerosols. As the proportion of these increases, the intensity of light reaching our eyes may decrease and the scattering of it may increase, impairing our vision. Whether or not a particular object is visible depends on the resolution of the eye, the transparency of the air, as well as certain properties of the object itself. If there are predominantly moist aerosols - essentially small water droplets - floating in the air, this is called mist (or haze, at lower humidity) at a visibility of 1 to 5 kilometres, fog below 1 kilometre, and is considered thick fog below 100 metres. Most fog persists until the temperature starts to increase, and in strong winds it should not be expected to form at all. The reduction in visibility caused by precipitation depends on its intensity and nature. In light to moderate rainfall, visibility can be between 3 and 5 kilometres, but in heavier precipitation it can drop to as short as a couple hundred metres. In the case of snowfall, visibility should be expected to only be a few hundred metres, and in this case not only horizontal but also vertical visibility is significantly reduced.

- **Mirages:** they are created by light passing through layers of our "atmosphere" that have different temperatures. Contrary to popular belief, they are technically not optical illusions, as they are actually happening natural phenomena. There are two main types, the inferior and the superior mirage, but there are also several subtypes, each of which affects visibility differently. Although some of them, unlike the others, are not able to obscure distant objects from below, they are often mentioned as a significant factor in the observability of the Earth's supposed curvature and must therefore be mentioned to avoid any misunderstanding.

Inferior mirage: the low-density warm air at the lowest level and the higher-density cold air above it have different refractive indexes, and this difference refracts the light passing through them. As a result, the direction of the light rays from the object changes, so that the object is not only seen in its true position, but also reflected back under itself. The reflection seems like it merges slightly with the object, always obscuring some of its underside. As it requires a warm surface and cooler air above it, it is mostly observed in deserts, on tarmac roads and occasionally on the surface of water, only near the horizon.

Superior mirage: similarly to an inferior mirage, it's caused by a gradient in atmospheric temperature, but in this case the colder air is at the bottom and the temperature increases going upwards. Accordingly, objects are seen mirrored above themselves, reflected upwards rather than downwards, also partially merging with the original image. Since it requires a cold surface, it is mostly observed in areas covered by ice or snow, and sometimes above the water surface, also exclusively near the horizon.

Fata Bromosa: a relatively rare variant of the superior mirage, whereby fog appears to be in the distance, even though it is not actually present. The apparent fog looks so real that ships passing through it can disappear completely from view. The term means "fairy fog" in English.

Fata Morgana: also a rarer, more complex version of the superior mirage. It can form when the temperature inversion of the "atmosphere" is not uniform. This phenomenon can result in a number of optical illusions, which often change over a short period of time. Often, underneath objects in the distance, a certain part of the surface will fade and become difficult to see, making it appear as if they're suspended in the air. It is also possible, however, that the fading is only partial, and instead there is a severe distortion and/or reflection on the object. The term is translated as "fairy Morgan", named after the fairy in the British legend of King Arthur called Morgan, who, according to folklore, could conjure up floating castles.

Compression and Towering: the results of a more complex form of atmospheric refraction, which causes the apparent size of individual objects to change asymmetrically as a function of the thermal profile of the "atmosphere". In the case of compression, the object appears to be compressed from the top down, whereas in the case of towering, it looks like it's stretched from the bottom up.

Sinking: a difficult-to-observe consequence of light refracting towards the Earth's surface. The effect is to make stationary objects, normally visible above the horizon, appear to be placed lower or disappear altogether. This is also the reason we often cannot observe the phenomenon at all.

Looming: a supposed phenomenon whose very existence is highly disputed. According to the official definitions, it also belongs to the subtype of the superior mirages, but it would often be observed even in the absence of an actual mirage. In essence, it would be the reverse of what the phenomenon of *sinking* is, and would mostly be seen in the polar regions. Theoretically, it is caused by the inverse temperature gradient making light bend along the Earth's "curvature" until it breaks away from it, projecting the image of an object - which has already disappeared behind the supposed spherical bulge – upwards as what would essentially be a hologram, allowing it to be seen from a distance much greater than under normal circumstances. The source of the problem is, of course, that all this requires us to first assume that the Earth is in fact spherical, then that light can actually bend along the arc of a sphere and project hologram images upwards on its own without their significant distortion. There is, of course, no verifiable example of this, because if only either the real object or its copy was visible at any given time, it would be virtually impossible to tell when we are actually seeing something in its true self and when is what we can see merely a projected hologram. Even if we grant the possibility of the existence of such a phenomenon, the question still remains: how do we know for sure that we are not simply seeing the object – as suggested by Ockham's razor principle - because it is just where it's supposed to be? Since we find often in reality that we can see significantly further than we would expect based on the globe model, if we accept this phenomenon as something that can happen, we can say that nothing within the model is where it should be and that essentially everything we see may just be the result of some dubious optical illusion or distortion. A further serious problem for this theoretical construct is that this hypothetical phenomenon would only be able to project objects into the sky, and would not be able to affect the position of the horizon itself, which, assuming a planet, would be the visible edge of it. Since the heliocentric model, by its nature, only ever allows for the calculation of physical curvature, this means that every single millimetre we can see further than "allowed" is essentially a fatal blow to it.

Of course, the more obsessive proponents of the solar-centric worldview have an answer for this, too; in the form of the conceptual - meaning not actually observable - "terrestrial refraction" mentioned earlier in connection with the curvature calculator internet application. The way its operating principle is imagined would be essentially the same as that of "looming", but made continuous and almost entirely predictable, thus decoupling it from its old self as a mirage and incorporating it into the mathematical equation used to model the theoretical sphere. Thus was finally born the equation 7/6*R for "terrestrial refraction", which means - as is implied - that an object at a distance, assuming the pressure of one "atmosphere" and a dry, adiabatic (upward cooling) temperature gradient, must be obscured by 1/6 of the "known radius" of the Earth divided by the measured distance. The application of this equation is now, of course, expected (by the sphere-model's proponents) of everyone for every attempt at curvature calculation, thereby undeniably admitting that their model will never reflect reality based on geometric calculations alone, and providing an excellent example of the practical application of the fallacy of begging the question: "proving" sphericity simply by assuming it.

But that's not the end of their series of tricks. Some curvature calculators now even allow you to increase the assumed amount of refraction or adjust the expected weather conditions until the result matches what you actually observe in reality. In many cases, this means virtually increasing the level of assumed refraction until we arrive at a result that corresponds to a completely flat Earth. Of course, they won't worry about this for a minute, because it doesn't matter to a fanatic how much their calculation distorts reality, the important thing is that the result matches the model's parameters, seemingly validating it *(fallacy of reification)*. Such baseless assumptions can lead to claims bordering lunacy from the above-mentioned camp, such as that *"in clear weather, with a large enough telescope you could possibly even see your own back thanks to terrestrial refraction!"*

But since we live in reality, not on a model, there is no real reason for us to rely on such - to put it mildly - mind-boggling statements or even the formulae on which they are based, which are also far removed from reality, in order to explain why we see what the model says we should not be able to.

One of the most experienced researchers on the subject, Nathan Oakley, started hosting a daily online discussion-show a few years ago on YouTube, which any listener can join as they wish, where participants sometimes analyse photos taken from a great distance. Often, some of his panelists with opposing views on the topic will suggest that a photo they think is inexplicable has objects on them that are only visible because it has been projected upwards as a hologram by some kind of a mirage. It makes no difference whether it is a building, a mountain range, a ship or - as will be referred to later - a hyena.

On one occasion, Nathan was asked in an interview by one of his fellows what was the most ridiculous excuse of a mirage he had ever come across. He then promptly replied with the following answer, which has since become quite famous among those who frequently debate the subject, and has been quoted countless times (found on the YouTube channel *NathanOakley1980*):

„This is probably one of my favorite points to make as a flat-Earther, especially when someone says there's no proof of flat Earth. So, I'll give you an example - we'll use (...) a picture of a clock tower at about 20 miles at Barrow-in-Furness. It's just a picture of a clock. As a flat-Earther, I look at this picture and say: "clock at 20 miles". That's the end of my explanation. As a flat-Earther, I can make that statement. Now, if you're a fundamentalist religious zealot, then that's not a clock at 20 miles. That would be a slightly looming, non-standard refraction hyena holographic projection of a clock from behind the reified edge

of a sphere, based on an R value and a begging-the-question, proof-of-nothing, perspective-hijacking curve calculator, to turn a clock which seems to be there into a clock which is not actually there. That's what you have to assert if you're a globe-head. As opposed to me; I say: "clock, 20 miles"."

The absurdity of the current official explanations could hardly be better expressed than that. This does not mean, of course, that the clock tower will always be visible in the same degree and quality under all circumstances, but even just this one example should be enough to justify further questioning the validity of the theoretical model Copernicus and his ilk imposed on us, and to expose its serious flaws.

Since our "atmosphere" is a heterogeneous mixture of different gases, it follows as a matter of law that its density varies with altitude, which can slightly refract the light rays passing through it. However, this generally has only an almost negligible effect on the way we can observe our surroundings, even from a great distance. Although the currently most widely accepted, official model of the world suggests that the Earth is an open system, in reality this would be impossible, as our atmospheric pressure would not have been able to be created under such conditions, let alone maintain itself at all – another astonishingly devastating contradiction that will be discussed in more detail later on. Logically, then, our "atmosphere" (which couldn't possibly be a "sphere", though, as it's a well-known fact that gases always take the shape of their container) must be a closed, dynamic (in which there is continuous motion) system, where the mixture of gases is heterogeneous and anisotropic (different in composition from one direction to the other). All these parameters vary from hour to hour, as does the distance to our horizon and almost all other factors that affect our ability to see into the distance. But regardless of all this, we can be sure that if we can clearly observe an object, it is indeed located just where we see it. In the following, we will illustrate this fact by the introduction of tools and methods that are regularly used in practice.

Sextant: a two-mirror protractor used for marine navigation, capable of measuring the position of celestial bodies relative to each other or to the horizon. It works on the principle of triangulation and can therefore only be used over a large, level surface, otherwise the bottom side of the triangle used for the calculation would not be a straight line. Since nothing would be where we see it in case the assumed terrestrial refraction of light was actually a real thing, this instrument would, of course, be useless - just as it would be over the curving surface of a sphere.

Military Grid Reference System (MGRS): a geographic coordinate system based on the Universal Transverse Mercator's special grid system, which is based on a flat world instead of a globe. It is a tool for determining geographic positions and allows any point on the Earth's surface to be marked with an alphanumeric datum to an accuracy of one square metre. The advantage of this flat projection system is that its miniaturisation allows it to be provided with grid lines of perfect kilometre length, thus rendering the - originally unnecessarily assumed - globe and its longitude and latitude completely obsolete.

Evolved Seasparrow Missile (ESSM): a naval weapon designed for use on battleships. There are several types, most of which are used for air defence, but the BLOCK-1 type can also target objects on the surface of the water. Its targeting system is an SPG-62 radio-frequency radar, which is located on the same ship from which the missile is fired. This marks the target with a dot of light, which must remain until the missile hits, in order to successfully guide it. The radar itself is located just 20 metres above the surface and has a range of more than 50 kilometres. This means that between the radar and the target that's 50 kilometres away, there should be a spherical bulge more than 90 metres high, according to the currently accepted model's curvature calculation. Of course, if we were to resort to the sneaky lifeline of terrestrial refraction, the situation would be no better, as the resulting hologram image would obviously be impossible to even target and mark, let alone hit.

Plumb bob: a weight with a pointed lower tip attached to a string, used since ancient Egypt to determine the verticality of various structures and buildings. Used by surveyors to determine the position of the nadir (the point on the celestial sphere that's opposite of the zenith). It can also be used to determine the centre of mass of uneven objects. The weight at the end of the string and the surface of the Earth always form a 90° angle, making it easy to determine the tilt of an object with the tool's help. Since a spherical Earth would assume that under natural conditions this closed angle is always slightly greater than 90°, it should be possible to observe from a sufficient distance how tall buildings are tilted relative to each other or at least to the person making the observation. However, we cannot find any credible example of this, despite the fact that it should obviously be even more noticeable if we assume terrestrial refraction to be a real thing.

Spirit level: a straight metal bar that has a glass tube with a yellowish-green mineral spirit solution in it embedded into it. The tube is first filled incompletely to leave a small air bubble in the liquid, and then welded at both ends. It is then placed inside of the instrument so that it lies either perpendicular, diagonal or parallel to it, with many of the tools having all three variations in them. When a spirit level is placed in the horizontal position, the bubble is always going to be at the top of the tube. A well-known fact that everyone has obviously experienced countless times throughout their lives is that - as long as no force is exerted upon them – bodies of liquids will always assume a horizontal position, regardless of the shape of the container in which they are confined. Webster's dictionary defines the word "horizontal" the most elegantly as "parallel to, in the plane of, or operating in a plane parallel to the horizon or to a baseline: level". And, since liquids always find their level, it is no surprise that if one wishes to mount a shelf on a wall in a perfectly horizontal position, for example, they would use a spirit level. With all this in mind, one might legitimately ask: how long would such an instrument have to be before the liquid would not be horizontal but instead start to curve along the surface of the spherical Earth? The question is a rhetorical one; of course, there is no example of such a thing, since the Earth's surface is clearly not curved, except occasionally due to special topographic conditions – which, of course, still doesn't change the way all liquids fundamentally and universally behave.

Natural mirrors: in nature, there are many instances of large surfaces that can provide a perfect, undistorted reflection. Obviously, this is only possible if the surface is perfectly flat and smooth. Probably the best examples of this (in calm conditions) are lakes and wet salt flats. The largest known natural mirror of these are the Bolivian salt flats. They are deserts that are dry at times, but after a period of rain, the water remains a few centimetres high for long periods. This allows its surface to be perfectly smooth, flat and reflective, just like a perfect, gigantic mirror. The reflection of the sky on it is so flawless that walking on it can make you feel as if you are not even walking on the ground at all. The plain covers an area of 10,582 square kilometres, which means hundreds of metres of missing curvature required by the Copernican model in every direction from its centre. This is why the mention of the place can be rather embarrassing for those obsessed with the theory of a spherical Earth.

Long-distance video recording: advances in technology over the last decade have made it possible for the average person to have access to high-resolution, extremely powerful video cameras with optical magnification of up to more than 100 times. As a result, more and more people have fortunately started to shoot video from a great distance, with the direct consequence that an ever-growing number of the population have started to realize the shocking reality of the situation: we can see "too far". Presumably, this was the most powerful catalyst which made large masses of people begin to question and scrutinize the heliocentric worldview and its model, only to discover its countless serious flaws and the collection of logical fallacies on which it was built. Typically, the better the viewing conditions and the further away one can see, the clearer and greater the size of the missing curvature that would be expected by the reified model. The best results are probably achieved by fitting an infrared filter, which allows one to filter out particles in their "atmosphere" that can impair their vision, so that they can see much further than ever before. Such a tool is particularly useful for shots made from a high altitude point. With a camera equipped in this way, it is not uncommon to be able to make high-resolution recordings of objects more than 1400 kilometres away from an aircraft, in which case, even at such a high altitude, we would need to be able to see behind dozens of kilometres of curvature, if it were indeed present. To try and explain this all away just by bringing up the usual "terrestrial refraction" argument would, no doubt, take a great deal of courage - or ignorance. However, that is still not the end of all the struggles for the model's proponents. These past few years several video clips have surfaced, showing a rather interesting and presumably relatively rare phenomenon. One in particular footage became rather famous among researchers, depicting two oil platforms at sea at a distance of many miles. First of all, the recording was created with the camera merely elevated to the height of one foot, which means that these oil platforms should, of course, be completely covered by the curvature, according to the model. Such "inconveniences" are, however, regularly encountered in this kind of research by most who decide to conduct them.

Nevertheless, what makes these pictures really special is that the horizon on them is located well beyond the objects that the model assumes should be nothing more than projected holograms risen from beyond the line of the horizon itself. This means, of course, that the idea of any kind of refraction as an explanation is out of the question, since even in theory it would require the horizon to be located at no further than the feet of the supposedly projected objects. Since in the recording it is clearly behind them far in the distance, and an assumed "terrestrial refraction" could only possibly project images of objects from behind the horizon, but not the horizon itself, it would be physically impossible for any supposed curvature to obscure anything - although the model would definitely require it to do so. As a result, there now seems to be an increasingly widespread consensus among researchers and critics that the horizon is not actually the physical, visible edge of a hypothetical sphere-Earth, but - as critics of the model (and anyone who has actually thought about it for more than a minute) have argued from the beginning - is in fact merely a kind of optical illusion, simply marking an apparent meeting point of the Earth's surface and the sky. Seeing this, arguably even the most hardened heliocentrist would have no choice left but to conclude that the model is clearly fundamentally flawed, the calculations based on it are wrong and it is all simply inconsistent with what we actually observe in reality.

But then where do they still claim we could possibly see that elusive curvature in all its glory, without the need for assumption of refraction where none can be? Opinions seem to be very divided on this question. Some people are convinced that anyone travelling on an airplane can observe it at any time, generally not taking the optical distortion caused by the slightly curved window of the aircraft into consideration. However, according to Neil DeGrasse Tyson, the famous American astrophysicist, you would have to go straight into "outer space" to even begin to see any kind of Earth-curvature.

He explained this claim in one of his presentations where he was talking about a base jumping event called Red Bull Stratos, organized by the multi-national company to set a new world record. This was performed by Felix Baumgartner, the Austrian-born, multiple world record-breaking base jumper, in 2012, from an altitude of 39 kilometres. Although, it claimed to be done at the "edge of outer space", that height cannot in any sense be taken to be the that, as it would otherwise be officially marked by the arbitrary Karman line at 100 kilometres, which was only even established to let authorities enforce various airspace laws. Despite this, the company and all its beneficiaries proudly proclaim that they jumped from the "edge of outer space" to perform this particular stunt, which was officially organized as a kind of mission, the aim of which, they claim, was "to improve airspace safety", and which was "preceded by years of work by a team of elites".

The comedy is, however, further enhanced by the footage of the jump itself. For the first roughly two-thirds of the fall, all we see on the screen is a more or less human-shaped blur that we can only assume is really Felix. This is somewhat surprising, because shortly after the parachute opens, the image suddenly clears and we can finally see everything crystal clear and much closer up - even if only for the last minute and a half or so. Maybe the camera lens was just very dirty and no one had noticed until then, but then suddenly, in a split second, it cleaned itself spontaneously? Perhaps so, although a much more logical explanation would, of course, be that the first two-thirds of the jump was just a pre-recorded computer animation that they simply started playing while Felix jumped out of an aircraft (or rather out of a metal capsule suspended from a helium-filled balloon shown in the ascent phase, but at a much lower altitude), then opened his parachute and began to descend, which they then actually started recording a little bit later on.

At any rate, if they were very careful about one thing, it was to get it into the viewers' heads that the Earth is in fact spherical. This was achieved by using cameras with, instead of a distortion-free rectilinear lens, a fisheye lens which creates a significant barrel distortion. The consequence of this optical effect is that the image appears to bend outwards from the centre, so that when the horizon is viewed through such a lens, it will often give the illusion of a very emphasized curvature being there. This in itself is, of course, not a particularly unique technique, as such cameras are very popular for making videos of this kind – whether with good or bad intentions. However, the editors of this broadcast that was advertised as "live" did not leave it to chance. Whenever they showed the control centre or Felix's worried family members, they made sure to always let them cover only part of the screen, with the rest being taken up by a computer animation, which, of course, depicted a huge, shiny, rotating spherical (model of) Earth. So, what exactly does such an animation have to do with a base jump from a height of a few tens of kilometres? Clearly not much, and yet, those who would like us to believe that we live on one of those things, apparently need no particular reason to shove it in our faces whenever they get a chance. Another, just as transparent attempt at manipulation was when Felix reached 29 kilometres during the initial climb, at which point the person who narrated the event said the following:

„There, again, you see the dark sky and the curvature, which is somewhat falsely accentuated by the wide-angle camera lens, but nonetheless, people who have been that high say that you can begin to

see the curvature of the Earth when you get up around seventy-eighty thousand feet (21-24 kilometres) above the Earth, and you certainly see that darkening of the sky."

The reason this is a rather odd claim is because, after a quick search on the internet, anyone can find video footage of cameras mounted on balloons, in one case even of one at a record altitude of 53 kilometres, which – with the camera giving no optical distortion - of course, still shows no sign of the Earth's supposed curvature. And why, one wonders, did the commentator feel it so important not only to mention the apparent curvature, but also to immediately try to explain its obvious falsity? It almost seems as if they have expected that sooner or later there would be those who would question it. This might not even be all that surprising nowadays, but in 2012 still almost no-one questioned the round Earth dogma, so this comment by the narrator might best be categorised as a method of mind manipulation called predictive programming, which aims to prepare the viewer for events that are likely to occur in the future and steer their minds about them in the way the programmer wants.

So now that we got to have a bit of the details of this world-record jump - or deception - let's return to Neil DeGrasse Tyson and his claim that we should only be able to see Earth-curvature from "outer space" in the first place. In one of his lectures, he used a beach ball with a globe pattern, roughly half a metre in diameter, to show how we have been fooled by the aforementioned recording. It was then that he made the next, very important and now famous, statement:

„Felix Baumgartner would have been about two millimeters above the surface of this globe. That's his "edge of space jump". Now, you know, I don't have a problem if he does it, but the honesty of it would greatly diminish what I think people thought he was actually doing. And not only that, but they made sure to photograph him standing there with

a really wide angle lens which curves horizontal lines, so in the photo you see this curvature of Earth's surface and – "wow, he's in space, look at that!" No, he's not! At that height you don't see the curvature of the Earth - if you are two millimeters above this beachball! You just don't! That stuff is flat! (...) There's so much to actually be impressed with in the universe, I don't want you to be distracted by things that are not - that's all I'm trying to say.

So even the highly esteemed astrophysicist says we shouldn't be able to see the supposed curvature of the Earth even from tens of kilometres above the ground, and he even took notice of the obvious attempt at deception during the making of the world-record jump video. But if this is the case, what exactly is the height from which we should – according to the "experts" - definitely be able to see this ever-elusive Earth-curve?

Almost everyone is probably aware that in cartoons, movies and even documentaries, the full-figured Earth or any celestial body – be that real or imaginary - is presented to us using computer animation or, especially in the case of older productions, paintings and models. However, what far fewer people know is that these methods are not only used to bring fantasy to life in the making of entertainment material or to enhance the spectacle of a supposedly educational film or presentation. A search on the internet for full-figure images of the Earth will quickly reveal to anyone that the shades of the colours of our so-called "planet" vary considerably from one image to another, which officials would, of course, try explain with the assumed use of light filtering units on the cameras that could therefore possibly provide different colours for the same shot. What would be much more difficult to explain in this way, however, is the significantly different size of the continents visible on some of them. In order to receive the most authentic explanation for this peculiarity, we're now going to invoke assistance from none other than the "experts" at NASA themselves.

One of their employees, Robert Simmon, a senior data visualizer and information designer working (at the time) at the Goddard Space Flight Center facility, and a colleague explain it step by step in a public information video officially released by NASA, how the most famous of all "Earth photos" (most often seen on television, posters, textbooks and the internet when looking up the word "Earth"), the 1972 and 2002 versions of the fancy Blue Marble image, were taken. This video can be found on the internet on many platforms using some of the above keywords (especially embedded into some of the content of the YouTube channel *ODD TV*).

Since the detailing of the methods of the fakery is done by the two of them in a rather odd way, with them taking turns reacting to each other's lines - and occasionally cutting into each other's words – in the video, it shall be quoted in its original dialogue form:

- *Colleague: "In 1972 we saw our home in a new way. Apollo 17 astronauts snapped this picture (the image here is of the 1972 Blue Marble).*

- *Simmon: It gave people the first look at their home planet as a single entity.*

- *Simmon: Last week, scientists at NASA released this (the image here shows a globe similar to the 1972 Blue Marble, mostly differing in just the shades of colours). The shot is compiled from data from NASA's VIIRS instrument, which orbits the Earth about every 100 minutes, taking measurements of light coming off the planet. That can be translated into ribbons of imagery like this (here you can see an elliptical, half-done globe made up of thin, irregularly curved strips) and then into one of these (here you can see the picture of the finished Blue Marble shown earlier). And this is just the latest in NASA's "Earth from Space" album, which may be one of the most mind-expanding collections of images of human history. Then in 2002, Blue Marble 2.0. NASA's Rob Simmon made this. Simmon's job is...*

- Simmon: It's primarily taking data and making pictures out of it.

- Colleague: That's what this is. A composite of data sets from several different instruments translated into a picture.

- Simmon: So we actually had to take clouds out.

- Colleague. They stashed the clouds for later, then went on to the ocean. That came from an instrument that measures phytoplankton in the sea.

- Simmon: Where it was low, I coloured it dark blue because they're low mostly in mid-oceans, and then where it's a little bit higher it was like a little bit brighter green.

- Colleague: Then add the clouds back in...

- Simmon: There's a small problem with it, because there's a very slight gap in-between each orbit...

- Colleague: So some of those are painted on...

- Simmon: It IS Photoshopped (a popular image editing software), but it's... it's... has to be!

- Colleague: Then...

- Simmon: There was another layer to sort of simulate the "atmosphere".

- Colleague: And then there is this little bright spot.

- *Simmon: It's called a specular highlight. So, it's the reflection of sunlight off of water.*

- *Colleague: Those are the pieces. But you can't just slap them all together...*

- *Simmon: Just didn't look realistic. It looks kind of flat, or the clouds are sort of too see-through, so I just take command-Z (the keyboard shortcut to undo a previous action on Mac computers) a lot.*

- *Colleague: There's artistry to creating the world.*

- *Simmon: What I imagine it to be (here's a draft of the image in question on one side, with the final version next to it). Unfortunately, I'm not an astronaut, I've never been to space, but I've looked at these images over and over again, trying to sort of get the essence of it."*

Simmon later said the following in an interview on the subject, as found on the nasa.gov webpage's "People" section under his name:

Questioner: "What is the coolest thing you've ever done as part of your job at Goddard?

Simmon: The last time anyone took a photograph from above low Earth orbit that showed an entire hemisphere (one side of a globe) was in 1972 during Apollo 17. NASA's Earth Observing System (EOS) satellites were designed to give a check-up of Earth's health. By 2002, we finally had enough data to make a snap shot of the entire Earth. So we did. The hard part was creating a flat map of the Earth's surface with four months' of satellite data. Reto Stockli, now at the Swiss Federal Office of Meteorology and Climatology, did much of this work. Then we wrapped the flat map around a ball. My part was integrating the surface, clouds, and oceans to match people's expectations of how Earth looks from space. That ball became the famous Blue Marble. I was happy with it but had no idea how widespread it would become. We never thought it would become an icon. I certainly never thought that I would become "Mr. Blue Marble".

(...)

Questioner: What lessons or words of wisdom would you pass along to somebody just starting their career at Goddard?

Simmon: You can discover wonderful things from satellites, but communication is just as important as what you discover. Even if you are talking to another scientist, unless they are in your exact discipline, they may not understand you. The public is even less likely to understand. What made the Blue Marble successful is that it appealed to the general public."

So, what these dialogues are actually about is the process of creating a so-called "composite image". However, the need for such a thing is, to put it mildly, odd and, of course, raises a number of questions. Firstly, according to an official NASA statement, new satellites have been launched into space since 1957, some of which are capable of taking photographs. In this very same communication, there is also what seems to be a photograph of an entire globular Earth, similar to the famous Blue Marble. In the article, there is no mention of an edited, composite image, so it seems to be is presented as an actual photo. This supposed photograph was allegedly taken in 1967 by the ATS-3 satellite that was launched the same year. However, if that is the case, why would a photo editing program be used in 2002 to tediously create composite images of the Earth? Moreover, why not indicate under the drawn images that they are in fact just artistic illustrations? Why are these and similar imagination-based pictures used in almost all of the related textbooks, documentaries, posters, advertisements, logos, billboards, etc. with never any mention of them not being real photos? Why do they allow all of humanity to remain under the illusion that these are in fact photographs taken from "outer space"? How is it possible that even the video feed from the ISS that's supposedly orbiting the Earth at an altitude of over 400 kilometres, all the imagery of our so-called "planet" is either clearly computer-generated or zoomed in so much that no horizon – straight or curved - is even visible? Does the necessity of all this manipulation also mean that, while technology in all other industries has advanced at an astonishing rate between the two above dates, the modernity of the equipment used in space exploration would have instead regressed drastically? If so, that certainly is a rather disheartening fact, especially if we consider the enormous amounts of government funding all of these institutions have been receiving continuously.

However, every sign seems to point in that direction. To prove this point further, let's just take a look at the disappointing fact that it seems like we as humans are no longer able to travel to the Moon, despite having supposedly done it easily on the first try in 1969, when technology was inconceivably less developed than it is today. In fact, the Apollo's guidance computer is claimed to have had barely more computing power than an average calculator. But to get some more clarity about this issue, let us now read the words of Donald R. Pettit, one of NASA's more famous astronauts, that he uttered decades after the supposed moon landing in an interview on the matter of returning to that particular luminary (found in some of the content of the YouTube channel *ODD TV*):

"I'd go to the moon in a nanosecond. The problem is we don't have the technology to do that anymore. We used to, but we destroyed that technology and it's a painful process to build it back again. But going to Mars should be one of the next series of steps that humans do. The first step should be going back to the moon for a number of technical reason and exploration reasons, and then after that, Mars, maybe high orbit in

Venus "atmosphere", maybe going to Europa, there's all kinds of targets to go to places of interest in our solar system. The only limit to human future is in our own imaginations."

Unfortunately, we don't get to find out who decided to destroy that "incredible" late 60's technology that's supposed to be so hard to build back again many decades later, not to mention having no logical reason for doing something so wasteful and pointless. At any rate, even if we could build computers as powerful as a calculator in our time – which we apparently cannot –, we still wouldn't be able to go to the moon due to the supposed Van Allen radiation belts. They are claimed to be zones of energetic charged particles around Earth, that – according to NASA's own engineers – are too dangerous to traverse and they have yet to figure out how to pass through them without the spacecraft and its passengers being severely harmed, limiting the highest reachable altitude for "space-travels" to only the so-called "low Earth orbit", meaning a height of 160 to 1000 kilometres above surface level.

But at least we still have our imagination to fantasize about all the wonderful destinations in our beloved "outer space" we can maybe go to, some day in the distant enough future...

Thus, the final conclusion seems to be that the Earth's supposed curvature cannot be seen even on (real) video footage made from an altitude of 53 kilometres, and all signs point to the fact that no real photo has ever been taken of the Earth from much higher than that, especially not from what's claimed to be "outer space", only some artistic illustrations produced in their place. The only reason we would ever even assume that this particular curvature truly exists is because we were all told so at school, and so were our teachers. It was taught to us as fact, by people who have also never seen it and never will. In the light of all this, the only way one could still think of the

Earth as a sphere is by hoping to prove this proposition in a logically extremely flawed way by mere mathematical calculations based on all sorts of desperately and haphazardly made up assumptions. Unfortunately, many people choose this path, because not everyone is able to just let go of all the ingrained, comforting lies and escape from a lifetime of deception. Sadly, such people often cannot even be convinced by any kind of overwhelming proof, simply because they just want to keep believing - almost as if this dogma was a religion to them. Therefore, after reading this chapter, it should be blatantly obvious to all that we have been living a lie from our birth.

How the deception took over the world

In order for us to fully explore and understand the fundamental flaws of the heliocentric globe-Earth model and other closely related theoretical constructs, and to be able to see through the depths of the brainwashing done to us using these tools of deception, it would prove essential to closely examine their history and the cornerstones of their development. Since most of the official, government-sponsored or government-run institutions of at least the Western world are fond of referring to the globular shape of the Earth as a "2500 years ago scientifically proven fact" - thus explaining why it should be taught in schools to everyone as such - with no alternative views allowed to be as much as mentioned in class -, this claim should be investigated with particular care. As we have already made clear, in order for anything to be considered scientifically proven, it is essential that it has to pass through the steps of the scientific method and be systematically validated by it. Unfortunately, however, it would be impossible to determine the shape of the Earth in this way, since it is not a matter of causality, but simply the attribute of an object; a yes or no question. Since most people are not aware of this basic prerequisite (most likely by design, as all signs seem to show), it is perhaps understandable why the establishment dares to present this story as scientific fact in their institutions, thereby greasing the skids to gain more influence for their word as if it was truly "scientific". However, pushing semantics aside for a short while, let us now see just how much their claims of 2,500 years of (clearly non-scientific) evidence could be worth.

Although the average person has already heard of some of the few main culprits of the great globe-hoax, however, there have been a large number of other astronomers, mathematicians and polymaths who had contributed - to varying degrees - to its survival and consolidation throughout history. Furthermore, even though the Copernican model was not completed until the middle of the 16th century, it is a fact that the con itself actually began its career much earlier. The reason for this is because it first required the Earth to be "established" as not flat but instead spherical, for which an important condition was that the sun must be located "very far away" from the Earth. If we consult official sources, we are likely to find it claimed that the possibility of the Earth being a globe was raised as early as the 5th century BC at the latest, and that it was already generally accepted in the 3rd century BC. However, a deeper research will show that even if this was indeed the case, the arguments brought up to convince the public about the legitimacy of the globe-theory back then were even weaker than what we get today (especially with no computer animations being available), and they were essentially meant to provide nothing more than mere mind-exercises for the philosophers of their time. Not only did the participants of the creation of the deception made the idea of a globe feasible, but they eventually made up so many - highly contrived - theoretical explanations in a seemingly never-ending struggle to mend the gaping holes in their speculations that, at this current point, it would not be a small feat to untangle it all and see through the countless layers of the lie. So let us examine how the chronology of this fabled story actually progressed, embedding itself milestone by milestone into the public consciousness, gradually transforming the way most of humanity view reality itself.

- 500 BC: Pythagoras, Greek mathematician raised the possibility of the Earth being spherical, based solely on a philosophical argument rather than measurements, insisting that the Earth must be spherical because "it is a perfect shape". It was from this unusual obsession with shapes that the simpleminded theory of the globe was born, according to some official sources, which is almost forbidden to question in our time. According to other sources, however, he based his suggestion on the fact that, since both the Sun and the Moon are seemingly spherical, the Earth must be too. This version of the story is however highly unlikely, because at the time there was obviously no suitable instrument available for making long-distance observations, so there is no way he could have unequivocally determined the shape of any of the celestial bodies. In any case, according to the mathematician's idea, the motionless, spherical Earth has the Sun and Moon orbiting around it. Unfortunately, the date of this highly questionable "discovery" is only an approximation, since even the existence of Pythagoras himself is supported by very few historical documents (which probably explains the existence of contradictory stories about the development of his theory), and thus even this claim is often disputed among the researchers of this topic. At that time, of course, everyone but him was aware of the obvious, self-evident fact that the Earth is in fact flat and motionless.

- **400 BC:** Although Pythagoras' idea did not manage to gain significant popularity with the ancient Greeks, a century later Plato, a Greek philosopher, also expressed his support for the theory of a sphere-shaped Earth, popularizing it further considerably.

- **350 BC:** Aristotle of Stagira, another Greek philosopher who was also Plato's apprentice, took the theory further and wrote his book *On the Heavens*. In it he makes a number of compelling arguments as to why the Earth is likely to be immobile and in a central position, and then - in the last chapter of it's second volume - he also describes why he thinks it could possibly be spherical in shape. In these arguments, of course, instead of empirical research, we are still merely presented with a number of multifarious presuppositions, speculations and biased philosophical thoughts. His first argument was that all mass is moving towards the centre of the Earth, so it could only be spherical - creating a kind of theory of gravity. How did he originally know that the Earth had a centre, meaning it's a sphere, before he could have even discovered this supposed fact? Of course, he couldn't have known, but he had already learned it from Plato, and by means of the logical fallacy of circular reasoning, he easily "overcame" the "difficulty" caused by the fundamental unprovability of the claim. His second argument was that he believed that it's the curved shadow of the Earth that's cast by the Sun's light upon the Moon which is visible during a lunar eclipse *(Affirming the Consequent)*. This assumption, of course, required a series of additional logically flawed presuppositions. First, he had to assume that the Sun would be positioned exactly in opposition to the Moon at the other side of Earth at every observation. Then, since – despite what the official diagrams show today - no object can cast a shadow smaller than itself, he had to presuppose that the Earth was smaller than or equal in size to the Moon, without him having had the slightest idea of their size (or their actual shape). Furthermore, he also had to assume that the Moon does, indeed, have a physical body that is in fact able to reflect light uniformly. However, he unknowingly invalidated this conjecture right away by theorising that, judging from the shape of the shadows cast on it, the Moon, just like the Earth according to his beliefs, must also be spherical. The reason this would be impossible is because it's a well-known fact that spherical bodies cannot reflect light evenly, as their curved surfaces scatter it. Aristotle's theory of the Earth was therefore developed on the basis of such and similar arguments, which are sadly all flawed to the extreme. However, because it was so convincing to many at the time, over the next few decades most philosophers adopted his proposed model and proclaimed it a "remarkable discovery".

- **300 BC:** Euclid of Alexandria, Greek mathematician compiled a series of books called the *Elements* from a number of works of earlier men. In these books he wrote about geometry, number theory, the general theory of ratios and proportions, as well as the examination of three-dimensional figures. The knowledge withing these books proved to be of major importance for many branches of human affairs and served as the foundation for a number of famous scientists and researchers in the future. *Elements* has since become one of the most studied and translated books produced in the Western world of all times. It remained the primary source of geometric reasoning, theorems, and methods for over two millennia.

- **276 BC:** Eratosthenes of Cyrene, Greek astronomer "calculated" the circumference of the Earth using a stick, a shadow and – the by now very familiar - circular reasoning. According to the official story, it was known at the time that in the Egyptian city of Syene (now Aswan), the sun was at its highest point at noon on the summer solstice, so that things on the ground did not cast visible shadows, while in the city of Alexandria, 800-900 kilometres (the exact length of the unit of measurement used at the time is not clear today) to the north, it did cast shadows at the same time. There, after measuring the angle of the shadow cast by the stick he had stuck in the ground, he, like the others, incorrectly assumed the shape of the Earth as a sphere and that the Sun is *"very far away"*, so that its rays are parallel to each other when seen from the Earth, and then used the acquired data to make his calculations. Since he knew that a circle encloses an angle of 360°, he calculated from the distance between the two points and the measured angle of the shadow projection, which was 7.2°, that the circumference of the Earth was (360/7.2)*800 (which could, of course, be (360/7.2)*900, if we interpret the unit of measurement he used differently), or 40,000 (or 45,000) kilometres. This figure is, of course, satisfactorily consistent with the 40,075 kilometres lie that is accepted today as the official propaganda. Which is no coincidence, since modern astronomical calculations are based on exactly the same logically flawed assumptions as those of the ancient Greek astronomers. But the reality is that it is just about impossible to know the distance of the Sun from the Earth until we know its exact size, which we would, however, need to know its distance to calculate. And without these crucially important pieces of data, it would also be impossible to determine the circumference of the Earth by way of trigonometrical calculations, as the result would always be different depending on what we decide to presuppose. For example, if we presuppose a much closer Sun and we use the surface of the clearly and observably flat (minus the topography, of course) Earth as the baseline, our calculation and everything we see will perfectly support our assumptions all the same. Not to mention that in this case we wouldn't need a series of logical fallacies to desperately try and legitimize our claims.

- **270 BC:** Aristarchus of Samos, Greek astronomer came up with the first model of the world in which the Sun, rather than the Earth, was at the centre, stationary, while all the "planets" revolved around it. His model showed the stars as also immobile, distant "suns", and based on these assumptions he believed that the universe itself is much bigger than his contemporaries thought. In his treatise On the Sizes and Distances of the Sun and Moon, he attempted to determine the diameters of the two celestial bodies, as well as that of the Earth. He sought to do this by, similarly to the others, assuming a number of things and then incorporating the speculative theories based on these assumptions into his model to make it seem more credible and robust. Unfortunately, however, even with the help of the usual plethora of logical fallacies, he was unable to put together a model that would have convinced the pseudoscientists of his day in the end. In this day and age it is, of course, only the figures extracted by his flawed calculations that are disputed by officials, never the patently flawed, unproven and unvalidated premises of the model (*Biased data collection, Confirmation bias, Status quo bias*). According to many historians of science, even Aristarchus himself may eventually have rejected his own theory after realizing that it simply did not match up with what he had experienced in reality. Thus, even after all the work done by him, the geocentric view of the world - for lack of convincing arguments for any other - still remained the dominant one worldwide.

- **150 BC:** Nicæan Hipparchus, Greek astronomer and mathematician discovered the potential of trigonometry and became the first in history to use this new method in a stillborn attempt to calculate the distance of stars from Earth. For a long time, this method, which is completely unsuitable for this kind of measurement, also provided the basis for modern astronomy's attempts to calculate the distances between different celestial bodies. The idea is that, since we know that the sum of the interior angles of all triangles is 180°, we can simply calculate the third angle if we know the size of the other two inside the triangle. Furthermore, if we know the length of the base line and the size of the angles at its ends, we can then also calculate the length of the triangle's stems. Thus, using these unique properties of this simple shape, we can easily calculate the distance to a point on a high elevation by just knowing the three numbers. Unfortunately, however, calculating the distance to a celestial body is far from that straightforward. In fact, the further away a given point with an unknown distance is, the longer the baseline you need to get a meaningful result. So using triangulation, we can calculate our distance from the top of a tree or a building relatively easily, but for celestial bodies we obviously need a baseline that is orders of magnitude larger, presumably at least a few thousand kilometres long, to get even a roughly accurate result - if we are to assume the physicality of these celestial points of light in the first place. In Hipparchus' time, the necessary technical background was, of course, not present, as high-speed travel or telecommunications were still some time away. Since there was no other person a few thousand kilometres away who could have dictated to him, to the second, the figure he had observed there, it is perhaps not surprising that his attempt failed. Nevertheless, instead of accepting the fact of total failure, he drew the far-reaching conclusion that *"the celestial bodies are infinitely far away"*. He also came to this same conclusion when he tried to determine the distance to the Moon using data collected from two observation points during an eclipse. While at Hellespont (now known as Dardanelles) a total eclipse was visible - according to his information -, only a partial eclipse was visible from Alexandria at the same time. Hipparchus explained this by the parallax (the apparent displacement of an object when viewed from different vantage points) of the Moon in relation to the stars in its background, including the Sun, and from this he once again drew the hasty conclusion that the stars, as well as the Sun, are *"infinitely far away"*. And this irresponsible and unfounded assumption has accompanied the history of astronomy from then until modern times. In fact, when hearing today's astronomers regularly talk about all the nearly incomprehensible distances in the heavens, it should make it clear to anyone that this conjecture from ancient times still remains the dominant and decisive idea in our cosmology, considered by most to be unquestionable.

- **140 AD:** Like Eratosthenes, Ptolemy also "calculated" the circumference of a presupposed globe-Earth, but instead of using the Sun's rays, he used the position of the stars. This seems to have been less acceptable to today's official propaganda-experts, since he only got 28,800 kilometres instead of the length accepted today, which apparently did not meet their expectations. Despite this significant numerical difference, the set of logical errors used in the calculation is, of course, the same as in Eratosthenes' method. At first, he "determined" the distances of the Sun and Moon from the Earth on the basis of practically nothing but guesswork, and then assumed the physicality and sphericity of the celestial bodies, thus reconciling the resulting figures with his model in order to make them fit (*Experimenter effect, Circular reasoning, Baseless assertion, Affirming the consequent, Confirmation bias*). With all this, he eventually created the most modern and widely accepted geocentric model (*Fallacy of reification*) for explaining what we can see on the sky, which slowly became the dominant cosmology and remained so for nearly a millennium and a half.

- **III. century:** Due to the spread of early Christianity, the theory of a spherical Earth was completely discarded in many areas, where it was then accepted as flat once again for the next nearly a millennium.

- **XI. century:** Al-Biruni, a Persian polymath who is also known as "the father of geodesy" was thought to have determined the "radius of the Earth" for the first time in history. According to the official story, knowing the size of the presupposed spherical Earth was becoming a pressing issue at the time, so our Persian hero took some "measurements" in the Abbasida Caliphate (now Pakistan) to help out a beleaguered humanity. Unfortunately, however, instead of real measurements, he too worked largely with mathematical equations based on nothing but assumptions. First, he calculated the height of a nearby mountain using an instrument called an astrolabe (the predecessor of the sextant) and trigonometry, then, by climbing to the top of the mountain and looking out to the horizon, he calculated the distance between himself and what he thought was the edge of the Earth, which he, of course, imagined to be spherical. Sadly, when he did this, he didn't take into account the fact that the horizon is not a fixed geometric plane, but an apparent point, whose position varies depending on weather conditions and other factors affecting vision, and that it cannot therefore serve as a basis for geometric calculations. Nevertheless, with the help of the imaginary triangles thus obtained and the Biruni-equation constructed by our hero, the polymath finally succeeded in calculating the imaginary radius of the imagined globe, a figure which, not surprisingly, is only a few percent off the figure propagated by modern pseudoscientists.

- **XIII. century:** Ptolemy's work reached the Christian parts of Europe via then-Islamic Spain, spreading the Greek astronomer-mathematician's geocentric but spherical model of the Earth across the continent.

- **1543:** Nicolaus Copernicus, Polish astronomer came up with the first solar-centred sketch of the visible world, now simply known as the heliocentric, or Copernican model, which has since been "perfected" to reflect the worldview currently accepted - although less and less so in recent years - in much of the world. Contrary to previous concepts of a motionless Earth, all the celestial bodies in his "solar system" orbited the Sun, including the Earth, the home of all mankind, which would have been just one of many points of light on the sky paying homage to a central Sun. All this was based, not too surprisingly, on the logic that the Sun and stars are "infinitely far away" from us, so that the Sun can be assumed to be much larger than the Earth, and the Earth therefore would be more likely to orbit the vastly greater Sun than vice versa. He also was likely influenced by the Platonic philosophy that, since the Sun is essential for all life, it should be placed in the center of the world. Although Copernicus rejected practically everything else in Hipparchus' cosmology, interestingly enough, similarly to his predecessors, he readily accepted this one premise, although he was unfortunately just as unable to prove its truth. Since Copernicus must have studied the theories and models of his predecessors in detail, it may be safe to assume that he had, in fact, found this most serious error in Hipparchus' work, but instead of correcting it, he decided to instead replace everything else and built a new theoretical model around the one retained faulty assumption. It is unfortunate that neither Copernicus nor the other astronomers were able or willing to apply Ockham's razor principle, which would have made it clear to them that heliocentrism (and, of course, the spherical Earth theory) had already failed beyond doubt even in the field of plausibility. That is because what's observed in reality can be illustrated with almost exactly the same amount of confidence by every single one of their theories. Therefore, the cosmology chosen remains a philosophical question, not a scientific one. But if it had turned out that the celestial bodies were significantly closer than they thought, not only their own world view would have collapsed immediately, but, of course, also that of everyone else who had first assumed a spherical Earth and then based their calculations on it. Like the others, this model was therefore just a drawing based on observations, supplemented by some numbers. All this has not changed to this day, so that the much-vaunted "Model" is still nothing more than a collection of scribbles based on the personal world views of "renowned" stargazers and all the figures they managed to derive from faulty equations. Although many praise its "predictive" capabilities *(Fallacy of reification)*, those are really just calculations of the next expected occurrence of previously observed, periodical natural phenomena, as opposed to actual predictions of unexpected events. These calculations can, of course, be made without the "Model", following simple observations, so it has no real role to play. Although a large part of humanity – mainly due to the authority of what they all too often consider to be a "scientific" society - accepted Copernicus' ideas as described in the new model, anyone who looked into his claims in detail would have been very reluctant to accept at least the proposition that the Earth is hurtling around the

Sun at an incomprehensible speed in a vast space, while none of the beings on Earth itself perceives any of this ever throughout its life. However, no matter how much this whole concept defied all human experience and common sense, the many logical flaws behind it were presumably recognised only by a few at the time, and hence – also largely thanks to the strong institutional backing it received - it still managed to survive the doubts that might have arisen in those that stopped to think about the whole of it for more than a minute.

- **1583:** Taking ideas from both Copernicus and Ptolemy, Danish mathematician Tycho Brahe - continuing a series of baseless and seemingly pointless conjectures where the "infinite distance" of celestial bodies is never questioned - created a model in which the Sun orbited the Earth and all the other "planets" orbited the Sun. He was a good friend of the German astronomer Johannes Kepler, whom he took on as a disciple after the church in Kepler's home country, according to the official story, began to persecute ideas contrary to earlier teachings.

- **1584:** Giordano Bruno, Italian mathematician, philosopher, astronomer and occultist wrote his dialogues called *The Ash Wednesday Supper,* in which he not only reaffirmed the reality of the heliocentric theory but also suggested the rather bold claim that the Sun is not even the center of the universe, which he thought was actually infinite and constituted of innumerable worlds quite similar to those of the solar system. These views – as well as his alleged meddling with magic and occultism - were, of course, met with great resistance at the time and he was eventually sentenced to death as a heretic.

- **1609:** Galileo Galilei, Italian natural philosopher, mathematician and astronomer improved on the telescope that had been invented shortly before, allowing him to see celestial bodies that no one had ever seen before and to get a better view of what had been observed before. The most powerful telescope he developed and used had a magnification of about 30 times. One of his most significant observations was that the surface of the Moon is not smooth and uniform, but looks like it is covered with mountains and craters, which he thought goes against Aristotle's assumption that the Earth is fundamentally different from the luminaries in its nature. He also discovered sunspots, Saturn's ring and four dots of light around Jupiter - which he then named its "moons" -, as well as the different phases of Venus. The implications of the assumptions he had based on these observations convinced him that there could be more than one center of motion within the universe, that the Sun might indeed be in the center of it, and that the Earth is just a "planet" like any other, as Copernicus proposed with his model. Thus, fully pushing him toward that system of belief, instead of also taking Aristotle's worldview into consideration as he previously did *(Confirmation Bias, Reification Fallacy)*. After his conversion to Copernicanism, he has written a book containing his theories and arguments regarding the model, which eventually ended up being a key turning point in the development of this branch of pseudoscience, as his fellow professionals praise his supposed "breakthrough achievements" - that greatly helped further the cause of heliocentrism - to this day. He was also the first to assume that, when looking through binoculars at receding ships, they could possibly disappear from the bottom up because - contrary to logic, common sense and the most basic laws of physics – we somehow live on a floating marble *(Affirming the consequent, Confirmation bias, Status quo bias)*.

- **1609-1618:** In less than a decade, Kepler came up with three arbitrary statements based on the fundamentally flawed Copernican model, which we now know as "Kepler's three laws". Without any real basis, he made an assertion about the physics of the celestial point of light called Mars, and then developed a concept of what the Earth's "orbit" would look like when viewed from there. He believed that such and similar conjectures could be used to calculate the motions of the "planets" with greater accuracy, and we could thus make "perfect predictions". Although the reality of the heliocentric model was then beginning to be accepted more and more as fact by a large part of the world *(Fallacy of reification, Appeal to authority)*, one question still held the worldview back from undivided success even in the circles of those that wanted to believe. Namely, that if the Earth is actually flying and spinning (at very high speeds), why don't we fall off it? This question, of course, continues to concern the pseudoscientific community to this day, whose members weave a series of wonderful stories to distract humanity from the inconvenient and inescapable fact that the theory of gravitation, which is given as an explanation, has exactly as little to do with science and reality as the heliocentric model itself. But at the time, for want of a better idea, Kepler simply hypothesised an "unknown force", one which the pseudoscientist assumed could also be responsible for the motion of all celestial bodies. His analema also implies that the Earth's orbit is actually not a perfect circle but actually elliptical in the model and therefore its speed is supposed to change daily - making it even harder for those who would want to try and explain why we don't feel any movement while standing on it. Although Kepler is claimed to have been persecuted and even excommunicated by the Lutheran Church, however, at the same time the Catholic Church, and particularly the Jesuits, not only protected but even encouraged him.

- **1653:** Christiaan Huygens, Dutch mathematician, astronomer and physicist came up with the assumed average distance between the Sun and the Earth, now referred to by the professionals as the "astronomical unit" (AU), which is used as a standard measure of the supposed distances between so-called "celestial bodies" in astronomy. This number has an absolutely crucial role in the solar-centred cosmology, since all celestial distances - and hence many of their other assumed properties – happen to be also based on this value. Since this was a prerequisite for the model to even just theoretically make any kind of sense, Huygens, like Hipparchus, had no choice but to assume "very distant" celestial bodies for his calculations by default. Hence, of course, his results can only be classified as guesswork and, unfortunately, the conclusions drawn from them are therefore also inherently flawed logically, and as such, utterly useless. His method consisted of drawing a theoretical triangle connecting the Earth, the Sun and - when it was only half visible - Venus, then calculating the luminary's assumed distance from Earth simply by – admittedly - doing nothing more than taking a blind guess at its size *(Confirmation bias, Baseless assertion)*. Once he had one side of the triangle he had just built up on this logically outrageously flawed foundation, knowing its angles, he could finally calculate the imagined distance of the Sun from Earth. Perhaps unsurprisingly, the enormous "logical leap" used to achieve this has proved too much of a strech even for today's pseudoscientists, so in most cases the credit for calculating our supposed distance to the Sun is not even granted to him. What is quite astonishing, however, is that despite the generally acknowledged – colossal - flaws in his method, the final result of his calculations was accepted, claiming that the assumed size of Venus, despite being merely a belly flop from his part, just happened to be correct by chance. It would certainly prove to be a difficult task to find better proof that the pseudoscience of astronomy is in fact based on a series of guesses and conjectures, while – in many cases - not even the slightest attempt is done in order to at least make it seem somewhat scientific.

- 1666: While sitting under a tree, an apple fell on the head of English mathematician and physicist Isaac Newton, leading to the first theory of gravity and, 21 years later, its mathematical formula as well - or so the story goes around the world. Which came in very handy at the time, as the spread of heliocentricity meant that there was a growing need for a new story to explain why certain things fall to the ground (and those that don't, of course, were easier to simply ignore) and how they can stick to the side of a sphere hurtling at almost incomprehensible speeds through an infinite space. Despite the fact that Newton's concept of gravitation could only have existed in the world of mathematics - which unequivocally implies that it was completely devoid of any kind of scientific validation - many people still believe that his theory was a "historical discovery", nowadays just – mistakenly - known as "gravity". However, the details of this so-called "discovery", as ridiculous as that sounds, will be examined in more detail in a later chapter, given its critical importance for the development of a large portion of all pseudosciences.

- 1669: Jean Picard, French astronomer became the first to make measurements that supposedly allowed him to determine the "radius" of the imaginary globe-Earth with what the pseudoscientific community considered "acceptable accuracy". For these measurements, he used a telescope attached to a quadrant (a measuring instrument commonly used before the invention of the telescope), with which he made triangulations based on the heliocentric model. Using the resulting imaginary triangles, he then calculated the supposed "polar radius" of Copernicus' model, which, like modern pseudoscientists, he believed to be the same as the actual parameters of our real Earth *(Fallacy of reification)*. The figure accepted today was changed by only half a percent, which certainly made it easier for humanity to accept the validity of the measurement. Newton later used the figures Picard had obtained to formulate his abstract theory, based solely on mathematics, that the Moon's pattern of motion in its "orbit" was due to the Earth's supposed "attractive force".

- **1672:** Giovanni Domenico Cassini, Italian astronomer with the help of Jean Richer, the French astronomer used the method of triangulation in yet another futile attempt to determine the distance of a celestial body - in this case Mars - for the first time since Hipparchus. In doing so, they thought they had obtained not only that, but also the distance of the Sun from the Earth (AU). Needless to say, all of their work was built upon the previously existing – by then dominant – cosmology of faulty assumptions, therefore it should also be considered inherently flawed. Their measurements were taken by sending Richer to Cayenne, French Guiana in the north of South America to look at the stars from there, while Cassini did the same from Paris. They then both measured the apparent distance between Mars and the position of the stars in its background, and used the resulting figures, together with the distance they already knew between the two of them, to perform the triangulation. Their assumption was that once they had our supposed distance to Mars, they could easily calculate the distance to the Sun. Because this method of Cassini is considered "more scientific" by modern pseudoscientists, he is often credited with defining the AU rather than Huygens. Due to the supposed success of these measurements, which are considered to be the first reasonably accurate ones regarding the dimensions of our assumed "solar system", it was henceforth believed to all be much larger than previously imagined. In that same year, Richer had also made an observation concerning pendulums at two different locations. He discovered that the one in Cayenne, near the circle that is everywhere equidistant from the geographic poles of the presupposed globe-Earth, called the "Equator", has a somewhat slower beat compared to the one observed in Paris. At the time he couldn't come up with an explanation for this, but later on his peers created an extraordinary theory around it.

- **1676:** Ole Roemer, Danish astronomer thought to have accidentally „determined" the speed of light to be finite. He had been commissioned to create a chart sailors could use to navigate while they were at sea, as the clocks of the time didn't work very reliably under such conditions. Roemer then thought about using Jupiter and the other dots of lights circling nearby, which he and his peers called its "moons", as a celestial clock. He had heard Galileo suggest that these so-called "moons" could possibly serve well for such a purpose, as they only took a few days to finish their supposed orbits "around" Jupiter, so Roemer planned to take advantage of this. He decided to use one of Jupiter's "moons" called Io, which had the fastest orbit with just under two days. He had been observing it's movement for a few months in an attempt to create a timetable of the phases of it's eclipses for his chart, but noticed that they aren't perfectly consistent with their schedules. Since he considered the Copernican model of the world and Kepler's laws of planetary motion factual and essential parts of our reality, it is perhaps not at all surprising that his conclusion from this discovery was just as illogical as those ideas. His assumption was that this inconsistency happened due to the Earth being at varying distances from Io as we are supposedly moving along in our orbit around the Sun, and – in addition - that light must also be traveling at a finite speed – explaining why it could take longer for Io's light to reach us when we're farther away from it and shorter when we're closer. This sight would have demonstrated what we today know as the Doppler effect, that in the astronomical world supposedly manifests as what they call a "redshift"; the shift towards "redder", longer wavelengths in objects that are assumed to be speeding away from us. However, since Roemer based all his calculations on the - by then already generally accepted - heliocentric model, he failed to find the much more realistic – and much more likely correct – explanation. Namely, that the differences in the so-called "satellite's" schedule were simply due to the fact that it was moving, therefore every time we would see it being eclipsed by Jupiter, it would be viewed from a different angle. Despite him having based his calculations on the usual flawed assumptions that automatically come with the utilization of the rickety Copernican model, because his conclusions implied that the Sun must be – simply put once again - "very far away", his contemporaries were, of course, more than happy to accept them without a question.

- **1678:** Edmond Halley, English astronomer and mathematician made the first observation of a transit of Mercury and thought that a similar transit of Venus could somehow be used to measure the "size of the solar system". He envisioned doing this by observing the luminary's movement across the Sun – which, however, did not occur within his lifetime - and hoped that the assumed parallax could be used to trigonometrically determine the distances between Earth, Venus, and the Sun itself. A few years later he and two of his colleagues visited Newton, then they went on to try and work out the mechanics of celestial motions. Later on he also made multiple sightings of what's today known as Halley's Comet, as well as looking into the historical data in its regards, then – after hearing the idea from Cassini – decided to make the daring assumption that it must be orbiting the Sun just because its movements are periodically repeated every 75-76 years. This is now considered history's first "evidence" that anything other than the supposed planets repeatedly orbit the Sun.

- **1687**: Newton published his to-be very famous and influential book *Mathematical Principles of Natural Philosophy* - funded and edited by Halley -, often referred to as the Principia, in which he made an audacious claim based on Jean Richer's discovery regarding the varied speeds of the two pendulums at different latitudes of the presupposed globe-Earth. He argued – without actually performing any experiments to determine the real cause of it - that the phenomenon must mean that the globular Earth-model's equatorial semiaxis would be $^1/_{230}$ longer than the polar semiaxis, which didn't quite match with the currently accepted value of just about $^1/_{300}$ *(Reification fallacy)*. Satisfied with their result, he and Huygens then together concluded that the Earth must, in fact, not be a sphere, but rather an oblate spheroid - also known as an ellipsoid. This wild guess apparently seemed like good enough evidence to convince the majority of the pseudoscientific community, so – astonishingly - that is what was officially considered to be the Earth's actual shape from this point on. The book also included the final version of his theory of gravitation, which largely utilized as well as significantly extended Kepler's second law of planetary motion.

- **1690**: Huygens published his Treatise on Light in which he attempted to actually determine the speed of light by building upon the "discoveries" of Roemer. Although he used the now admittedly overestimated time delays and the - since then revised but at the time accepted - figure for the diameter of Earth's supposed orbit for his calculations, his 211,000,000 m/s result is by many considered "reasonably close" to today's accepted value of 299,792,458 m/s.

- **1704**: John Locke, English philosopher coined the term "solar system" in his book *Elements of Natural Philosophy*. Not challenging authority, he just elegantly described it as "the Sun with the planets and comets moving around it".

- **1720:** Measurements of the presupposed globe's arc were made again, this time done by Domenico and his son Jacques Cassini in France. They were continuing what they thought was an "arc" of Picard north to Dunkirk and south to the boundary of Spain. Their results ended up the length of a so-called "meridian degree" north of Paris being 111,017 metres, which was apparently 265 metres shorter than one that would be measured south of Paris (111,282 metres). From this data it was then assumed that the presupposed globe-Earth is actually a prolate spheroid that is not flattened, but in fact elongated at the poles, with the equatorial axis shorter than the polar axis. This new illusion of a discovery – unfortunately for the time's professionals - was completely at odds with Newton's previous conclusions.

- **1728:** James Bradley, English astronomer announced the finding of what is claimed to be the first ever actual evidence for Earth's orbit around the Sun, while also coming up with our supposed distance to the Sun, as well as an updated value for the speed of light. He was originally trying to calculate the "parallax" of a star called Gamma Draconis, however the amount of displacement he measured over the span of three days seemed too large and was in the wrong direction to fit into the Copernican model, so he decided that there has to be a different cause for it from what he had initially assumed *(Confirmation bias, Status-quo bias)*. According to the official story, he was then sailing on a river and looking at the wind vane of his boat when a realization suddenly came to him, resulting in his explanation - one that is, of course, as fallacious as can be. He postulated that the phenomenon with the previously observed star must have been caused by something called the "aberration of light"; an apparent displacement of star positions supposedly caused by the Earth's motion around the Sun, assumed to be possible due to light having a finite speed *(Affirming the consequent)*. Furthermore, once he decided this was good enough evidence of Earth orbiting the Sun, he also extrapolated its average supposed orbital velocity by using the observed displacement of the star over time and the assumed speed of light. The latter of which he – based on merely his guesswork regarding earlier ideas - miraculously calculated to be 295,000 kilometres per second, a value almost matching today's official figure. The result of his mess of an equation ended up being the - perhaps not-too-coincidental - figure of 66616 miles per hour, or 29.78 kilometers per second for Earth's average orbital velocity, which remains the accepted value to this day. Using trigonometry, he then related the angular shift he noticed earlier to the supposed velocity of Earth in its "orbit" around the Sun, and the presumed speed of light, thus calculating the alleged distance to the Sun. His estimation ended up being approximately 93 million miles (150 million kilometers) for the mean distance, a figure that essentially matches what's accepted today. Later he had also come up with a theory regarding an assumed nutation, or oscillation, of the Earth's presupposed axis, which he believed would have been caused by the Moon's "gravitational pull". Despite all of Bradley's guesswork clearly being – to say the least - quite a long shot, the lovers of the heliocentric model were overjoyed by his so-called "discoveries" and he was eventually awarded the prestigious Copley Medal by the Royal Society for his "outstanding achievement" of helping the world's acceptance of the Copernican worldview, which was still highly controversial at the time.

- **1735**: The French Academy of Sciences decided to send out two expeditions in order to settle the controversy caused by Newton's theoretical derivations and the measurements of the Cassinis. One team traveled to Peru and – a year later – another team made its way to Lapland to measure the length of what they believed to be a meridian degree. Both parties determined the length of their given presumed "arcs" by using the method of triangulation. A 12.2 and a 10.3 kilometres long baseline were used in Peru, while only a single 14.3 kilometres long one was measured in Lapland. Once they had these numbers, they believed they've determined these imaginary triangles' latitude by the usual method of looking at dots of lights in the sky and fallaciously presupposing their distance, from which the size of their angles was then calculated. The expedition to Lapland reported that the length of one degree of the meridian over there was about 111,947 metres. This result, when compared with the corresponding value near Paris, made them think once again that the assumed Earth-globe was flattened at the poles. Despite major errors being admitted today regarding the way the measurements themselves were done, they are still claimed to have been in the "right direction."

- **1791:** The French National Assembly came up with a new unit of measurement called metre, which they defined as 1:10,000,000 part of the meridian quadrant that's running from the imaginary globe's equator all the way to its pole through Paris. This has been since changed to be the distance supposedly traveled by light in a vacuum in 1/299,792,458 of a second, a value adjusted in accordance with the estimated two-way speed of light.

- **1796:** Pierre Simon de Laplace, French mathematician, astronomer and physicist made up a story known as the "nebular hypothesis" as an explanation of the supposed solar system's cosmogony *(Baseless assertion)*. According to his idea, the creation of Earth and all the other so-called "planets" all began with a giant cloud of rotating gas flying through nothingness for some reason, then eventually beginning to somehow cool down and shrink while also rotating faster, the centrifugal force of its spin, as well as what he thought was "gravity", making it leave behind rings of gas that would then inexplicably condense into planets and their satellites, while the remaining part of the nebula is supposed to have formed the Sun. As hard as it is to believe, this asinine little story has quickly become widely popular and remained the favored cosmogony among pseudoscientists for over a century.

- **1798:** Henry Cavendish, English chemist and physicist conducted a procedure in an attempt to determine the so-called gravitational constant and "measure" the mass of the Earth, today known as the Cavendish "experiment". For this, he used a torsion balance apparatus consisting of two small lead spheres suspended from a horizontal rod, originally built by his countryman, geologist and astronomer John Michell. By measuring the miniscule twisting force which he assumed was exerted on the rod due to the gravitational attraction between the small lead spheres and two larger ones, Cavendish was believed to have calculated the gravitational constant and provided an estimate of Earth's mass. The so-called "experiment", which, of course, had no control variables and therefore should have been deemed inconclusive, is perceived as having played a crucial role in understanding the nature of gravity and advancing our knowledge of the universe *(Confirmation bias, Status-quo bias, Experimenter effect)*. The result obtained for the supposed density of Earth is within one percent of the currently propagated figure, which is quite odd if we consider that the entire concept of "gravity", which was allegedly an essential part of the whole endeavor and the thing that allowed for all its conclusions, has been since completely redesigned and redefined. Nonetheless, since the pseudoscientists at play don't even seem to care about their own made up rules, the procedure is celebrated by them to this day as an experimental proof of whatever they decide to describe "gravity" as at the given moment.

- **1824:** Johann Franz Encke, German astronomer made the first recognized attempt at the blunder of trying to find the distance to the Sun with nothing but the transit of Venus and Kepler's third law as his tools. Instead of making the observations himself, he examined previous data recordings from two different occurrences from a few decades earlier to carry out his calculations using the method Halley advocated in his time. Sadly, the baseline for the attempted triangulation created by the two spots of the observers was not ideal, so "allowances" had to be made, as in numbers were changed to match the globe-model's diameter, retroactively putting the observers onto much more favourable locations at the opposing poles to create a baseline with a known (assumed) value that also happens to be perpendicular to the Sun. Although in reality this never could have possibly worked, since – due to the sight-limiting property of a sphere's bulge - it would have been impossible for the two observers to look at the transit at the same time, but nevertheless, his contemporaries accepted it all without a question, the calculations were made and Kepler's third law, one that's based on the model and designed to support it and all of its assumptions and implications, was applied. Not too surprisingly, this number he had acquired (97,000,000 miles) through all his blatantly and absurdly faulty calculations aimed to take a guess at our supposed distance to the Sun was so satisfactory for the so-called "experts" that it only required a few percent "correction" to get us today's accepted value.

- **1827:** Laplace finished the fifth and last volume of his book *Celestial Mechanics*, which contained his astronomical research that were largely inspired by Newton's ideas. The book quickly made him famous, as he proposed in it – among others - the hypothesis that the perturbations of planetary orbits that were thought to be caused by the interactions of so-called "planetary gravitation" may well be periodic. This would have meant that the assumed solar system is already perfectly stable on its own and therefore requires no assistance from a higher power to keep it functional. Since this suggestion fit the worldview of his fellow professionals so well, it is not hard to understand why he became so popular once he published it. However, due to the fact that he based this idea on the pillars of the arbitrarily conjured up and completely unfalsifiable – and therefore unverifiable - theory of gravitation, it should be considered no more than mere fairy tale, similar to most others within the profession.

- **1838:** Friedrich W. Bessel, German astronomer attempted to use stellar parallax to calculate our distance to a star other than the Sun for the first time in history. His choice fell upon a luminary called 61 Cygni and the bi-annual method of stellar measurement, a legacy of Halley. The way this is supposed to work is that the person doing the calculations first assumes that every tenet of the Copernican view of the world is a full and correct representation of reality *(Status quo bias, Reification fallacy)*, then makes the observation of the star at a given spot to note its position compared with a star adjacent to it, then waits exactly 6 months to do the same thing right there once again. The idea of this would be that, since the baseline of any two points on Earth seemed still too short for stellar measurements, the baseline of Earth's presupposed orbit around the Sun had to be used instead. Since this requires the knowledge of our distance to the Sun, it couldn't have been attempted before, but now that Ecke supposedly figured it out, the road was clear and this so-called "pioneering work" could finally commence. So, after conducting the expected calculations, Bessel concluded that the parallax angle of 61 Cygni is 0.31 arcseconds (or 0.31") and therefore it must be a bit over 10.5 light-years, or in other words, 63 trillion miles away from Earth. However, it should be noted that this angle size equals merely 11,613th part of a single degree, which is so incredibly subtle that no-one could realistically hope to ever as much as notice it, let alone accurately measure it, and therefore should be considered nothing more than simply the result of error *(Experimenter effect)*.

And, unfortunately, this was far from being the only issue with the venture, as Bessel also applied a number of basic astronomical tenets to acquire the desired results, such as the theory of perpendicularity, geocentric parallax and sidereal time – all of which together would in fact make it impossible to acquire any kind of parallax angle with the bi-annual method of stellar measurement. Regardless of the obvious blunder of the whole endeavor, however, astronomers were in awe and so impressed by the - clearly completely worthless - results that even in these modern times they consider this to be the first "experimental proof" of heliocentrism and praise Bessel for this so-called "historical breakthrough" – as outrageous as all of that might sound.

- **1849:** Hippolyte Fizeau, French physicist and his professional colleague, Léon Foucault made an attempt at determining the velocity of light. Fizeau had built a device that had a beam of light focused by a lens on to the edge of a wheel with 800 teeth and 800 gaps on it. The way it worked was that the light passed through the gaps between the teeth and on to a second lens, which produced another beam of light parallel to it. This then traveled to a third lens to next reach a concave mirror placed 9.5 kilometres away from the wheel, which reflected it back into the eyepiece to be observed. The wheel was rotated until a speed was reached at which the pulse of light leaving through one gap could no longer return before its way was blocked by a tooth and therefore no light would be able to reach the eyepiece anymore. This was the first terrestrial method of trying to measure the speed of light, and its result is claimed to have been extremely close to today's accepted value. However, it is important to note that this – just like every other - was merely a two-way speed measurement, therefore the actual one-way velocity of light remains unkown even to this day, with seemingly no hope for a reliable way of accurately determining it.

- 1851: Foucault created a device that consisted of a 28 kilogram iron ball attached to 67 metre long wire today known as a "Foucault pendulum" for the purpose of trying to demonstrate the supposed rotation of the Earth. The way the ball swings on the wire above the clearly unmoving Earth is claimed to prove that the so-called "planet" is actually rotating on its presupposed "axis", although this is highly debatable for a number of reasons, which are to be explained in a later chapter in great detail.

- 1859: Charles Darwin, English naturalist published his book *On the Origin of Species*, in which he describes his ideas of a possible evolution of living organisms by natural selection. This conjecture was not welcome by everyone, but it had the potential to deceive humanity into thinking in a much more materialistic and nihilistic way by implying that humans are not much more than mere animals and that the Earth must have been at least millions of years old to allow for their transformation. This way of thinking is, of course, exactly what an establishment interested in controlling the masses would be looking to spread. Therefore, the theory eventually became popularized and thus the foundation for an endless spiral of speculative guesswork, as well as the basis for the creation of a number of new branches of pseudoscience were set up.

- 1871: George Biddell Airy, English astronomer conducted a procedure with the goal of examining the aberration of light coming from the luminaries. To do this, he first attempted to observe a star with a telescope that was set up perfectly vertically, but the light from the star ended up coming in at an angle, so he tilted the device just enough for it to hit its bottom. Once that was achieved, he decided to fill it up with water so that the light is slowed down, and – if the Earth is indeed moving and the stars are stationary relative to it – it will once again be unable to hit the bottom of the telescope. He had conducted two sets of such observations about six months apart, each set spanning at least a month, at dates when the aberration of stellar light was supposed to be the strongest. However, he was shocked to find that this did not go as expected; the beam of light still came in at the same angle every time, despite being slower due to water being a denser medium than air. The self-evident conclusion of this result would be that it is actually the stars that are on the move relative to a motionless Earth, although Airy – most likely due to his deep trust in heliocentrism that was by then accepted and taught as fact just about everywhere in the world - didn't quite dare to make this claim at the time, despite realizing that things just don't quite add up for the Copernican model when compared with reality. Perhaps not too surprisingly, this experiment and the astonishing, fundamentally game-changing implications of its failure to find any aberration of stellar light - and therefore Earth-based motion - were not popularized at all. They also seem to be hardly mentioned or even known today by most (even in the field of astronomy), likely due to the fact that – despite being more than worthy of mention - they are also not being taught in any of the schools to begin with. Not to mention the fact that there is, unfortunately, little information from a relatively small number of sources to be found on the topic anywhere, which would rightfully lead researchers to the conclusion that there may have been in fact a deliberate attempt to scrub it from history as much as possible. Even the few official sources that do make a brief mention of it, generally fail to take note of the research's obvious implication that the Earth stands still, and instead make the claim that the only goal of it would have been to prove that we're flying through a conceptual medium called the "ether", thus simply referring to it all as "Airy's failure".

- **1877:** David Gill, Scottish astronomer attempted to measure our distance to Mars with the intent of verifying or correcting the previously supposedly found distance to the Sun. His method of choice was the so-called diurnal measurement by parallax, yet another legacy of Halley. The advantage of this technique was that he could do both observations not only on his own, but also within a mere day's time. The disadvantage was, of course, that it was just as riddled with devastating issues, errors and fallacies as all the other methods tried before – if not more so. The concept was quite simple: all he had to do was first assume that the whole of the Copernican worldview is without a flaw *(Status quo bias, Reification fallacy)*, then make his first observation of Mars, then, to let Earth make half a turn around its presupposed axis and thus allow him to use its diameter as a baseline, repeat it 12 hours later, and lastly, as one might have guessed, apply Kepler's third law to the result. So Gill set out to Ascension Island, made the observations and the calculations, then finally concluded that the angle of parallax of Mars is around 23", which made its distance to be roughly 35 million miles, which would place the Sun about 93 million miles away from the Earth. Needless to say, this number had promptly become and still remains the officially accepted and propagated number to this day. It does, despite the fact that this method not only contained just about all of the problems of Bessel's and Ecke's, but it is also very likely that Gill couldn't actually afford to wait 12 hours for his second observation, as it would have been almost certainly no longer visible in the morning, but only on the first occasion which took place in the evening. However, even if we were to assume that he somehow managed to do it exactly as planned, the fact that Earth would have supposedly moved to an entirely different position in Sun's supposed orbit during the night, or that, more realistically, it was actually the observed luminary that moved, making it the only reason for finding any apparent angle of parallax – if it was in fact present -, was dutifully ignored. Since the knowledge of our distance to the Sun (AU) - whose final value was ultimately derived from our assumed distance to Mars - is so crucially important even just for the perceived operability of modern astronomy and all its branches, we should always remember that it was this preposterously blunderous process that's claimed to have led us to find it. So blatantly erroneous, in fact, that there has been at least one other grandiose - and very expensive - organized attempt to get more accurate results regarding our distance to the Sun – by the already repeatedly failed method of the transit of Venus - a few years later. However, that was admittedly unsuccessful, therefore it was simply decided that Gill's value will be settled upon for the foreseeable future.

- **1882:** Simon Newcomb, American astronomer and mathematician, along with Albert Michelson, American physicist carried out a procedure in an attempt to verify the previously established value for the (two-way) speed of light, as astronomers believed that the number was crucial for them to be able to accurately determine the AU. Although such trials have been done before on several other occasions in history with similar results, but none this elaborate. Just as with another – claimed to be - relatively successful attempt by Foucault two decades ago, the contraption they built for this purpose consisted of mirrors set up at a long distance from one another. In this case, there was one setup with a four-sided mirror made of solid steel to avoid breaking, which was made to spin by compressed air operating on fan wheels at each end of the device. This was placed on the main site at Fort Myer, while one fixed mirror was placed on the grounds of the Naval Observatory and another one near the northwest corner of the Washington Monument - the former being 2,551 metres and the latter 3,721 metres from the Fort Myer station. Once all set, they could supposedly calculate the two-way speed of light by measuring the angular velocity of the spinning mirrors, the angular deviation of the light transmitted and reflected, as well as knowing the distance between the sites. The result is claimed to have been 299,810 kilometres per second in a "vacuum", which is a bit of an odd conclusion to make, considering that the endeavor didn't take place in a vacuum at all. Nonetheless, this has remained the accepted value for over four decades, and has only been adjusted very slightly ever since, despite many more attempts at its measurement even utilizing more advanced technology.

- **1887:** Michelson, along with Edward Morley, American chemist performed a test that would later become known as the Michelson-Morley experiment. The goal of the test was to detect the supposed motion of the Earth (or as it's officially claimed, the "ether wind", despite the medium having been deemed already debunked by Airy), if it was in fact not a fixed object, but one that's somehow flying aimlessly through an infinite nothingness for no reason. To conduct it, the two participants used an instrument called the Michelson interferometer, constructed by its namesake. This device splits up a beam of light into two, which are then reflected back and measured for speed by the observers. The premise was that – as per the beliefs based on classical Newtonian physics - the beam that was parallel to the supposed rotation of the Earth should return with a certain delay as it's being slowed down by the drag of the movement, while the beam that was set up perpendicular to it would experience less delay. However, they were shocked to see both of them return at the same time, no matter how many times the test was done. This was quite possibly one of the most significant procedures in the history of science that ended up forever changing the way the average pseudoscientist approaches certain basics tenets of the Newtonian so-called "laws of physics" they've previously established for themselves. This result, of course, shook the whole of the pseudoscientific community, and a number of rather odd explanations were conjured up along the following years and decades in a desperate attempt to somehow salvage what little was left of what now seemed to be a woefully wrecked Copernican view of the world.

- **1888–89:** Gill and a number of other astronomers conducted a program whose aim was to extensively observe certain luminaries with a heliometer. This device consists of a telescope with its objective lens cut in two along its diameter so that they can move independently, thus letting the observer see two different images of the same object. It was thought that the supposed angular separation of two stars – as well as, in the case of the Sun, its diameter - can be measured by moving the two pieces of lens just the right way. Unfortunately, such a method could clearly not be relied upon to acquire such intangible data and only have any perceived use with the usual fallacious assumptions of a heliocentric model of Earth. Including, of course, the belief in "very distant" luminaries and all the previously acquired defective figures. And yet, the results of these observations are somehow still claimed to have led to the first determination of the alleged solar parallax with what they like to refer to as "modern accuracy" within the next years.

- **1889:** George FitzGerald, Irish physicist came up with the borderline insane idea that moving objects might be able to somehow shorten along the direction of their motion relative to an observer, while – conveniently - dimensions in other directions are not contracted. He did this in a desperate attempt to try and explain the results of the Michelson-Morley (M-M) "experiment" - which seemed to have proved that the Earth is at rest – and thus save the Copernican view of the world *(Baseless assertion)*. This completely made up "phenomenon" of his has also sparked the interest of Dutch physicist Hendrik Lorentz, who decided to independently study and developed it further over the next few years. Finally, he came up with a set of equations known as the "Lorentz transformations", which aimed to relate the space and time coordinates of two systems moving at a constant velocity relative to each other. The made up phenomenon thus received the name "Lorentz-FitzGerald contraction", also known as "space contraction". The two physicists attempted to preserve the classical concepts of heliocentrism by hypothesizing how this "space contraction" of the measuring apparatus could possibly reduce the apparent constancy of the speed of light. Although it may seem like an absolutely ludicrous idea, but it did provide a heliocentrism-compatible explanation to the results of the M-M measurements that were otherwise simply baffling to most pseudoscientists, and therefore it was eventually – reluctantly - accepted as a feasible theory.

- **1904:** Forrest Moulton, American astronomer and Thomas Chamberlin, American geologist proposed a far-fetched idea for a new cosmogony for our supposed solar system and called it the planetesimal hypothesis, which they based on barely more than their imagination *(Baseless assertion)*. Their theory stated that the so-called "planets" were formed by the accumulation of pieces of rocky and/or icy bodies called planetesimals. These were assumed to have been produced when a passing star went very close to the Sun and their "gravitational fields" pulled out hot gas particles from one another, which then eventually somehow condensed and turned into the aforementioned solid objects. This ridiculous story they came up with was apparently more convincing than the previous one made up by Laplace back in his time and ended up replacing it as the mainstream cosmogony of our world for over three decades.

- **1905:** Albert Einstein, German physicist came up with the idea of "special relativity" for the sole purpose of trying to help out the pseudoscientific community that was hell-bent on clinging to the Copernical model of the world, but had an increasingly difficult time doing so after receiving the devastating blow from the M-M "experiments", its explanation by a "Lorentz-FitzGerald contraction" not being fully satisfying. In this new theory, Einstein postulated that the velocity of light could just be a fundamental constant that no object can ever exceed, and that the laws of physics (whatever he deemed them to be at any given moment) have the same form for all observers. These ideas ended up completely overhauling the way the world – to this day - views physics, letting such concept-based theories take over the place of empirical, scientific ones that didn't quite fit into a certain worldview well enough anymore. The ether-theory was now hoped to be definitively laid to rest by these theories, as they implied that light could propagate even without a medium. Space and time were no longer absolutes, changing within objects depending on their speed (or as pseudoscientists needed them) – an idea that goes against the experience of all humans since the dawn of time. Humanity was actually encouraged by Einstein himself to accept that a railway station is just as much of a moving object as the train is, from the point of view of someone on the train that's leaving the station. Evidently, this was merely a preparation of the masses for the predictable claim of Earth actually being on the move, despite all of our own experience. These made up phenomena of his – perceptible by none – were the called "length contraction" and "time dilation"; the "improved" versions of the Lorentz-FitzGerald contraction-theory. Later on – to add to the craziness – he also proposed that the mass and the energy of objects must also change with their speed and that these two properties are interchangeable. Of course, pseudoscientists – although not quite understanding any part of them – were all too happy to accept these unprovable conjectures as fact. This was helped by Einstein creating a number of highly contrived equations to "explain" it all - or to bamboozle everyone -, knowing well that the layman would take one look at the monstrous piles of mathematical jargon and conclude that they're probably just not smart enough to understand such complexities anyway, thus giving up on ever even trying to look behind the proverbial curtain. So, while the world was struggling to make any sense of the thing, the so-called "professionals" already started using it as a blank check which allowed them to make claims that previously would have certainly had them end up in a mental asylum. One of these was the idea that the Earth might actually be on the move, it's just that whenever someone tries to measure any of its motions, their device of measurement ends up changing its size and sabotages their otherwise flawless plan for proving Copernicus right. And so seems to have died the last shred of perceived sanity within the so-called "scientific community" - as if making a Faustian bargain - in exchange for keeping heliocentrism and its branching models on life support.

- **1911:** A handful of professors held a series of lectures in Petrograd, where they proposed yet another collection of theories that they hoped would be helpful in better explaining why all the experiments done earlier pointed in the direction of a stationary Earth, despite the fact that – as they still kept on steadfastly insisting – the Copernican view of the world must be correct *(Status quo bias, Confirmation bias)*. Their ideas included one which states that the light from luminaries can never come in at a straight line due to the ether somehow causing it to follow the Earth as it moves along its presupposed orbit, therefore we can never be entirely sure where they actually are, only that not where we think. As one would expect, they followed by making the claim that this must have been the reason none of the experiments could detect any movement of Earth. Another one of their postulates was a conclusion of this, namely the idea that nothing we can observe in the universe has a fixed place, as all of it – including the stars, the Moon, the Sun and the entire solar system and whatever else that may be out there – is somehow continuously drifting through nothingness. These ambiguous, muddy assumptions turned out to be of great help to their fellow pseudoscientists, serving as more blank check excuses they could use to explain to the layman how anything that seems to go strongly against heliocentrism actually fits into it perfectly. Clearly, at this point all the professionals have realized that they can make up just about anything and not only get away with it, but become part of history as long as their stories push the right narrative.

- **1913:** Georges Sagnac, French physicist carried out another test similar to the Michelson-Morley one, with the main difference being that this was done on a horizontal rotating turn-table, in an attempt to verify his predecessors' results. At first there seemed to have been no change in light velocity, however, once the table was rotated around during the test, the expected shift in speed did appear – which Sagnac, as well as many researchers today, interpreted as proof of ether wind. The result of the procedure therefore ended up not only contradicting Einstein's theory of relativity, but also the whole of the Copernican model itself. The pundits of heliocentrism, of course, couldn't accept this and tried to explain it away by claiming Sagnac later having also attempted to develop a new theory to restore the more classical understanding of not only the ether, but also space and time somehow diminishes the implications of the results acquired. Alas, because he and his work dared to contradict the official narratives, they never became popularized or even mentioned in the majority of schools, therefore today's professionals seems to have generally never had the chance to learn about them.

- **1915:** While Einstein was sitting in his office, a man washing the window of the building appeared outside, and he imagined what that person would feel if he were to fall off the ladder, leading to the physicist coming up with yet another far-fetched theory known as general relativity – or so the story goes. At any rate, he likely made up this new contrivance with the primary goal of attempting to patch up one more bothersome gaping hole in the heliocentric plot, namely the fact that if the Earth was in fact spherical, then – according to special relativity – the shortest path on geodesics for freely falling objects as well as light rays would be a curved line. In order to cover up this unresolvable contradiction between his theory and reality, he imagined a new kind of so-called "gravitation" in his conjecture. Perhaps not too surprisingly, this was one that was – just like everything else he proposed – even further removed from reality and is no longer even claimed to be some mysterious force acting at a distance, but instead merely the bending of a conceptual medium he called "spacetime". The whole of Euclidian geometry with its straight lines was replaced by a new kind of geometry where only curved ones exist, and the concept of time itself was turned into a so-called "fourth dimension". As nonsensical and preposterous as all of this was, he was celebrated for it and it ended up forever changing the way our world is viewed by supposed scientists. Because of its generally perceived significance, we shall take a deeper dive into it in a later chapter to further expose its faults and discuss why it is deemed a brilliant discovery by the pundits of heliocentrism.

- **1917:** Einstein made up yet another hypothetical thing that he called "cosmological constant", a kind of cosmic repulsive force which he introduced into the equations of his theory of general relativity. He felt this necessary as a desperate attempt to conjure up something that could counteract the supposed attractive force of gravity (despite it not even being assumed to be a "force" anymore) and account for a universe that he still believed to be neither expanding nor contracting.

- **1919:** Arthur Stanley Eddington, English astronomer, physicist and mathematician, along with Frank Dyson, English astronomer and Andrew Claude Crommelin, French astronomer made a number of observations of the total solar eclipse in May with the hopes of proving Einstein's so-called "law of gravitation" as described in his theory of general relativity. These were carried out by two expeditions, one of which went to the island of Príncipe in West Africa, and the other to the town of Sobral in Brazil. Eddington argued that during the eclipse the bending of light - due to the Sun's supposed gravity - could be measured. Based on the "law", the amount of bending should have been twice as much as it would be under the assumption of classical Newtonian physics. Although, the expeditions have had a number of technical and logistical difficulties and Eddington was even accused of manipulating the process on his part for more favorable results, the values gained were still ultimately accepted by most. To probably nobody's surprise, the numbers were closer to what was expected based on the assumption of relativity, and thus the procedure was deemed a success and is today referred to as the first "observational proof" of the theory's validity *(Experimenter effect, Affirming the consequent).* Since this event occurred right after the end of the first world war, its alleged success, and the fact the Einstein was German while his accomplishes English, also ended up turning him into an international superstar, which – despite all his fallacies - eventually led to his name becoming synonymous with being a genius.

- **1921:** Crommelin made a prediction that a comet named Pons-Winnecke might hit the Earth within a few months, possibly setting a large part of our world on fire – a forecast founded on nothing but calculations based on mere observations and the arbitrarily established astronomical theories from the past. A part of the world's population was, of course, sufficiently frightened by this conjecture, living in the false belief that such methods so popular with astronomers actually have some kind of value when it comes to predicting things - or anything else, for that matter *(Appeal to authority, Herd mentality).* Needless to say, when the time of its supposed arrival came, the comet was nowhere to be seen. This was the first big – and completely unfounded - scare of this kind. One that was, of course, followed by many more in the future as the upper echelons of society realized they can instill a constantly lingering fear of death into the unwitting masses - and thus control them with much more ease - by telling them scary stories about ways their doom could arrive at any given moment from the "dangerous and unpredictable" realm of so-called "outer space".

- **1924:** Aleksandr Friedmann, Russian mathematician came up with the idea of a dynamic, time-dependent universe and used Einstein's general theory of relativity to also formulate the mathematics for it. In this, he imagined that the average mass density is constant over all space but may change with the supposed expansion of the universe as time goes by. Continuing his string of baseless speculations, he then also attempted to calculate the time back to the moment when a supposed expanding universe would have been a mere point with his newfound equations. His result ended up at tens of billions of years, which has been since modified significantly to better fit the more modern cosmology. Regardless, his rather nonsensical assumptions were deemed "valuable" and contributed greatly to the creation of the first Big Bang theoretical model.

- **1925:** Michelson, along with Henry Gale, American astrophysicist helped by an assistant called Fred Pearson, conducted a procedure to try and measure the Sagnac effect they assumed to be caused by Earth's supposed rotation, and thus also test the theories of special relativity and the so-called "luminiferous ether" along the "rotating" frame of Earth. The process was very similar to that of the Michelson-Morley version of the test, but this time it was done on a significantly larger scale to make the magnitude of the expected effect much greater to allow for more accurate results. As one might have guessed at this point, they were once again disappointed to see that the result was essentially null this time around, too. Although they did acquire varying degrees of deviations throughout the many repeated attempts, but it was all very ambiguous, as the numbers went both ways and weren't significantly prominent anyway, therefore the whole endeavor was deemed inconclusive. Of course, the so-called "scientific community" may have realized at this point that this could very well mean that the Earth does not actually move, and could have admitted the obvious failure of the Copernican model. However, they chose a different path as they apparently wanted to keep hanging onto it at all costs, and thus decided to instead conclude the one thing that could have let them keep their beloved model despite all evidence to the contrary. Namely, they asserted that Einstein's special theory of relativity must have been proven correct by the endeavor; setting a precedent for a recurring way of explaining things that would otherwise clearly disprove the model in the future *(Experimenter effect, Confirmation bias, Status quo bias)*. With the use of this little trick, they thought they should be able to salvage the ruins of the heliocentric worldview, and consequently, they would now even make the bold claim that the procedure in fact proved that the Earth rotates *(Affirming the consequent)*.

- **1927:** Georges Lemaître, Belgian astronomer and cosmologist came up with an updated version of the Big Bang theory. In this elaborate guesswork, he proposed that the universe somehow began from what he called a "primeval super-atom" by way of a cataclysmic explosion. Oddly enough, a large part of the world went with it, and thus it was made possible that his fairy-tale would live to this day as a widely accepted and propagated "discovery" *(Baseless assertion)*.

- **1923-1936:** Edwin Hubble, American astronomer made a number of observations and supposed discoveries using the largest telescope of the time, eventually also publishing his book *The Realm of the*

Nebulae, in which he detailed his speculations regarding the universe. In this, he made it seem like it's not only much larger than anyone could have thought before, but also continuously expanding – meaning in essence that empty space would somehow keep creating more empty space. Most of his assumptions were, of course, based on practically nothing except his imagination. In essence, he was merely looking into the telescope, noticing the same milky blur on the sky that has already been discovered by others before him - which he called a "nebula" -, and finally coming up with conjectures on what it may, or may not be made of, and how big or how far it could be. This so-called "nebula" was named Andromeda, and Hubble noticed a number of what he thought were pulsating stars inside of it, which he thought he could use to calculate its distance from Earth. He assumed that the apparent pulses of these stars are caused by their periodically fluctuating luminosity, whose intervals he could measure and make a guess on how far they might be away based on that value. Utilizing this highly questionable, seemingly arbitrary method, he ended up coming up with a mind-bending number of 900,000 light years, which is claimed to be much further out than the edge of our own entire so-called "galaxy", which is estimated by the pundits to have a diameter of no more than 300,000 light years. This supposed finding of his managed to convince his fellow professionals that the "nebula" was actually nothing less than another galaxy. In addition, since he had later on also discovered a number of other milky blurs on the sky, they just assumed that there must in fact be a myriad of galaxies similar to ours out there. He eventually also noticed so-called redshifts in the spectra of these supposed galaxies and arbitrarily decided that they should be interpreted as the result of Doppler shifts, meaning they might be constantly moving away from us *(Baseless assertion, Confirmation bias, Affirming the consequent).* Thus, the belief held by a significant part of humanity in an expanding universe, as well as the theory of its origination from a Big Bang were reinforced, making even Einstein relinquish his belief in a static universe and remove the "cosmological constant" from the equations of his theories.

- **1933:** Fritz Zwicky, Swiss astronomer came up with a new theory regarding the composition of the universe. When studying Hubble's supposed discoveries, he made the bold assumption that the mass of all stars in a certain cluster of so-called "galaxies", which he thought move too fast and should have been flung off, provide only about 1 percent of what's needed to keep those galaxies from escaping the cluster's supposed gravitational pull. As a haphazard band aid for this newest of inconsistencies in the model, he tried to account for what he believed was missing mass by "inventing" a hypothetical component that he called "dark matter" - due to the fact that it cannot be observed. Although his theory was not widely adopted at this time, it established what was to become more wiggle room for pseudoscientists who needed newer and newer things to insert into the gaping plot holes of their ever-rickety worldview.

- **1948:** George Gamow, American nuclear physicist and cosmologist, with the assistance of a few of his colleagues published a paper called The Origin of Chemical Elements, in which they attempted to explain some of the details of the Big Bang model, essentially updating Lemaître and Hubble's ideas. They fully adopted the concept of an expanding universe and elaborated on how they assumed atomic nuclei were built up after the explosion, which they claimed to have been thermonuclear. Their speculations apparently seemed convincing enough to their peers and were used as the foundation for a more modernized version of the theory.

- **1965:** American physicists Arno Penzias and Robert Wilson built a microwave antenna that they intended to use for communication, however, they kept hearing a noise in the sky with the device, which they eventually decided must be due to so-called "cosmic microwave background radiation". From this highly questionable supposed finding, they conjured up the asinine conclusion that the universe must be about 13.8 billion years old. Their alleged discovery was perceived by the pseudoscientific community as proof of the farcical "big bang" theory, and thus the two researchers were eventually awarded the Nobel prize. From this point on, this clearly unprovable and entirely speculative theory was - for all intents and purposes – accepted, used and taught by its pundits as if it was just about fully proven fact. The implications of this idea are very far-reaching in regards of humanity's perception of the world today, therefore it will be analyzed in detail in a later chapter.

- **1970:** American astronomers Vera Rubin and Kent Ford claimed to have confirmed the existence of dark matter simply by the observation of a phenomenon similar to what Zwicky had seen in his time. The updated supposition they came up with was that the stars observable in a typical galaxy only have a mass that is merely 10 percent of what is needed to maintain their orbital motion around the center of the galaxy. They had to make this assumption because they noticed that the speed with which stars move around the centre of their supposed galaxy is either constant or increase slightly with distance rather than dropping off as they previously expected. Therefore, they thought that the mass of the galaxy within the "orbit" of the stars must increase linearly with the distance of the stars from the galaxy's centre in order to account for this. All of these presuppositions were, of course, based on nothing more than the calculations relying on figures from the earlier guesswork of others, which Rubin and Ford clearly had no problem accepting without a question *(Confirmation bias, Status-quo bias, Baseless assertion)*. As the idea of this new, magical, invisible matter allowed the professionals to keep their beloved theoretical models, they were, of course, more than willing to go along with the story and take its reality as a given; inserting it into the official cosmology for all foreseeable future *(Affirming the consequent)*. Since the supposed discovery of the hypothetical substance, it has been already used to explain multiple phenomena not fitting well enough into the mainstream theories, including the occasional distortion of light, which they call "gravitational lensing" - matter acting as a kind of lens by "bending space" –, as well as the heat and motion of gas molecules that may give rise to X-rays.

- **1971:** Joseph C. Hafele, American physicist and Richard E. Keating, American astronomer carried out a number of observations involving eight cesium-beam atomic clocks - in an attempt to validate the theory of special relativity and especially that of time dilation -, which became known as the Hafele-Keating "experiment". They placed two of the clocks on an airplane flying westward, another two on one flying eastward, while the last four remained stationed in the United States Naval Observatory. Based on Einstein's concepts, the clocks were expected – when compared to the reference clocks at the observatory - to lose a few nanoseconds eastward, while gaining some when going westward; a supposed phenomenom which was simply referred to as the "clock paradox". These deviations were supposed to happen due to a number of the usual baseless assertions, including the Earth's rotation, the effects of the gravitational field originating from Earth's presupposed center, as well as the theorized influence that an object's velocity is thought to have upon the concept of time. Although they did end up getting the (barely noticable) figures they expected within the limits of their predetermined margin of error, the test was clearly ill-founded, as there were no control variables, thus there could have been a good amount of reasons for any deviation of the clocks. Not to mention that rather drastic - and arbitrary - "corrections" of the results were admittedly made afterwards to try and account for the unintentional bumps of the clocks that occur during flights, which unfortunately means that the entire outcome was obviously nil and it couldn't have been used as proof of anything *(Experimenter effect)*. Nonetheless, the endeavor was still considered nothing less than a great success and an "unambiguous evidence" of the ridiculous idea of time dilation *(Affirming the consequent)*. Alas, this is somewhat overclouded by the fact that "increasingly accurate" - but similarly uncontrolled and therefore just as unreliable - tests were later conducted in an attempt to acquire more precise results *(Confirmation bias)*.

- **1998:** Two independent teams of American physicists and astronomers claimed to have found evidence of what is now called "dark energy" in the universe through nothing more than mere observations. They were aiming to measure the rate at which the universe is supposedly expanding, so they were looking at a certain type ("Type Ia") of what they thought were exploding stars – supernovas-, whose maximum luminosity was believed to be uniformized and therefore usable as what they call a "standard candle". Upon studying the apparent brightness of the dots of light on the sky, they noticed that these particular ones were somewhat fainter than expected, which meant to them that they must be further away than predicted by the existing Big Bang model. Furthermore, they also noticed that these "supernovas" took on a reddish hue – thought to be a sign of "redshift". They then – based on the estimated two-way speed of light – tried to calculate the time it takes for the light from one of these "supernovas" to reach us, from which they thought they can indirectly estimate the "cosmic time" elapsed since their supposed explosion. From all of these wild assumptions, they concluded a number of asinine ideas, such as that these luminaries must not only be moving away from us, but doing so at an increasing rate since about 5 billion years ago. As the Big Bang model of the time was built on the assumption that the expansion of the universe is slowing down over time due to the supposed force of gravity pulling everything towards the center, these new "findings" forced them to modify this story. Then, to jump from one conjecture to another, they concluded that there must be some kind of counteracting repulsive force – similar to Einstein's discarded idea of a "cosmological constant" - at play, which fights against the supposed gravitational attraction and somehow fuels the acceleration of all matter in the universe indefinitely. This new, mysterious and very hypothetical invention was supposed to be a form of energy that they believed permeates all of "space" but – conveniently for the profession, similarly to "dark matter" – never observable, and thus, it eventually got its "dark" attributive as well. It is postulated to possess negative pressure, resulting in the desired repulsive force that the newfound Big Bang model desperately craved, while also somehow multiplying itself to fill all of the newly created space of the imaginary expanding universe. Even to this day, there are quite a few speculations circulating among the pseudoscientific community about what dark energy – existing clearly only in the minds of its most devout believers - may, or may not be and in what ways could it possibly affect our world – which is certainly a testament to their vivid imaginations, if nothing else. Nonetheless, this so-called "discovery", leading to an updated Big Bang theory, was considered such a saving grace for the models of 'The Deception' that three of the teams' leading researchers were eventually awarded the Nobel prize for it.

- **2012:** The Higgs boson, also known as the "God particle", was allegedly "discovered" by researchers using the Large Hadron Collider at the European Organization for Nuclear Research – a facility whose goal is claimed to be figuring out what the universe is made of and how it works. According to the official story, the existence of the Higgs boson has been confirmed by merely analyzing the data collected from millions of attempts where particles made to fly at high speed inside the device collided and a plethora of other particles were somehow produced, then sophisticated detectors were employed to measure the properties and trajectories of the resulting particles, searching for the "telltale signatures" of the boson's decay. Its supposed discovery was deemed a significant milestone in particle physics, as it's claimed to have provided insights into the mechanism of mass generation for elementary particles. Although this event was, of course, nothing more than the result of calculations based on data derived from vague observations as well as figures based on earlier conjectures and blunders of the profession, it should still be considered worthy of mention, if only because it can potentially let pseudoscientists finally give some kind of an explanation regarding the paradox of the Big Bang model where things are supposed to be created out of nothing, by nobody.

The forceless gravity

The topic of gravity is quite possibly the most interesting one when it comes to the world of pseudoscience. It is one of the few so-called "scientific ideas" that permeate our everyday life so deeply that we consider it an absolutely fundamental bedrock of our very existence. While, for example, few people ever think about the shape of the Earth, and even fewer talk about it on a daily basis, gravity is reasonably often mentioned, especially in regards of supposed scientific discoveries and, of course, in the different branches of the entertainment industry, such as motion pictures or video games. In fact, of all the kinds of metaphorical glues that are used to hold together the decaying pieces of the horrible abomination that the Copernican view of the world has become over the centuries, gravity is perhaps the most essential – and arguably also the most farcical. It is something that's required in order for the model to have things stick where no sticking should be possible, it's supposed to (selectively) move or hold things in ways that should not be possible, it's claimed to form celestial bodies – including the Earth – as well as keeping them stable. It is also assumed to cause tide forces, create black holes, and, of course, dilate time itself. It's even held responsible for the growth of large-scale structures in the universe, such as the so-called "galaxy clusters" and "superclusters" - and more. Indeed, it would prove difficult to find a fundamental part within the models of deception which doesn't rely on this specific theory in some significant way. Which is why it's such a shame that a mere concept, which is what gravity has officially become since the worldwide acceptance of Einstein's theory of general relativity, cannot actually do any of these magical things.

Not to worry, though. If we were to ask a teacher or decided to look up its definition, we shall quickly realize that a good portion of the answers still simply define gravity as a kind of force, or even as the long-superseded, archaic "mass attracting mass" even to this day, while, at best, making just a quick mention about it "also being interpreted" as the curvature of spacetime "in the context of Einstein's theories". Of course, we all know that it can't possibly be an actual force and also merely just a concept at the same time, but let's face it: the "authorities" of the matter desperately need it to be both at the same time. Therefore, they have no other choice than to muddy the waters, make things as confusing and convoluted as possible and hope that no one looks behind the curtain to notice the glaring contradiction. The reason for this great necessity is, of course, that gravity needs to be a force in order to be usable as an explanation for certain phenomena that we can actually observe, while at the same time it must also be a concept for when it's needed to explain things that are only imagined but just as necessary for their models to appear "functional".

The ambiguity of the matter at hand is in fact stretched to the extent where students of elementary and high schools are generally just taught the Newtonian version, while those attending relevant classes in colleges and universities are taught Einstein's theories instead. This is very convenient for the establishment for a number of reasons. First of all, it means that everyone who only learns about the topic at a base level will live their whole lives believing that gravity is a force and that all mass can indeed attract mass. Furthermore, it also means that those who have been "more initiated" will likely feel compelled to defend the dogma they've learned that much more, as they would now have much more time, effort and money invested in acquiring the apparent knowledge. As British mathematician and astronomer Fred Hoyle once said about his fellow professionals:

"They defend the old theories by complicating things to the point of incomprehensibility."

However, the jumble of misinformation doesn't even stop at that level. Once one reaches a high enough level of indoctrination in theoretical physics, yet another layer of confusion is bestowed upon him as he is introduced to something called "quantum mechanics". The main purpose of this discipline and the reason for its creation appears to be providing additional explanatory stories about imaginary things such as the assumed conditions in "the early moments of the universe" or the area near so-called "black holes". In those specific cases, the effects of "gravity" are claimed to become significant at the quantum level, and the classical framework of general relativity supposedly "breaks down". In essence, this means that trying to combine the conventional ideas with the ones based on quantum mechanics directly lead to mathematical inconsistencies and infinities, thus giving rise to the need for a theory of "quantum gravity". This would, of course, open up the path to yet another string of baseless assertions and conjectures that could provide sufficiently smart-sounding explanations for the use of the pseudoscientists who may want to try and patch yet another batch of gaping holes in all the officially accepted and propagated theoretical models supposedly depicting our world.

One of the most poignant examples that showcase just how much of a made up, convoluted mess the whole topic of "gravity" really is, may be an over 36 minutes long "educational" video on YouTube uploaded onto the highly popular channel *Wired,* with the title of "Astrophysicist Explains Gravity in 5 Levels of Difficulty". In this video with nearly 10 million views at the time of writing, Janna Levin, PhD astrophysicist essentially guides us through the different historical milestones of the theory, except they're offered to us as if somehow they were all equally viable and valid descriptions of the same thing – despite being mostly fundamentally different. And frankly, if one were to think that such a basic thing as what "gravity" is supposed to be should definitely not require over 36 minutes to explain, they would be right. Ironically, it is none other than Newton himself that the following – rather wise - words are generally attributed to:

"Truth is ever found in simplicity, and not in the multiplicity and confusion of things."

If such was in fact his creed, he would certainly be quite disappointed to find out what a convoluted heap of tangled mishmash his relatively simple and stringent - although almost just as baseless - ideas have been turned into.

In regards of the aforementioned video, I will let everyone decide for themselves whether such a lengthy salad of words would qualify as "simplistic", or rather as deliberately confusing.

Nevertheless, there are actually a few interesting points brought up in it that are worthy of mention. For example, when Levin asks Lisa, her third interlocutor what she learned from their conversation (about theoretical nonsense regarding the ways gravity is or isn't supposed to work), she replies as follows:

"Well, I learned more about the intuitions behind the concept. 'Cause we already just do the problems, but sometimes you get lost in the math, but speaking like this really helps build my intuition."

Well, dear Lisa, that is essentially the whole point; you *are* supposed to get lost in the endless strings of overly complex math problems, so that you have less of a chance to figure out what you may now begin to get a grasp on. Namely, that, as you even mentioned, gravity is just a *concept* and nothing more.

The fun doesn't end here, however. Later on, near the middle part of the video, when Levin lectures Will, her fourth subject about other fairy-tales such as the attributes and behavior of "neutron stars" and "black holes", Will eventually asks her:

"So, is there a sensible way to talk about what's inside a black hole, or should you think of it as there is no spacetime inside a black hole?"

To which, astonishingly, she reveals things that she may have even ended up later regretting:

"There isn't a sensible way to talk about it yet. And that probably means that's where Einstein's theory of gravity as a curved spacetime is beginning to break down and we need to take the extra step of going to some kind of quantum theory of gravity. And we don't have that yet."

This should really make one think. After all, what kind of theory is that which falls right apart and requires a complete overhaul when we observe certain types of objects or events? Not a very solid one, I would say. And definitely not a scientific one that's gone through rigorous testing.

At any rate, Levin eventually asks Will what he took away from the conversation, to which he replies:

"Well, I've definitely taken away that the way that we think about gravity today is very different from how Newton thought about it and that even though we have a very good understanding, there's lots of things that we don't fully understand."

See, this is the issue with pseudoscience. While actual science provides us with clarity, definitive answers and proofs, theories that are only based on conjecture, such as that of gravity, give us nothing but even more questions, as well as a good amount of confusion.

Anyhow, in the last part of the video Levin's conversation partner is Matthew Kleban, a PhD theoretical physicist. Once they establish that his expertise is quantum mechanics (which he claims is *the most successful theory in the history of science*", which – for "some reason" – *"many people would say we don't understand even the basics of"*), Levin details how certain things are supposed to function within this theory, then compares Einstein's ideas to it as follows:

"And the language that Einstein gave us is so different. It's completely geometric, it's all this spacetime. And it's also unnecessary."

Now, that I can agree with, although *unnecessary* is probably not the word I would find best to describe it. Furthermore, the only way it's "geometric" is if we consider the made up, conceptual fourth dimension real.

Then Levin goes on to ask Kleban a surprisingly honest and direct question:

"Is there really spacetime, or are we just using unnecessary language because it's elegant and we like it and it's beautiful?"

Although I have a feeling that Levin (as well as most of my readers) already knows the answer, we're in luck, as Kleban makes sure to clarify things:

"Well, I think there's really spacetime in the sense that it's a description that works really well, so there has to be something right about it."

Indeed, there has to be. Of course, even the experts don't really seem to know what that something actually is, or what the concept even describes, but it "works" mathematically for models which it was built up to support in the first place, so why not pretend it's real? Well, other than wanting to be honest to one's self, but pseudoscientists rarely care about such things...

Oddly enough, however, Levin doubles down on the idea a few sentences later, as she says:

"So when we're talking about the multiverse or the Big Bang, we are really talking about gravity ultimately, and we're talking about how a theory of gravitation which we now think of as a theory of spacetime has a quantum explanation, has a quantum paradigm imposed on it that will help us understand these things, and we don't have that yet. One of the things that I think is so amazing is that the terrains in which we're going to understand quantum gravity are very few. It's the Big Bang, because that's where we know that quantum and gravity both were called into action. And there's black holes."

In case someone wasn't sure what the multiverse theory is, it's essentially a desperate attempt at a cosmogonical explanation that - combined with the Big Bang theory – aims to provide a pseudoscientific alternative to Creationism; one that, of course, involves no creator. It suggests that our universe might be just one of many universes, often referred to as a "multiverse". These imaginary universes could supposedly have different physical constants, laws of physics, and even dimensions, making them vastly different from our actually existing universe. Naturally, the idea of this particular fairy-tale arose from various theoretical models in cosmology and quantum mechanics. It is apparently also something that Dr. Levin and her ilk can tell us all about, but at least the fact that – just like most other just-so stories conjured up to support their worldview – it must fundamentally have something to do with "gravity". They also seem to have time traveling abilities, since they make definitive claims about what played what kind of role during the supposed Big Bang. Not to mention the so-called "black holes", which they must have studied up close to know such details about them. Unless, of course, they've just built it all up on assumptions, in which case all they have to do is sit in a studio and chat about how they have it -mostly - all figured out, and hope that the audience doesn't ask any uncomfortable questions...

In any case, nearing the end of the video, Levin does manage to ask yet another shockingly revealing question:

"Do you think it's possible that gravity is really ultimately just quantum mechanics and doesn't exist at all in the fundamental ways that we've been talking about so far, like the Newtonian way and the spacetime way, that those are just these kind of macroscopic illusions?"

No, dear Dr. Levin, I don't "think" it's an illusion, I know for a fact that it is one. Or, should I rather say, a delusion.

Then, after her almost worryingly above-board question, comes the no less appalling answer from Kleban:

"If we buy the idea of holography, then absolutely, that's for sure, that's what it's telling us. (...) so I guess with the holographic description we've got two sides, which are actually secretly the same. On one side, there's definitely no gravity. On the other side, well, it's a quantum theory of gravity, whatever that means."

Well, I certainly don't buy such ideas as the holographic universe (a concept that suggests that all the information about our three-dimensional universe might be projected from and encoded on a two-dimensional boundary that surrounds it), nor would I suggest anyone to do so. At any rate, it's certainly reassuring that even the so-called "experts" don't seem to know what the quantum - or any other - theory of gravity actually is, or whether it even exists. Of course, this wouldn't even be such a massive problem if it weren't for the fact that it's being taught in just about every school of the world as a valid scientific theory.

Alas, make no mistake, even when we refute the idea of a holographic universe – or any other fabricated quantum-nonsense -, gravity still remains just as untenable and decidedly fictitious.

Another good example of an honest attitude toward the topic from a person of authority is a lecture from PhD theoretical physicist and string theorist Erik Verlinde in the YouTube video "Erik Verlinde: Gravity Doesn't Exist" on the *Big Think* channel. In this, he's asked "why gravity is an illusion", to which he answers the following:

"Gravity, of course, is something that have, well, many people have already thought about. It's something that we see every day and it's not like it's not existent in our ordinary life. But what I mean by that it's an illusion is that one would eventually like to know where it comes from, an explanation. Up to now we have, well, descriptions, I mean, Newton, of course, is the one famous for first writing down a theory of gravity and he described why apples fall and why the Moon goes around the Earth (...). He had to assume that gravity was there and then had to write down a law that described that when two masses are a certain distance, how they attract each other. But he was also not very happy with the fact that we should just, well, assume that these things, these objects, attract each other and without even anything in between. So if there are two masses and empty space, there's nothing that really happens between them, but still, they're attracting each other. And he thought that was kind of mysterious and that it was something he would have liked to explain in a better way. So later came Einstein and (...) wrote down a theory where he thought about space and time together and then his explanation of what gravity would be is that there's masses which curve space, and time. And then motion of planets and (...) the reason they go around then in circles is that space and time itself is curved, in the sense that things don't move in straight lines anymore (...). So what

I've done in my paper is try to start from a point of view where you don't assume gravity to be there, (...) but then just follows from a certain logical reasoning."

As tiresome as all this gibberish may have been to process, it's certainly interesting to hear it from a professional. Furthermore, besides it obviously being a confession of how unproven and speculative the whole idea is, it also tells us just how much of a convoluted mess it ended up to be and just how hard it is even for an expert to make it seem somewhat sensible when trying to walk us through its historical development.

Once the matter is considered concluded, he's asked how we should think about the "forces that exist to create the illusion of gravity", to which he answers:

"If you think about particles, very tiny particles, and it turns out that things like positions and velocities are not very precisely defined, you have to take into account the fact that there's an uncertainty in when we look at something (...). So taking gravity into account then gives us a bit of a problem because then we have to talk about spacetime and then these quantum certainties give us another way of looking at spacetime at the short distances. (...) people have studied the problem of quantum mechanics in gravity from various perspectives; from string theory, but also by thinking, for instance, about black holes, what happens with black holes. And I've taken some of the things we've learned about it and seen that there is some explanation of maybe where gravity then comes from, from those new ways of thinking about quantum mechanics and gravity together. (...) it has to do with the fact that this at the microscopic scale, a certain information about how you describe this, which we don't see ourselves, we forget about that. And it turns out that if you take that into account in some appropriate way (...) you can understand where gravity comes from."

These words of the highly esteemed Dr. Verlinde may not exactly have been clear and concise either, and it's certainly not easy to find the bits of real information among them - let alone the part that is supposed to answer the original question. Although, at this point I doubt anyone would have expected too much intelligibility from a theoretical physicist anyway. At any rate, it's worth noting that he, similarly to Dr. Kleban and Levin earlier, also essentially established that a new kind of gravity needs to be invented; one that's more compatible with the number of other new theoretical contraptions that their fellow professionals have come up with over the past few decades. And just like the others, he also mentioned the assumed but not even observable "black holes" as an integral part of the foundation of this new and updated version of "gravity". So it's probably safe to say that this new one will stand about as "strong" as its predecessors, and may even live quite a few decades before another "update" is needed to make it better fit yet another bunch of conjectures.

Unfortunately, since even these highest of authorities couldn't truly deliver when it came to comprehensibly explaining what gravity would actually be if it existed (or why we need to pretend that it's real when it admittedly can't be substantiated), we will just have to try and figure out what it definitely isn't. Coming to our aid are excerpts from a few of the more up to date definitions of the word strictly from some of the highest profile sources:

- California Institute of Technology's website, written by Jacob D. Bekenstein, professor of theoretical physics: *"After a decade of search for new concepts to make gravitational theory compatible with the spirit of special relativity, Einstein came up with the theory of general relativity (1915), the prototype of all modern gravitational theories. Its crucial ingredient, involving a colossal intellectual jump, is the concept of gravitation, not as a force, but as a manifestation of the* *curvature of spacetime, an idea first mentioned in rudimentary form by the mathematician Ceorg Bernhard Riemann in 1854. In Einstein's hands gravitation theory was thus transformed from a theory of forces into (...) the geometry of four dimensional curved spacetime."*

- Universetoday.com, written by Brian Koberlein, astrophysicist: *"While general relativity is an elegant theory, it's a radical departure from the idea of gravity as a force. (...) In general relativity, gravity is not a force between masses. Instead gravity is an effect of the warping of space and time in the presence of mass. Without a force acting upon it, an object will move in a straight line."*

- Space.com, written by Elena Giorgi, assistant professor of mathematics: *"According to general relativity, the spacetime is a 4-dimensional object that has to obey an equation, called the Einstein equation, which explains how the matter curves the spacetime. (...) General relativity explains gravity, and in this theory, it is not really a "force" anymore. The gravitational field comes out of the description of general relativity as a result of the curved spacetime."*

- Phys.org, written by Matt Williams, space journalist and science communicator: *"(...) Einstein's General Theory of Relativity (...) remains the best means of describing gravity's behavior. According to this theory, gravity is not a force, but a consequence of the curvature of spacetime caused by the uneven distribution of mass/energy."*

- Physics.info, written by Glenn Elert, science research coordinator: *"Gravity isn't a force, it's the curvature of spacetime caused by the presence of mass-energy."*

- Newscientist.com, written by Pedro Ferreira, professor of astrophysics: *Albert Einstein's general theory of relativity is one of the towering achievements of 20th-century physics. (...) it explains that* *what we perceive as the force of gravity in fact arises from the curvature of space and time. (...) So although Earth appears to be pulled towards the sun by gravity, there is no such force.*

- Scientificamerican.com, written by George Musser, theoretical physicist: *"(...) Einstein created his general theory of relativity - which provides our modern understanding of gravity - with the express purpose of expunging nonlocality from physics. Isaac Newton's gravity acted at a distance, as if by magic, and general relativity snapped the wand in two by showing that the curvature of spacetime, and not an invisible force, gives rise to gravitational attraction."*

In the case of the last quote, it's worth mentioning that - partly due to its peculiar way of phrasing – it sparked great interest in the circles of independent researchers a few years ago, and debates were started on how to best interpret it. This eventually culminated in George Musser himself being invited for an interview by the owner of the YouTube channel named *FTFE* to clarify things once and for all. Musser decided to accept the invitation and expanded on his position on the subject in what became a roughly 25 minutes long video called "An interview with George Musser" on the channel. In this, when the interviewer asks him what he meant when he wrote that "general relativity snapped the wand", he gave the quite elaborate answer as follows (with only the most relevant parts quoted):

"(...) Newton developed this law of gravity that we're all taught, but even Newton and his contemporaries had a real problem with that law, namely that it (...) described gravity's effect, but it didn't really describe how gravity works, and Newton actually, in his own life, tried to develop – unsuccessfully as it turns out – an understanding of how gravity works, what is actually communicating the influence for instance between the Earth and the Moon or between the Sun and Mars, et cetera. And it really fell to Einstein. Einstein's role here was to

really fill in that mechanism. He explained how is it that massive objects exert what seems to be a force on one another. Now, literally it's not a force. (...) Newton had various ideas on this, but generally it's thought that Newton did not take his own law that literally that there is a force reaching from one object out to another. However, you can act as if there were one. And it's perfectly valid for the applications of Newton's laws to act as though there's this force that's operating. (...) there was really no way that the force got from one place to the other (...) – that was the magical component of Newton's law recognized by him and the others in his time. And I used the word magic in a couple of senses here. First of all, it's magic in the sense of, you know, supernatural, but it's also magic in the sense that it actually did come from a very particular scientific tradition that was, by modern standards, magical. So Einstein came along and he said (...) what could cause this apparent force, this action that gravity exerts, and he developed this whole theory of spacetime and its distortions and how masses distort spacetime which in turn exerts what we perceive as the effects of gravity. So that's the breaking of the magic wand; it's in the sense of filling in a mechanism that had not been there. (...) science, as you know, operates on multiple levels of explanation and often we speak in an approximate way to kind of make progress and understand phenomena that we observe, even though we kind of know deep down, it doesn't quite work that way. (...) we can and do and we must think of Newtonian gravity as a force. That doesn't mean it really is, but we don't necessary need to work at the "really is" level. (...)"

Well, that was a much longer way than one would expect of saying that there is "kind of a force of gravity", but not so much in reality, rather it just exists in its believers' imagination. And, of course, also in many of the arbitrary calculations used in support of certain theoretical models, in an abstract way.

So, to once and for all summarize all of the best available information gathered on the subject which we've fought ourselves through here: gravity is indeed officially no longer considered a force today, merely the curving of the conceptual - non-existent – medium of spacetime. How something that not only isn't a force, but also doesn't exist, can move objects or make "orbiting" – or anything - possible, of course, remains anyone's guess – including the experts, who are, lucky for us, still "working it out". And, as to never let anyone make the mistake of conflating – or even comparing as counterparts - the old version of the theory with the newer one, we should note that they are completely mutually exclusive. While Newton's was supposed to function within the three-dimensional realm and surmised an instantaneous action at a distance, for the Einsteinian variant a four-dimensional world was assumed with its effects limited to the speed of light. Moreover, the principle of superposition - the net force on an object being the vector sum of the individual forces on the object - applies to the former theory, but not the latter one. Therefore, we can conclude that the two interpretations truly have nothing in common, apart from being unfortunately referred to with the same word. A word that thus has no real meaning anymore and should be abandoned once and for all.

Now that that's settled, we shall carry out a damage assessment on the solar-centred model of the world to see just how badly it's doing with the glue that used to hold it together now officially missing from it. First of all, let us be reminded that what happens whenever someone uses the word "gravity" is that they inexorably invoke a supposed cause for an effect. One which they could, of course, never hope to prove or verify by any means. However, this is usually done unwittingly and goes unnoticed even by those that are aware that one should not carelessly invoke a cause for a natural phenomenon without knowing if it has been previously validated through the scientific method, or at least if such a deed would even be possible.

Indeed, the only reason the idea of gravity being something real even survived this long is that the largest part of humanity has been convinced by the perceived authorities that mathematical equations are able to substitute the scientific method and provide proof of such causes. Unfortunately, as was already mentioned in regards of the method itself in an earlier chapter, this could not be farther from the truth. As a slightly more unconventional inquest than what we're used to, let us read a few lines from a satire titled *Gravity: It's Only a Theory* found on the website of the National Center for Science Education, written by American physicist Ellery Schempp:

"Even Isaac Newton, said to be the discoverer of gravity, knew there were problems with the theory. He claims to have invented the idea early in his life, but he knew that no mathematician of his day would approve his theory, so he invented a whole new branch of mathematics, called fluxions, just to "prove" his theory. This became calculus, a deeply flawed branch having to do with so-called "infinitesimals" which have never been observed. Then when Einstein invented a new theory of gravity, he, too, used an obscure bit of mathematics called tensors. It seems that every time there is a theory of gravity, it is mixed up with fringe mathematics."

Although this was meant as only a joke overall, there is a surprising amount of truth to it, and it further illuminates just how unfounded these theories actually were and how they were substituting the process of the scientific method with mere equations as a so-called "new method of proof".

So, then what about the models of deception now? What if we still just kept pretending that gravity is in fact a force? Wouldn't that solve all their problems? – one might ask, and we shall look into it.

Originally, the invention of gravity was needed as a way to explain why we don't fall off the presupposed "globe" while it's spinning wildly and flying at breakneck speeds. According to the current definition by Webster, "weight" itself – in regards of an object's mass - just means *the force with which a body is attracted toward the earth or a celestial body by gravitation and which is equal to the product of the mass and the local gravitational acceleration".* Which is, of course, quite useless, as it utilizes the antiquated force-based idea of gravity. And even if we were to disregard that "difficulty" and decided to pretend that a concept can somehow create some kind of attraction between masses, the model would still be in just as big a trouble, suffering from countless inconsistencies and self-contradictions.

One of the best examples may be how the Moon is claimed to cause such a powerful attraction upon the presupposed "globe-Earth" that it makes seas bulge out from it, creating high tides in them – ironically, both on the side closest, as well as farthest from it – while the Sun is also claimed to have a slight effect on them. As the Moon's "gravity" pulls at Earth, it's supposed to "shift its mass" and thus distort its shape slightly, elongating it at the equator and shortening it at the "poles". Of course, this brings up numerous questions that are very poorly – if at all - answered by official sources, such as: how is it possible that a force that comes from a single point uniformly reshapes the whole of the Earth and not just the side that is closer to it, as it would logically follow? If the attraction is supposed to be that strong, how come other objects in those areas aren't affected by it? Why doesn't it also tug on things like the "atmosphere", seeing how it somehow defeated the – claimed to be much stronger – "gravitational pull" of the Earth when it comes to its solid materials? Furthermore, when the Sun, the Moon and the Earth are presumed to line up twice a month, their so-called "gravitational power" is claimed to combine to make exceptionally high tides, called spring tides. In this case, should the tides not be even more one-sided during these times, seeing how both the Sun and the Moon would be pulling on them from the same direction? Not too surprisingly, even Newton himself is said to have considered the tides to be "the least satisfactory part" of his theory of gravitation, no doubt for many of the above reasons. Also, it should be mentioned that research has shown that tides are actually most likely caused by the gentle movement of the seabed, not by some kind of an external force.

Another blatant issue that would then come to mind is how an "orbiting" celestial body and the one being orbited are supposed to attract each other. It would only make sense that this should result in them being pulled toward one another gradually – and rather quickly -, just like two magnets would. Of course, their "force of gravitational attraction" toward one another and the inertia of the orbiting body trying to move in a straight line are claimed to be in just the perfect balance to allow for a perpetual movement in a curved path, which we would perceive as an "orbit". However, even if we were to push a magnet of any kind at the exact right angle and at the perfect speed into the proximity of another, there would still be no way to ever make one orbit the other, as they will promptly stick together and come to a rest. Furthermore, even if such a thing as an orbit was somehow in fact possible, during the spring tide periods the Earth would be pulled in the direction of the Moon not only by it, but also by the Sun, meaning the delicate conditions that could allegedly allow for the "orbit" to be maintained would be broken, making the Earth fly right into the Sun. Inversely, when the Moon is on the other side of Earth, it would have both other celestial bodies pulling on it from the same direction, inevitably crashing it into the Earth. In addition, it is also worth noting that if the presupposed globe-Earth does in fact spin on its axis, the purported gravitational attraction exerted from its centre would not be able to uniformly counterbalance the centrifugal force of such rotation, since the directions of the two forces wouldn't be aligned in perfect opposition. It would therefore result in us either experiencing an exceptionally strong force pulling us toward the ground near the "polar circles", where the rotational speed is very low, or being thrown off the "globe" as we're moving toward the equator, where the velocity of the spin is the highest. Not to mention that things would naturally be tilted in one direction or another almost everywhere in the world, due to the disparate vectors of the two forces.

These few examples were really just a small demonstration of how easy finding holes in the plot of heliocentrism could be, even if we granted feasibility to some kind of a "force of gravity". The list of discrepancies and contradictions could, of course, go on forever – some of which will need to be dealt with in later chapters as they become relevant.

At any rate, the good news is that in reality there's no involvement of any such force required for something heavy to drop down to the gound from a height, just like it's not needed for something lighter than the air to rise toward the sky; a phenomenon which the proponents of gravity - more often than not – tend to forget about.

Thus, let us now examine what exactly happens in everyday scenarios where most would believe that the so-called "force of gravity" is at play. First of all, we should note that everything on or around the Earth that we know of is created on the ground level. Once that happens, most things will remain relatively close to the surface, while a few things start to rise – depending on their density relative to the medium they are in, or in more official terms, their "buoyancy". Let's take the example of the apple tree whose fruit allegedly gave Newton the idea of a downward force. The apple didn't come into being and reached a certain height by itself; it needed the tree to first grow out of the ground from a seed until it was big and strong enough to bear fruit. At that point, apples would slowly begin to grow on its branches and remain there, hanging in equilibrium until becoming ripe enough or an outside force, such as a strong gust of wind, detaches them from their branch. As that happens, the apple ceases to be in a state of equilibrium and thus, it will begin to seek it once again. Since it's much more dense than the air – the medium that surrounds it -, it will start moving back towards the ground, where the tree from which it originates has started its journey years ago. Once the apple hits the ground, it will once again rest in equilibrium until a force displaces it yet again.

Similarly, if we take a balloon and blow it full of air, we can throw it in the air and see that – as light as it may be – it will also drop to the ground, since its overall density is still somewhat higher than that of the medium surrounding it. However, if we were to instead fill it up with helium, which is much less dense than air, we shall see it starting to rise toward the sky to seek its equilibrium at a higher elevation. Once it reaches a height where the air is sufficiently thin, enough so that its density matches its own, it will have found its equilibrium once again and its vertical movement stops. We may also fill it up only partially with helium, in which case its point of equilibrium will be at a lower altitude, although still not on the ground. All of this, of course, provides clear and irrefutable proof of there not being any "downward force" that's acting upon all things. And yet, an argument from the faithful believers in a force of gravity still often arises: "it's the molecules of the surrounding air that are being pulled downwards, which is what's pushing the balloon upwards in these cases". Of course, we all know that gas molecules aren't actually affected by any universal downward force either. Generally, they just move freely and randomly in all directions, filling up all available space – as per gas law. Another argument from such zealots comes in the form of something even more unnatural. They argue that if we were to put the balloon filled with helium inside of a vacuum chamber, it would fall to the ground, thus demonstrating the effect of a downward force. Hopefully the dear reader already sees the fault in this logic; since a vacuum is a medium that even less dense than helium, we would expect the balloon to drop to the floor either way, even with no mysterious downward forces acting upon it.

Further, even more sophisticated evidence against their idea is the operating principle of a submarine. To control its own overall density, or buoyancy, it has ballast tanks and trim tanks, that can be alternately filled with air or water. When the submersible is on the surface, the ballast tanks are filled with air and thus the surrounding water's density is higher. As the u-boat dives, these tanks are flooded with water and the air in them is vented from the submarine until its overall density is greater than that of the surrounding water, letting it sink. To keep the submersible level at any set depth, a balance of water and air is maintained in the trim tanks so that its overall density is equal to the surrounding water's.

There are even a few actual scientific experiments simple enough that anyone can do them at home if still not convinced that the density of something relative to the medium that surrounds it is in fact the only circumstance that needs to be taken into account when trying to explain a vertical motion generally attributed to whatever "gravity" is thought to be at the moment. Perhaps the most accessible among these is the one involving two hard-boiled eggs, two large glasses of water and three tablespoons of salt. All one needs to do is pour the salt into one of the cups of water, stir it until it's fully dissolved, then put an egg in each cup. It will be apparent that the egg in the clean water drops to the bottom, while the one in the salt solution floats on the surface. Since the only physical difference between the two cups of water is their density, which we increased by adding the salt, we have just validated the hypothesis that the only thing that fundamentally determines the vertical placement of objects within any medium is their density relative to it. No "gravity" needed whatsoever – neither from the Earth, nor from a luminary.

135

And yet it doesn't move...

According to a number of dubious sources, Galileo, either on his death bed, or when the inquisition finally set him free, uttered the words *"And yet it moves..."* with fervent conviction, reassuring everyone of his firm belief in the mobility of the Earth. Although, we ultimately have no way of knowing whether or not such a thing actually happened, it is a phrase that has since then become widely popular in the world of pop culture as well as that of literature, using it as a way of dramatization. Thus, we shall now look at irrefutable evidence of just how wrong such a statement (and worldview) as Galileo's would be.

Since one of the most frequently brought up pieces of supposed evidence of Earth's motion to date remains the first one ever claimed to have been presented, the Foucault pendulum, it is what we shall examine first. The rate of the pendulum's apparent rotation would be expected to change depending on the latitude of the location where the device is set up; at the North Pole, it should complete a full rotation in 24 hours, while at the equator, it would not appear to rotate at all. In the Northern "Hemisphere" of the presupposed "globe-Earth", it should appear to rotate counterclockwise if one is looking at it from above, while in the Southern "Hemisphere", the rotation is clockwise. This phenomenon is supposed to occur due to the Coriolis effect, a result of the Earth's rotation in this case. This means that as the Earth turns beneath the pendulum, the plane of its swing creates an apparent rotation over time. Although the Earth is claimed to not only be spinning but also moving around the Sun, with the Sun orbiting the galaxy, while the galaxy itself also flying through "space" at a mind-bending speed, a Foucault's pendulum apparently somehow manages to ignore most of it and is claimed to only ever demonstrate the effect of Earth's spinning motion. This inconsistency in logic is often explained away by claiming that the so-called "gravitational forces" involved in galactic motion are much weaker than those involved in the Earth's rotation, so the pendulum is just not sensitive enough to detect these effects, and that the the Earth's orbit around the Sun cannot influence the behavior of the pendulum because its plane of oscillation remains constant relative to the local vertical direction. Nonetheless, even if we were to accept these rather contrived explanations, a number of issues still remain with the device.

First of all, as far as its modern version – the one including electromagnets - is considered, it is admittedly "very tricky" to properly set one up, because even the slightest mistake or the lack of perfect adjustment of its every tiny part can and will generally result in failure to get the expected outcome. As for the pendulum's original, more authentic version with no magnets, it would most likely prove to be a hopeless endeavor to even attempt getting it to work as expected, as - more often than not - it tends to be extremely unreliable, and, of course, since perpetual motion is not possible, it will stop moving after a while; the duration of its swinging depending on the legth of the wire that's used to suspend the plumb. Which is a problem, since even the modern version's user guide advises that one should keep it going for at least a few days in order to find out whether it has been set up "correctly" *(Experimenter effect)*.

Those who did try to set one up throughout history found that the pendulum would usually either show no oscillation, show it in the "wrong" direction, at the wrong rate, or at an uneven frequency. In just about every case, multiple attempts were required before results even somewhat close to what was expected could be seen, and even then, it was often distorted when the plumb received the push that was needed to keep it going after a few hours, while at least a few days of uninterrupted swinging would have been necessary for the endeavor to even have a chance of being perceived as conclusive. Not to mention that the angle of the initial push, as well as the way the screws at the two points of connection of the wire are set up also seem to play a major role in determining exactly how the oscillation will appear - or whether it will at all. As for other factors, there are, of course, the possible wind currents – which may even influence indoor procedures to a certain extent -, the Earth's seismic activities, the changes in air pressure and humidity, electromagnetic radiation, and, as some researchers speculate, the dragging force of the supposed "ether".

And then there is the rather fascinating phenomenon called the Allais effect, named after French physicist Maurice Allais who is credited for observing and taking notes of it for the first time. This occurrence appears to show a correlation between the motion of the Moon and changes in the behavior of pendulums during a solar eclipse. The exact cause of this effect remains controversial and is admittedly "not well understood" by professionals to this day, contradicting their expectations based on their preconceived physical theories, and thus challenging the current paradigm of "gravitational" and physical interactions. The variations in a pendulum's behavior caused by this effect can include such things as changes in its amplitude and frequency, as well as its direction of oscillation. Knowing this, it should be clear to all that no pendulum can therefore be used as a distinctive proof of any single kind of celestial movement, and especially not Earth's rotation.

Today we may see many "sophisticated" Foucault pendulums displayed in science museums and universities, all of which are, of course, of the "modernized" variety with plenty of electromagnets carefully placed in them all around to not only keep the plumb moving indefinitely, but also control the direction and rate of its apparent rotation. For this reason, just like their older version, they are obviously just as incapable of proving anything other than either the ignorance or deceitfulness of their inventors and – just as importantly - their operators.

Another device that purports to present evidence of Earth's rotation is the ring laser gyroscope, which is essentially a consumer device version of the Michelson-Gale-Pearson "experiment". Unfortunately, however, this means that the exact same issues arise with it as with that, which also happen to be the Foucault pendulum's problems: the results always seem to vary and are thus greatly ambiguous and unable to provide conclusive proof of anything. Furthermore, mechanical gyroscopes, on the other hand, offer conflicting evidence, as these should clearly detect any kind of Earth-based rotation, but they show no such signs. Of course, we may hear counterarguments such as that their free rotation may be prevented by too much weight being put on their bearings, or that they must not be sensitive enough. However, these accusations are negated by the fact that they have been also tested in artificial situations where they were placed on a revolving platform with a rotational period of 24 hours, in which case they managed to successfully detect the motion. Since this process is perfectly analogous to the way the imagined globe-Earth is supposed to be rotating, the only conclusion that could be drawn from the endeavor is that the Earth in reality simply must stand still.

Yet another phenomenon that is frequently brought up as proof of a spinning Earth is the way storms tend to rotate at different latitudes. It is claimed that in the presupposed globe's Southern "Hemisphere" wind systems always rotate clockwise, while in its Northern "Hemisphere" they rotate counter-clockwise. This is presented as proof of the alleged Earth-based Coriolis effect, and consequently, as proof of the Earth's daily rotation. While it is true that this "correct" rotational direction can be observed in tropical cyclones and hurricanes that develop from specific wind patterns near the equator, it's important to note that other kinds of storms do not necessarily follow this so-called "rule". As for these tropical storms originating near the equator, their direction of spin can be easily explained by the robust and permanent easterly-flowing wind current, known as the Equatorial Counter Current. This airstream flows in the opposite direction compared to the westerly currents located directly to the north and south of it, and it's known for creating so-called atmospheric Kelvin waves, which then cause the counter-rotating vortexes that turn into the storms we can see emerge from that area.

Some may also bring up the idea that sinks, toilets and tubs drain counterclockwise in the Northern "Hemisphere" and clockwise in the Southern "Hemisphere", providing evidence of the Earth-based Coriolis effect, however, even the more serious official sources admit that this is merely a (very common) misconception. In fact, what actually determine the way of drainage of liquids are simply just the angle from which they were poured into the drain pipe, as well as the shape of the receptacle itself. Another, less frequently heard argument for a supposed Earth-spin is that objects weigh slightly less at the equator compared to other latitudes due to the centripetal acceleration experienced by objects on the Earth's surface as it rotates. Of course, this is based on the idea that the so-called "gravitational force" – which has already been proven not to exist in the previous chapter - is slightly weaker there than at the poles, therefore we could just disregard it. Nevertheless, let it be said in the spirit of full disclosure that the alleged reduction in weight at the equator is typically less than 0.5% compared to the weight at the poles, which is admitted to be usually not even noticeable in everyday situations. So, even if the phenomenon is indeed real, such a miniscule difference can easily be explained by other factors, as it is known that a scale, and therefore the measured weight, is affected by properties such as air pressure and humidity. It is known that the pressure is lesser at the equator and greater at the "poles", while it's also greater at lower altitudes and decreases as one goes higher. Unfortunately, the scales used to do the weighing during the tests are simply not calibrated for such environmental influences, therefore the whole of the argument of them proving Earth's rotation is invalid.

Other than the above examples, there are also most of the so-called prevailing winds, ocean currents and anything that is detached from the Earth – which the proponents of heliocentrism usually tend to conveniently forget or ignore - serving as clear proof of there being no Earth-based Coriolis effect present anywhere. Knowing this, the only defense we may frequently hear from them that could – at least at first glance - possibly seem somewhat rational is that we are actually not even supposed to see this effect, because the whole of the "atmosphere" is in fact attached to the Earth and rotates along with it. Indeed, when all else fails, they'll have no choice but to resort to making such a contradictory claim, as there are simply too many holes in their plot to fill.

This is because when someone claims that the Earth rotates, but allows the air to behave as we well know all gases do - their unbonded molecules moving freely and randomly in all directions -, that means it constitutes a second frame of reference, or system of inertia - making the appearance of the Coriolis effect possible. The first frame of reference being, of course, the Earth underneath it, which would continue to rotate at a high speed – over a thousand miles per hour at the equator - while the air above it moves at its own pace, completely disconnected from it. Unfortunately for the proponents, as the more adept readers have probably already figured it out by now, this would also mean that anyone who stands near the equator would always have to experience winds of roughly 1000 miles per hour, which would be gradually getting slower as one moves further away from that line of latitude, making the biggest part of our world entirely unfit for living for most lifeforms.

Not to mention that everything that detaches from the surface of the Earth would immediately become part of that second frame of reference, resulting in the most insurmountable and chaotic conditions. For example, if an airplane tried to fly from west to east, the same direction as the Earth should rotate, the time required to reach its destination would drastically increase, while those flying from east to west, against the rotation, would find it drastically reduced. Not only that, but it would also be nearly impossible for them to land without crashing, unless every single runway was perfectly aligned to be parallel to the Earth's spin direction, and even then it would only be possible by approaching them eastward – if at all. Furthermore, we should keep seeing a plethora of obvious proofs of Earth's rotation, with clouds, birds, butterflies, hot air balloons, drones and whatever else can fly or float in the air rapidly moving away laterally from the observers on the ground as soon as they leave the moving reference frame of the Earth and enter the one that is fixed. But alas, we see no such thing, ever.

That is precisely why the sort of reasoning which includes an "atmosphere" that's somehow attached to the ground and moves along with it in perfect unison is inescapable if the followers of the Copernican faith would ever hope to reconcile such a contradiction in logic as well as physics. Of course, an argument like that will, in turn, immediately destroy all claims for an observable evidence of Earth's rotation, as it removes the second frame of reference that's required for the only possible way of clearly showing the effects of Earth's revolution. Yet, interestingly enough, the currently accepted official, mainstream standpoint is that the so-called "force of gravity" does indeed attach the air to the surface of the Earth so that it spins along with it, however, at the same time there is also somehow an observable Earth-based Coriolis effect, but only in a select few examples - such as what have been detailed earlier. We could assert that this massive, glaring, irresolvable contradiction is actually a necessary part of a dogmatic theory such as heliocentrism, which tries to convince everyone that it should be trusted more than one's own senses. Its believers at the higher levels seem to simply hope that humanity won't ever discover this uncomfortable antilogy on a large enough scale, and thus they may be able to keep getting away with just about any claim they feel like making regarding our world.

Luckily, though, there have been quite a few among them who were – at least on occasions - unusually honest about the ambiguity of the professions which happen to be closely related to the models of deception. An interesting take can be read in Arthur S. Otis, American psychologist's book *Light Velocity and Relativity* which he wrote in 1963, where he analyzes the rather irrational reasoning behind the final conclusions of the highly controversial Michelson-Morley "experiment" (p. 58):

"In the effort to explain the Michelson-Morley experiment (...), the thought was advanced that the earth might be stationary (...). Such an idea was not considered seriously, since it would mean in effect that our earth occupied the omnipotent position in the universe, with all the other heavenly bodies paying homage by revolving around it."

It is thus obvious that the official conclusion had nothing to do with science or even observations, but rather with the worldview of those in a decision-making position who felt the need to remove humans from a central location at all costs. This very same point was made by Dennis W. Sciama, English physicis who wrote the following lines in his book *The Unity of the Universe* in 1961 (p. 102-103):

"Whether the Earth rotates once a day from west to east, as Copernicus taught, or the heavens revolve once a day from east to west, as his predecessors believed, the observable phenomena will be exactly the same. This shows a defect in Newtonian dynamics, since an empirical science ought not to contain a metaphysical assumption, which can never be proved or disproved by observation."

Yet another example of such an admission can be read in the 1976 book *The Relativity Explosion* by Martin Gardner, American mathematician (p. 86-87):

"The ancient argument over whether the Earth rotates or the heavens revolve around it (as Aristotle taught) is seen to be no more than an argument over the simplest choice of a frame of reference. Obviously, the most convenient choice is the universe. (...) Nothing except inconvenience prevents us from choosing the Earth as a fixed frame of reference. (...) If we choose to make the Earth our fixed frame of reference, we do not even do violence to everyday speech. We say that the sun rises in the morning, sets in the evening; the Big Dipper revolves around the North Star. Which point of view is "correct"? Do the heavens revolve or does the Earth rotate? The question is meaningless. A waitress might just as sensibly ask a customer if he wanted ice cream on top of his pie or the pie placed under his ice cream."

A similarly intriguing thought was put forward by Bertrand Russell, British philosopher and logician in his 1925 book *The ABC of Relativity* (p. 13):

"Before Copernicus, people thought that the earth stood still and that the heavens revolved about it once a day. Copernicus taught that "really" the earth revolves once a day, and the daily rotation of sun and stars is only "apparent" (...). But in the modern theory the question between Copernicus and his predecessors is merely one of convenience;

all motion is relative, and there is no difference between the two statements: "the earth rotates once a day" and "the heavens revolve about the earth once a day."

Phil Plait, famous American astronomer, blog writer and author has also written such words of wisdom (even if his last statement in this is debatable) in his blog on Slate.com back in 2010:

"I have two things to say that might surprise you: first, geocentrism is a valid frame of reference, and second, heliocentrism is not any more or less correct."

Yet, perhaps one of the most shocking revelations of them all comes from an article of Wayt Gibbs, science journalist, editor and former senior writer at the prestigious Scientific American. In the October 1995 issue of the scientific magazine, on the last two pages of his article Thinking Globally, Acting Universally, he explains the professional work of George Ellis, famous South African cosmologist – and also president of the Royal Society of South Africa at the time. In these lines, Gibbs shines light not only on the unprovable nature of heliocentrism, but also the duplicity of the discipline of cosmology itself:

"More remarkable is the fact that his analysis (...) seems to undermine the rationale for continuing to fund his own highly theoretical work in cosmology. Lately that work has taken on a familiar pattern: drawing connections among disparate facts and ideas in order to change people's perception of what is real and what is possible. Within cosmology, Ellis has been exploring alternatives to the so-called standard model. (...) Ellis says his aim is to counter a recent trend "of researchers being very dogmatic, almost to the point of discounting the astronomical evidence." (...) "People need to be aware that there is a range of models that could explain the observations," Ellis argues. "For instance, I can construct you a spherically symmetrical universe with Earth at its center, and you

cannot disprove it based on observations." Ellis has published a paper on this. "You can only exclude it on philosophical grounds. In my view there is absolutely nothing wrong in that. What I want to bring into the open is the fact that we are using philosophical criteria in choosing our models. A lot of cosmology tries to hide that.""

Indeed, hiding the truth seems to be the main purpose of the entire discipline, along with, of course, the other branches os astronomy. Nevertheless, the lack of any observational evidence for the Earth's orbit around the Sun – and therefore its own rotation - was also pointed out by I. Bernard Cohen, history of science professor at Harvard in his 1985 book *Birth of a New Physics* as follows (p. 78):

"There is no planetary observation by which we on Earth can prove that the Earth is moving in an orbit around the sun. Thus all Galileo's discoveries with the telescope can be accommodated to the system invented by Tycho Brahe just before Galileo began his observations of the heavens. In this Tychonic system, the planets Mercury, Venus, Mars, Jupiter, and Saturn move in orbits around the sun, while the sun moves in an orbit around the Earth in a year. Furthermore, the daily rotation of the heavens is communicated to the sun and planets, so that the Earth itself neither rotates nor revolves in an orbit."

Even Einstein made remarks acknowledging the lack of any actual evidence of Earth's motion, all while supposedly knowing that devices such as the Foucault pendulum exist. The following was part of his famous lecture in Kyoto (called the Kyoto Address) in 1922 where he talked about how he created the theory of relativity:

"(...) I came to know the strange result of Michelson's experiment. Soon I came to the conclusion that our idea about the motion of the Earth with respect to the ether is incorrect, if we admit Michelson's null result as a fact. This was the first path which led me to the special theory

of relativity. Since then I have come to believe that the motion of the Earth cannot be detected by any optical experiment, though the Earth is revolving around the sun."

Of course, he, just like Galileo supposedly did, also had to add those last few words to reaffirm his belief in heliocentrism, thus making sure nobody thinks for a second that he would actually dare to challenge the status quo. Newton must also have had similar thoughts when he decided to no longer include his Proposition 43 in the second and third editions of the Principia. This barely known proposition of his, which tells us how even in his theories geocentrism would be a valid consideration, reads as follows:

"In order for the Earth to be at rest in the center of the system of the Sun, Planets, and Comets, there is required both universal gravity and another force in addition that acts on all bodies equally according to the quantity of matter in each of them and is equal and opposite to the accelerative gravity with which the Earth tends to the Sun (...). Since this force is equal and opposite to its gravity toward the Sun, the Earth can truly remain in equilibrium between these two forces and be at rest. And thus celestial bodies can move around the Earth at rest, as in the Tychonic system."

So, to summerize it all, those who want to claim that the Earth is in fact moving will only have two choices, both of which are absolutely damning for their worldview one way or another. There is simply no escaping the uncomfortable dichotomy: they either have make the claim that the air over the Earth is somehow attached to it, in which case there's no Earth-based Coriolis effect and all of their claims of "observational evidence" go right out the window by default, or they can insist on such a Coriolis effect and be left with no rational way of explaining why it can supposedly be seen only in a select few cases, but never in others. Indeed, if one has any humility, this would be the point to admit to himself that he has been deceived and it is simply no longer possible to deny the obvious fact that the Earth stands still. Consequently, as it's claimed to have been formed into a globe by "gravitational forces" as well as its own rotation, both of which are now debunked, we can conclude once again that it can't possibly be a sphere, an "oblate spheroid", or anything of the sort.

Outer space, the hoax of a century

Now that it has been established that there is no such thing as gravity or Earth-based movement, it's time to look into the portion of the deception that's just as big as those claims were, but perhaps even more significant in regards of our daily lives. Namely, the idea that the sky above our head is an endlessly expanding vacuum called "outer space". Although even ancient civilizations, such as the Greeks and Babylonians developed cosmologies that included the idea of a celestial realm beyond the Earth, it was the so-called "Copernican Revolution" of the 16th century that would truly separate us from that region and contribute to the concept of "outer space". Then later on, Kepler's laws and Gelileo's telescope observations further reinforced the idea of such a place as a distinct realm, and finally, the first known use of the phrase "outer space" with the currently accepted meaning of *the space immediately outside the Earth's atmosphere*" was recorded in 1842. While there is claimed to be no clear boundary between our "atmosphere" and "space", a working definition - established for practical purposes - called the *Kármán line* marks the official boundary between aeronautics and astronautics at an altitude of 100 kilometers. The density of the air that's supposed to be "wrapped around" the Earth is claimed to simply decrease gradually as the altitude increases, eventually reaching the point of "intergalactic space" - the physical space between supposed galaxies -, where there are hardly any gas molecules to be found at all, becoming the closest possible approximation of a perfect vacuum. In fact, while the air we breathe contains about 10^{19} (ten quintillion) molecules per cubic centimeter, giving us a pressure of 14.7 psi - pound per square inch (or 760 Torr) -, this farther region of the sky above us is claimed to be so extremely rarefied that it only has a single molecule in a cubic centimeter on an average, resulting a pressure of roughly 10^{-17} (one hundred-quadrillionth) Torr, allowing all the supposed celestial bodies to move freely with effectively no friction.

And this brings us to exactly what the issue with the whole concept of "outer space" is: it's supposed to be a system that is essentially void of gases, but somehow takes place adjacent to our pressurized system with plenty of air to breathe – with no barrier between the two realms to separate them. As incredible as such an idea might seem, unfortunately, it would be a physical impossibility, as it would violate the most fundamental and universal of all natural laws; the second law of thermodynamics. This law of nature states that *the total entropy of an isolated system tends to increase over time*. Although in practice, a perfectly isolated system – one that does not exchange energy or matter with its surroundings - does not actually exist and it is merely a concept often used in physics to simplify the analysis of certain physical phenomena, however, the law applies to all of the natural world nonetheless. In short, it means that heat always has the tendency to flow from hot to cold, energy invariably transitions from a state of concentration to one of dispersion, and - most pertinently – high gas pressure always moves to low gas pressure, without exception. The reason this is considered a natural law in the first place is, of course, because there has never been a single example of it being violated, and the moment it would be, it should cease to exist as a law. As even the famous and exceptionally highly esteemed British astronomer, astrophysicist, and mathematician, Arthur S. Eddington wrote about it in his 1928 book, *The Nature of the Physical World* (p. 74):

"The law that entropy always increases holds, I think, the supreme position among the laws of Nature. If someone points out to you that your pet theory of the universe is in disagreement with Maxwell's equations - then so much the worse for Maxwell's equations. If it is

found to be contradicted by observation - well, these experimentalists do bungle things sometimes. But if your theory is found to be against the Second Law of Thermodynamics I can give you no hope; there is nothing for it to collapse in deepest humiliation."

Indeed, that is precisely all that the concept of "outer space" could ever hope to do in light of this most basic law of nature. It is a widely known, basic fact that nature inherently abhors vacuums, which is why it cannot be found anywhere and can only be created artificially. This simple fact that's observable for anyone used to be so obvious that for most of human history, the very idea of even just a tiny space that has nothing in it was completely unthinkable. Not to mention that the idea of any vacuum being right next to a region of non-vacuum also violates the universal gas laws. According to Encyclopædia Britannica, general gas behavior is as follows:

"The remarkable feature of gases is that they appear to have no structure at all. They have neither a definite size nor shape, whereas ordinary solids have both a definite size and a definite shape, and liquids have a definite size, or volume, even though they adapt their shape to that of the container in which they are placed. Gases will completely fill any closed container; their properties depend on the volume of a container but not on its shape."

Furthermore, it is of the utmost importance that we understand and remember that the very definition of *gas pressure* implies that it cannot possibly created, let alone maintained without containment. Let us now examine the definitions from some of the highest profile sources to have this crucial point made perfectly clear for us:

- Grc.nasa.gov, written by Nancy Hall, Research Scientist/ Aerospace Engineer at NASA Glenn Research Center: *"The molecules of a gas are in constant, random motion and frequently collide with each other and with the walls of any container. (...) As the gas* *molecules collide with the walls of a container, (...) the molecules impart momentum to the walls, producing a force **perpendicular** to the wall. The sum of the forces of all the molecules striking the wall divided by the area of the wall is defined to be the **pressure**."*

- Bbc.co.uk, written by an anonymous state-approved science journalist: *"As the particles of a gas collide with the walls of their container, they exert a force on these walls. Gas pressure is the name given to the force exerted by gas particles colliding with the wall of their container."*

- Inspiritvr.com (founded by Stanford University researchers), written by Shrinithi Mahadevan, science journalist: *"In the case of a gas, pressure is the force exerted by the gaseous molecules on the vessel that holds them. Gas particles move quickly and randomly in straight lines, colliding with both each other and the walls of their container. The greater the number of collisions that occur with the container walls, the higher the pressure of the gas."*

- Shiken.ai, written by AI built by official data: *"To understand gas pressure and temperature, let's imagine a closed container with gas particles flying around inside. Sometimes, these particles hit the walls of the container and bounce back inwards, creating a force outward on the container. This force per unit area is called gas pressure (...)"*

- Tec-science.com, written by anonymous Tec-science journalists: *"The pressure of gases is caused on a microscopic level by collisions of the gas molecules with its container walls."*

- Techtarget.com, written by Robert Sheldon, technical consultant and technology writer: *"A gas has no fixed shape or volume. The atoms or molecules that make up the gas fill the container* *that holds them. The gas expands until it is uniformly distributed throughout the container,* **even in the presence of gravity. If not confined to a container, a gas disperses into space.**"

Additionally, the popular AI application, Chat Generative Pre-trained Transformer (ChatGPT), will give us the following, surprisingly instructive answer when asked *"can there be gas pressure without a container?":*

"No, gas pressure typically requires a container or some form of confinement to exist. Gas pressure is a measure of the force exerted by gas molecules as they collide with the walls of their container or with other surfaces. Without a container or some form of confinement, gas molecules would disperse freely into the surrounding environment, and the concept of pressure as we understand it would not apply. Gas pressure arises due to the random motion of gas molecules. When gas molecules move, they collide with each other and with the surfaces of their container. These collisions result in a net force that we perceive as pressure. The more frequent and energetic these molecular collisions, the higher the gas pressure. In the absence of a container or confinement, gas molecules continue to move freely and disperse into the surrounding space, leading to an equilibrium where their concentration is uniform throughout the available volume. In such a scenario, there is no localized pressure that can be measured because the gas molecules have no boundaries to collide with. Therefore, gas pressure is a property associated with confined gases, and it requires a container or enclosure to exist in a measurable and meaningful way."

Hopefully at this point it is needless to say that the aforementioned *"surrounding environment"* that the gas molecules would admittedly disperse into - in the world of heliocentrism - is called "outer space". The existence of which would therefore mean that the pressure of our "atmosphere" would equalize with that of the endless, expanding void of "intergalactic space" and we would have an extremely strong vacuum of 10^{-17} Torr even at ground level, leaving us with no air to breathe. This fact is further proven by Boyle's law, developed in the 17th century by English natural philosopher Robert Boyle, who conducted experiments with air pumps to investigate the properties of air and the effects of creating a vacuum. His law describes the inverse relationship between the pressure and volume of a gas, meaning that the larger the container that a given amount of gas is confined within, the lower the pressure will be. Consequently, the simplest way to create a vacuum artificially is also by increasing the volume of a container; for example, by blocking the tip of a syringe with no needle, then pulling on its plunger. This in turn, of course, means that an expanding universe would also dilute its own air density rapidly, including that of our own, which, however, we know has always remained stable.

In order to reconcile the rather uncomfortable contradiction between these basic facts of physics and modern cosmology, pseudoscientists invoke none other than, of course, the usual trump-card; the "force of gravity". Not knowing - or not willing to admit – that it is not actually a force but merely a concept, a figment of imagination, they claim that it is in fact pulling all the gas molecules downward. Which consequently begs the rhetorical questions: why isn't all of the air being pulled down right to the very surface of the Earth, why is there a pressure gradient, and what determines which molecules get to escape into "space", as some of them are claimed to do? Unfortunately for the model's pundits, as even the last lines of the quote from Mr. Sheldon emphasized it for us, there is simply no saving grace for the model even if we accepted the assumed presence of so-called "gravity". This is mainly because even the paradigm that would have us accept it as a "force" still describes it as an especially weak one, whereas the opposing law of entropy is possibly the strongest, most fundamental rule in existence, which cannot be violated by any means. Perhaps to combat this obvious fact, some of the more persistent zealots of the model also make the claim that the "weight" of the gas molecules form a sort of "column of gas", which is somehow pushing down on itself to keep itself from dispersing into the "vacuum of space". This idea is so essential for the model that the phrase "atmospheric pressure", defined as *the force per unit area exerted against a surface by the weight of the air above that surface*, was even invented in support of it. Alas, this assertion is not at all plausible, and those who have been paying attention so far might have already figured out the issue with it: gases simply don't behave like that. As stated earlier in the definition, they have neither structure, nor a definite volume, nor a shape. Gas molecules are in constant motion, simply moving in random directions in a straight line at a high velocity, always filling up their container – the necessary antecedent of gas pressure – thus taking its shape.

Yet another claim they often make in a feeble attempt to defend the impossibility that is "outer space", is that the pressure gradient that's present in the air is by itself a sufficient argument to counteract entropy and all known gas behavior. They would claim that the air that's otherwise also supposed to be "wrapped around the Earth" gets so rarefied as we move up in altitude that it simply reaches out into the nearly perfect vacuum of "space" until it essentially becomes one with it. However, not only does this contradict their assertion that there is a "force of gravity" somehow pulling down on gas molecules and preventing them from dispersing into "space", but also goes against the official narrative of "atmospheric" behavior. Which is to say that the ability of a "planet" to retain its "atmosphere" depends on factors such as its mass, temperature, "gravitational force", and the composition of the "atmosphere" itself, meaning that "planets" with stronger "gravitational forces" are supposed to be better at retaining their "atmospheres", while smaller bodies, like some moons, may lose gases more readily. The escape of gases from a "planet's" "atmosphere" into "space" is a process known as "atmospheric escape" or "exoplanetary escape".

Specifically in Earth's case, the "atmosphere" is claimed to be held in place quite firmly by its "gravitational force", which is apparently strong enough to prevent the majority of gases from escaping into "space". A few exceptions exist to this rule, which we shall now examine. Firstly, there are the trace amounts of hydrogen and helium in Earth's "atmosphere", which are very light gases and thus a small fraction of them can gradually escape into space over geological timescales. The primary mechanism for their loss is supposed to be what they call "thermal escape", where some gas molecules gain sufficient kinetic energy from high temperatures to overcome Earth's "gravitational pull". However, the loss of these kinds of gases from Earth is extremely slow and has a negligible impact on our "atmosphere" overall. There are also some heavier gases, such as oxygen and nitrogen, which are claimed to be able to escape from the "upper layers" of the "atmosphere" under certain conditions as well, eg. during solar storms or intense solar activity, when high-energy particles from the Sun can supposedly help them in the process of leaving our airspace. Of course, this loss is still claimed to be relatively slow and have a very minor impact on Earth's overall "atmospheric" composition. Lastly, a small fraction of the water vapor that's created at surface level is also claimed to be able to reach the "upper atmosphere" and be dissociated by the way of solar ultraviolet radiation, leading to the escape of a small amount of hydrogen and oxygen atoms. Other than these miniscule changes, the Earth's "atmosphere" has supposedly remained stable and supportive of life for billions of years.

Both the – official - *"column of air"* idea and the *"gradation into a nearly perfect vacuum"* idea are inherently based on the notion that the "atmosphere" consists of "layers of air" that are somehow built upon one another, pressing mostly just downwards. Of course, knowing how gases actually behave in reality, we can state that this is obviously a ridiculous claim to make. They don't form layers, but instead they always fill up all of the available volume, even if there is gradation in them. So the fact remains that the gas molecules still require the walls of a container to press upon in order to let them create gas pressure, and that they are also bouncing off each other constantly and rapidly. This simply means that the highest pressure measured at ground level inevitably needs even the much lower pressure measured at a high altitude to be supported by the wall of the container as well, in order for any pressurization to be possible.

Many would find this hard to imagine, as they believe that any kind of pressure gradient can in fact only be the result of "the vacuum of space" being above us, however, they could not be more wrong in this assertion. The fact is, nearly all of the gases on Earth are produced at ground level, whether they are created by geological, or by biological means. This simple fact alone would already provide a sufficient explanation for the gradient in the pressure, but there's also the gradient in the air's temperature - which is another obvious cause for it - that should be taken into consideration. Luckily, all of this can easily be demonstrated to anyone, as there are even some small-scale examples of gas pressure with a gradient in it, such as inside of a bottle garden, or any container that's being heated from one direction – both of which are also analogous to how it all works in nature.

Another reason there can be no "column of air" pushing downwards is that such a notion would imply that objects weigh more when in a pressurized environment, however, in reality they actually weigh more in a vacuum – a fact that can be tested in any home-made vacuum chamber.

The thing for which there is unfortunately not a single example, nor can there be, is gas pressure without a container - its necessary antecedent.

Unfortunately for the fanatics of the model, if the Earth or any other so-called "planet" or "star", along with the air that is supposed to be "wrapped around it", was actually located inside of an endless, vacuous void, there wouldn't just be some occasional loss of a few gas molecules. In fact, there would be an instantaneous, almost explosive dispersion of all gases into "space", followed by an immediate equalization of the "atmospheric" pressure to the nearly perfect, 10^{-17} Torr vacuum of "intergalactic space". That is, if any kind of pressure could even be created with no containment in the first place, which it couldn't.

For those who might still have a hard time accepting or visualizing just how quickly we would lose all of our air, there are a number of simple examples that can demonstrate it. Perhaps the most available and well-known of these are vacuum cleaners, whose operating principle is creating a pressure differential that draws air and particles into its cleaning mechanism by the apparent "sucking" force that's generated. While the created vacuum itself does not technically "suck" in the way we commonly think of it, as there is no actual force of attraction pulling things into it, the law of entropy is employed to make objects in the higher pressure environment rush into the tube of the appliance. To make things worse for heliocentrism, the average strength of the vacuum created by such a device is only around 11.6 psi (600 Torr), a pressure that is merely a bit over 20% lower than that of the "atmosphere" surrounding it. If we were to compare this to the 19 orders of magnitude stronger, 10^{-17} Torr vacuum of "intergalactic space" that supposedly surrounds our entire known world – not to mention expanding endlessly -, we can easily imagine just how quickly we would lose all of our air, along with most objects, too. Another fairly simple example would be thermos bottles, which can have a vacuum strength of up to 0.00002 psi (10^{-3} Torr) in them, which would, of course, instantly and fully get filled up with air as soon as they're opened up. Inversely, one could use a vacuum chamber to test out what happens if a sealed container with any gas in it is placed inside and opened up. Needless to say, there will be no slow trickling of the molecules or gradient of any sort as the model would suggest, simply an explosive burst as all of the gases immediately vacate the small container to rapidly and evenly spread out to fill the larger volume of the chamber. Although some of them would clearly have to find their way into the smaller container as well, as that is now part of the bigger one, the pressure would be equalized throughout the entire chamber. This means that if its volume is large enough – just like in the case of an Earth that's placed in "outer space" -, the released gases will essentially make no difference and the original vacuum of the chamber will be what's measurable throughout all of the available space.

All of these rules do, of course, also apply to other supposed "planets", and especially "nebulae" and "stars" - which are actually claimed to be primarily composed of gas. Obviously, this is yet another massive issue for the model, especially without the magical glue of "gravity" that is supposed to somehow hold them together, defying the law of entropy as well as basic gas laws.

Therefore, as uncomfortable as it may be for many with a certain belief, we have to conclude that the realm of this Earth cannot possibly be an open system, and must have some kind of containment around it to make pressurization possible and obey the most universal law of nature – regardless of how much some would want it to be different "just in this one case" *(special pleading)*.

Fearmongering cranked up

Fear is a natural and adaptive response to perceived threats or danger, but chronic, excessive, or irrational fear can lead to a range of negative consequences in a human's life. Living in fear can have profound and detrimental effects on an individual's physical, emotional, and psychological well-being, not to mention that it makes its victim more susceptible for manipulation, especially if one were to promise the alleviation of the perceived threat to him. With the advent of the globe-Earth theory, as well as the whole of the Copernican worldview and especially the idea that the sky is an infinite vacuum, a plethora of new narrative opportunities opened up for oppressive governments that were looking to instill as much fear into the public as possible without openly waging war against them.

As we have already touched on it in the preface, proven by numerous quotes from various authors and people in high places, there is currently a hidden power at play in the world which wants to conquer it. This power is often referred to as the *global power elite,* the *shadow government,* or the *deep state* and consists of less than ten thousand well-connected and mostly extremely wealthy and influential people who are scattered across the world. The reason this group of people received such names is because they are in fact so powerful that even nation states bow before them, meaning that they don't need to obey the laws and rules like a regular citizen does - and therefore no one can hold them responsible for any of their deeds. Not only that, but they also made sure to actually subdue leading politicians either by promising them massive financial gains, a chance to become "immortalized" by getting into the history books, or by putting them into a sort of incriminating situation, making a record of it, then using it to blackmail them. For these world-wide supergovernmental powers it has become increasingly important to keep humanity in a constant state of fear by any means necessary.

Having learned over the centuries that the more violent dictatorships – especially in the West - tend to collapse relatively quickly due to their subjects revolting against them, they have been working on the "more sophisticated" and much more durable fearmongering-based methods of mass control for some time, which they have been continuously testing on us all. As a result of this, over the past few centuries, and especially these last few decades, we've been forced to experience various propagandas of fear, which managed to reach us mainly through the monopolistic media network empire owned by the powers that be. However, making it possible for them to push a large part of humanity into a constant state of fear and thus having them make irrational decisions much more often while also becoming more easily influenced are not the only advantages of this insidious method. It can also allow the governments in question to gain significant popularity, apparent credibility and - probably the greatest advantage of all – legitimacy for the existence of the state itself, by successfully "averting" a fictitious disaster which, "thanks to the leadership's skilled and timely efforts", did not end up happening as predicted. Such methods of reinforcing the illusion of the usefulness and efficiency of the state have always been exploited more and more as even some of the otherwise very obedient and gullible taxpayers started to completely lose faith in the whole of the ruling class due to their increasingly blatant, immeasurable greed, corruption and dishonesty. Not to mention the fact that a major, impending – and very much imaginary - catastrophe conjured up by a government can easily serve as a highly effective distraction in a situation of political distress and possibly even restore the public's faith in an otherwise failing government, thus saving them from getting dismantled.

What serves as the basis of this method of mass manipulation is known as the Hegelian dialectic, often referred to as the "dialectical method" or simply "dialectics". It is a philosophical approach developed by the German philosopher Georg Wilhelm Friedrich Hegel in the late 18th and early 19th centuries, working as a method of inquiry and a way of understanding the development of ideas and reality through the process of contradiction and resolution. To put it into practice, government officials would simply need to come up with a partially or fully made up problem which their lackey media will be tasked to propagate nationwide, then wait for the fear-based reaction of the public, and finally, provide their own so-called "solution" for it. The core of this method of scaring people into obedience is also often referred to as *fear-based mind control*. If successful, this endeavor will allow the government to steer the given political narrative as they see fit, letting them achieve things that their people would have otherwise never agreed upon or accepted. In the most heinous cases - just like we've seen during the most recent so-called "pandemic" from 2020 to 2022 -, this can lead to such convincing-power which may even have a large part of the public willingly give up most of their basic human rights, essentially letting themselves become completely enslaved, just for some fleeting illusion of "safety".

This is one of the main reasons why so many governments rely frequently on scare-tactics, telling their people what they should be afraid for the next few months or years and why they should put all their faith and trust in their leaders. They would always have us fear the possibility of a "nuclear war", the effects of so-called "global warming" or "climate change" (the three of which are to be detailed in other chapters), the ever-looming "terrorism", those elusive "alien visitors", asteroids, comets and, of course, the gravely dreaded "viruses" (yet another example of pseudoscience - a topic for a whole different book) and "pandemics" that somehow always seem to come and go with far less impact on human life than most of the governments' reactions to them. Of course, they will make sure to remind us "just how much worse it could have been" if they had not intervened by forcing us to obey their newest Draconian edicts that generally push us into more poverty and rob us of our freedom, and one will only see through their lies if he's willing to take a good look behind the proverbial curtain, or at the countries where no such tyranny took place, and see that those places were actually much better off in every way.

Another, lesser-known "danger" that they occasionally like to scare us with is "gamma-ray bursts", extremely energetic and highly luminous explosions that are claimed to be among the most powerful phenomena in the universe, releasing intense bursts of gamma-ray radiation. Certain types are assumed to be the result of the "core collapse" of massive stars, while others are thought to be generated by the merger of compact objects such as neutron stars or black holes. A single burst of this kind, they say, can emit as much energy as the Sun will over its "entire 10-billion-year lifetime", capable of frying everybody on Earth. An "entertaining" fairy-tale, indeed, but nothing more.

Speaking of fairy-tales, there are also the so-called "wandering black holes", which are claimed to be such "black holes" that are not bound to a specific star or galactic center and are instead moving through "space". As we are told, if one of these should come too close to the Earth, it would cause mile-high tides in the seas that could "kill millions". Not to mention that, being a black hole, it would naturally be invisible – bad news for anyone who would want to see this phenomenon.

THE GLOBAL DECEPTION

I even have personal experience when it comes to falling for pseudoscientific duplicity from the part of the powers that (should not) be. Decades ago, during my childhood, I once had the misfortune of watching the TV when a "news report" was on, where they told us all about how it "seems likely" that the Earth will be hit by a giant asteroid within a few years, most likely destroying all life on it. Hearing this, I suddenly felt a kind of deep, burning, consuming fear that I've never known before. For the next few weeks, I felt depressed, lethargic and could hardly sleep – until someone finally told me that there have been many such "predictions" in history, but not once did any of them actually come true. Upon hearing this baffling fact, my fear soon started to dissipate and it may well had been the first time I realized that I've been deceived. From that point on, I always took anything I've heard on the "news" with a huge grain of salt, lest I become fooled again by a scientific-sounding but nonetheless fictional scary story. Evidently smartly so, because as it turns out, essentially the whole of commercial media has been taken over by the United States Central Intelligence Agency (CIA) during the Cold War era within an operation called Mockingbird. It was a covert program that involved the recruitment of journalists, media organizations, and other individuals in the media industry for the purpose of influencing and manipulating public opinion, both domestically and internationally. Today it's all out in the open, mainstream historians don't even deny it all happened. It's claimed to have started in the early 1950s and remained hidden for a long time, only to be revealed and turned into the subject of public scrutiny and controversy in the 1970s, when investigations into various intelligence agency activities, including those of the CIA, happened to take place. However, many details remain classified to this day, and the full extent of the program's activities may never even be known. Nonetheless, one thing is certain: their disinformation efforts did not end there, which is a fact that's also proven by the 1981 remarks of William J. Casey, as quoted in the preface.

Of course, one does not even need to be fed blatant propaganda from the news to become scared of certain pseudoscientific claims, thanks to the existence of science fiction movies and television series. Similarly to the fear of asteroids, getting startled by every little noise or flashing light in the dark, thinking that aliens have come to abduct us, has certainly caused many of us quite a few sleepless nights as children after watching some programming about such occurrences in a film the previous day. But that is, after all, why it's called "programming".

This is also why it's important to keep in mind that most of the "scary scenarios" listed earlier could not even theoretically exist without the heliocentric globe-model and all its related speculations and stories, as well as the branches of pseudoscience created just to support them. When it comes to incoming asteroids, comets, space invaders, gamma ray bursts or wandering black holes, their plausibility obviously relies heavily on one's trust in the mainstream cosmology of the world. Fortunately, after reading the previous chapter, we already know that there is no such thing as "outer space", which - to the regret of science fiction fans – is where all of these alleged "dangers" are purported to come from, therefore we can simply disregard them as hoaxes without further ado. Which is, of course, not to say that the ruling class won't do everything in their power to try and convince us otherwise. Other than the decades-long bombardment of the public with space-propaganda through the whole of the entertainment industry, they often use more tactile methods of deception as well.

The most prevalent of these are the so-called "meteorites" that are often presented as irrefutable proof of objects being able to drop in from "outer space" and hit the Earth. A "meteorite" is claimed to be a fragment of a meteoroid (a small celestial body, often a fragment from a comet or asteroid) that survives its passage through Earth's "atmosphere" and lands on its surface. These objects are called "meteoroids" when they are in space, "meteors" when they are streaking through the Earth's "atmosphere", and "meteorites" when they have landed on the Earth. They are categorized as either "stony meteorites", composed mainly of silicate minerals, "iron meteorites", composed of iron and nickel, and "stony-iron meteorites", a combination of the other two. Although "meteorite falls" are claimed to have been witnessed and recorded by humans for centuries, there have been few examples of what would allegedly be physical evidence of it over the past few decades. The origin of such rocks and hunks of iron is highly questionable, and not only because we know they simply couldn't possibly have come from the sky. The larger ones among them are supposed to have created massive craters - that can range from tens of meters to multiple kilometers in diameter - upon their impact. However, if this was the case, there should obviously be a huge meteorite in the middle of the crater, with countless smaller, but still gigantic chunks scattered around it. Yet, all that is ever claimed to be found at these sites are no more than a few, relatively small pieces of rock or metal, while the rest of it is said to have – conveniently – either buried beneath the surface, bounce "back to space", or somehow become "vaporized". The only pieces found are claimed to be what's known as "meteorite shrapnel"; small chunks that broke off the meteorite upon impact.

The biggest issue is that there has never been an uncut, verifiable footage of someone observing one of these falling balls of fire as it hits the Earth, then immediately getting to the impact site and showing the object to be a piece of rock or iron and nickel. It is true that there have been at least a few sightings of objects flying through the sky while emitting smoke and fire, then hitting the ground, throughout the past decades, however, they all seem to have proven nothing more than either some sort of military experiment or a - rather elaborate - conspiracy being afoot. Instead of actual meteorites, all that had been ever found were what looked like some kind of spherical, or in some cases cylindrical, firework with a hole on it to emit the smoke and fire as it's shooting through the sky. Some of these were shown to be made of solid metal, while others looked like some type of coil wire that could be heated up to the point where it glows red, similar to the one in a car's cigarette lighter, but much larger. These apparent "meteors" always come down from the same direction at very similar angles, as if they were being shot out from planes just for the sole purpose of creating the illusion of something actually falling into our earthly realm from "outer space". Needless to say, if that actually were the case, we should be able to see them move in every possible direction - including upwards, due to the supposed occasional "bouncing" upon impact. Which, of course, doesn't mean that we definitely won't see such a thing sooner or later - as the perpetrators of the hoax clearly have the means to do it - to better convince the onlookers, but alas, the fact remains that the verifiable evidence of actual meteorites is still missing. Which is clearly something that also bothers "them", which must be the reason that there are entire museums dedicated to the cause, presenting pieces of rocks or metals that are claimed to be real meteorites, seasoned with wild, often fear-inducing stories and computer-generated simulations telling and showing the details about the supposed "meteorites" and the circumstances and consequences of their impact. Unfortunately for us, though, we wouldn't possibly have a way of verifying most of their claims, and neither do they.

An excellent example of how this hoax can be utilized by the establishment a recent asteroid mining mission was claimed to have been helpful as it may well hit the Earth in a few 100 years and studying it can help us find ways of stopping it) (the idea of outer space is also a great opportunity for the powers that be to get infinite funding for any space-related project as long as they manage to convince the taxpayers that it will eventually greatly benefit them – or at least their great-granchildren's grandchildren.

Then there's the case of so-called "meteor showers", which are claimed to be large numbers of tiny, mostly no bigger than pebble-sized pieces of comet-debris (often referred to as "shooting stars") appear to radiate from a specific point in the night sky. As the story goes, the occurrence of such "meteors" are caused by the Earth passing through the debris left behind by a comet as it "orbits" the Sun. Alas, apparently they all get vaporized – which is the process that is claimed to make them glow, too - and therefore there is – conveniently – once again no physical evidence left for us to examine. Which brings us to the problem with this supposition, that is the same as it is with the idea that the luminaries are something physical; there's simply no way for us to know if that is indeed the case, and that they are not simply just mere dots of light on the sky.

Yet another scare-tactic, which is more of a philosophical one, stems from the powers that be feeding us the notion that we live on a "planet". Namely that they can tell us that our world has water covering about 71% of its surface, which inherently implies that both space and resources are quite limited and will become increasingly scarce for us all as the population grows, and therefore our reproduction needs to be stopped at a certain point - otherwise worldwide mass starvation and overcrowding could occur. Regardless of how unfounded this assumption is, it is in fact what fuels the whole of the depopulation-agenda that most major governments and so-called "philanthropists" are so very fond of nowadays. An especially important aspect of this scare is the claim that there's only so much so-called "fossil fuel" available in the world before it runs out for good, and thus the governments have "no choice" but to limit what kind of vehicles a citizen can purchase and how often or how far he should be allowed to drive it. However, the idea of "fossils" itself, as well as fuels supposedly originating from them, are a part of yet another sizeable hoax, which will be detailed in a later chapter. Let is just be said here that what's known as the *abiotic oil theory* – the notion that crude oil is not a product of the decayed remains of ancient plants and animals, but purely chemical processes deep within the Earth, involving inorganic substances like carbon and hydrogen - has proven to be the most likely explanation, as old oil wells that have already dried up tend to produce again later.

Finally, there is also a kind of psychological warfare that's being waged against us by making us believe the aspect of heliocentrism that we are in fact "insignificant on the cosmic scale" and should think of ourselves as nothing more than a meaningless speck of dust drifting aimlessly through the endless "space". Needless to say, this lie has a great use for an oppressive regime as long as they can successfully feed it to their subjects, since those that do believe it tend to become much more docile, embittered, nihilistic and apathetic because of it, making it far less likely that they would ever want to rebel against their tyrants.

All things considered, in reality it is safe to say that we hardly have any rational reason to be afraid of anything nowadays, except for, of course, the rampant fear-campaigns of the governments, as well as their actions which often border insanity and cause nothing but pain and suffering to us all as their subjects. Although, sadly enough, these days many people seem to find their lives to be so dull and sterile that they actually welcome any propaganda of fear with open arms, and often even hope for a previously prophesied disaster to happen just so that they get to experience something out of the ordinary and sufficiently stimulating.

The nuclear weapon hoax

As it was referred to earlier, it is not only the notion that objects or alien beings can enter our world through the sky which relies entirely on pseudoscientific speculations, but, no doubt to the surprise of many, just as much the idea of so-called "nuclear weapons". Before going into the details of how the nuclear bomb-hoax was built up, it's important to note that the fact that they don't exist doesn't mean that nuclear power plants cannot either. Although they are both claimed to be based on nuclear reactions, they would operate in fundamentally different ways and serve very different purposes. Nuclear power plants utilize controlled nuclear fission reactions, typically using enriched uranium or plutonium as fuel. In these reactors, the rate of fission is carefully controlled to maintain a steady release of heat sustained over a long period, which is then used to generate steam and drive turbines connected to generators, producing electricity.

Nuclear bombs, on the other hand, are said to utilize uncontrolled nuclear fission or fusion reactions. In fission bombs (like atomic bombs - A-bombs), a critical mass of fissile material is supposed to be rapidly brought together, leading to an uncontrolled chain reaction, resulting in a sudden, massive release of energy in the form of an explosion. Compared to that, in the case of fusion bombs (like hydrogen bombs - H-bombs), the tremendous heat and pressure generated by a fission bomb would be claimed to initiate a secondary fusion reaction, resulting in an explosion many times greater than those created by A-bombs.

Perhaps not too surprisingly, the idea of nuclear weapons was conceived in a work of science fiction, namely the short story *The World Set Free* by British author Herbert George Wells, first serialized in 1913 and later published as a novel in 1914. In this, Wells imagined a future where "atomic bombs of indefinite power" were used in warfare, leading to significant changes worldwide, exploring the consequences of this new and devastating form of - imaginary - weaponry.

While it is easy to imagine how one would research and test the process required to make a nuclear power plant work, it would be obviously impossible to do the same in the case of nuclear bomb, as even the smallest amount of ingredient would supposedly destroy everything and everyone in a large radius when experimenting. This is clearly the reason why nuclear power plants had been built and are constantly operating and creating electricity all across the world, while there's little evidence of even the attempted production of more than a couple nuclear bombs in all of history, and even less of their actual usage – although, the façade of their mass production is undoubtedly ever-present.

In fact, there seems to be no scientific evidence supporting the claim that "nukes" are by any means a plausible idea. However, the powers that be work hard to make us believe it, since inventing and selling the story of a bomb so powerful that it's capable of wiping out an entire city in the blink of an eye, leaving nothing but a huge crater and lethal amounts of radiation in its place, is the perfect scare-tactic for any empire that wishes to reinforce its prestigious position in the world. And the best part is, there's absolutely no need for the actual weapon in question to even exist for the scare to be successful. In fact, all that's needed is to make the common folk believe that it is real by building facilities and creating taskforces that are claimed to serve the purpose of the research of projects connected to it, along with creating conventional explosions far away and obscure enough to sell it as "nuclear". By doing that, as a bonus, they will also get to pump unfathomable amounts of the taxpayers' money into such facilities – something that governments never seemed to have any issue doing in the case of other state institutions anyway – thus laundering and stealing most of it.

Gigantic industrial facilities were therefore built with hundreds of millions of taxpayer dollars for the sake of the "top-secret" Manhattan Project (starting in 1939, originally named "Manhattan Engineer District") – the research and development project undertaken by the United States, the United Kingdom, and Canada – during World War II. The goal of this project – costing the taxpayers a total of more than $2 billion (not adjusted for inflation) by the end - was to create the first A-bomb as a hasty response to the (false) rumor that the Germans have already started building one, which itself originated from a small group of Jewish refugees who fled Germany. These included Leó Szilárd, Hungarian physicist and inventor, and the also Hungarian theoretical physicist and mathematician Eugene Paul Wigner (originally Jen' Pál Wigner). The two of them informed Einstein himself (who happened to hate the Germans and non-Zionist nationalism in general), who then "warned" the U.S. government by sending their historic letter (of lies) to President Franklin D. Roosevelt.

Carrying out the Manhattan Project also served the purpose of convincing the world that building such a weapon is not something that is replicable by just anyone, as it would be extreme costly to even hope to make an attempt at it. Which is, no doubt, a notion that would beg the question for any critical thinker: wouldn't it be easier, faster, and safer to just use all that time and all those invaluable resources in the middle of a massive war to simply fuel the conventional war machine that has already been proven to work for decades, as opposed to trying something so new and conceptual that it can barely even hold up in theory? In fact, it was deemed so unlikely to succeed that some of the scientists working on it even noted that they would be surprised if a workable bomb came out of the whole of the research when they were approaching its date of testing.

As Akio Nakatani, Japanese professor of applied mathematics and statistics wrote on the topic in his 2017 book *Death Object - Exploding the Nuclear Weapons Hoax* after detailing just how difficult and complicated it would have been to initiate the supposed explosive fission process required to even theoretically have a chance at making an A-bomb function as intended (p. 36-37):

"The pre-bang checklist requires incredibly elaborate and precise calculations to insure that a sufficient quantity of fast neutrons, going at 'fast' enough speeds as they blast through the material, are likely enough to hit a target nucleus, with a high enough proportion of those encounters of the right type (breaking apart the target nucleus rather than being captured by it or any of a number of other possible sub-optimal outcomes) resulting in enough neutrons being liberated in the collisions to propagate the process onward. And, most crucially, that all this will happen in just the right amount of time for an explosive outcome. It's a real Goldilocks problem because the target nuclei are few and far between (...). I don't mean to shirk the hard labor of stepping through all the analytical details and unraveling how or whether 'they' (the past and current bomb scientists) got all the stuff above just right. But now a conceptual roadblock rears up against us. It's a fundamental tenet of science that results are described openly, in sufficient detail for replication by skilled readers. But for safety reasons this standard protocol doesn't apply to nukes. And the tight security leaves us with no way to probe the truth and resolve the workability of these claims (...)"

In essence, this is what *compartmentalization*, the concept related to information security and the organization of sensitive or classified information, is all about; no one can spill the secret, because no one gets to see the big picture as a whole. This is precisely the tool they used to allow for the employment of as many people in the Manhattan Project as possible while still being able to keep the fakery an airtight secret. Only the top few scientists and military leaders had to know about it being a fakery, everyone else just received a smaller, much more mundane part in it, so they could be made to believe that they're actually helping to build the bomb without ever getting close enough to the leadership to have a chance to start asking uncomfortable questions about the details. Although the exact number of people who participated in the project is difficult to determine precisely, it is estimated to be around 130,000 at its peak, spread out over a complex network of facilities and organizations across multiple locations in the United States. Amassing such a large number of employees and thus having a significant part of the U.S. population know someone that's working on the project was an important part of letting the public feel much more related to and connected with the program. This, of course, also made it far easier to convince them about how "real" all of the purported nuclear technology is, even if the majority only got to work on smaller, less insignificant parts that weren't directly related to the building of the bomb.

Interestingly - and suspiciously -, the Manhattan Project has also become one of the very few "secret" government endeavors that is officially admitted and proudly taught today, while many other, provably real weapon technologies are being kept in the shadows as much as possible – which is what one would expect in such cases anyway. Perhaps just to give more credence to the project, it is today said that the very first computers were mainly used for the calculations of the endeavor, and that the first nuclear reactor - towards the end of 1942 - was also invented and built with the sole purpose of proving the concept of a nuclear chain reaction – even if it's fundamentally different from those supposedly taking place inside of an A-bomb.

Furthermore, there is the much-repeated – and very convenient - excuse that if any government were to start a nuclear war, the enemy might respond in kind, and both countries would surely be reduced to ashes in the end, which they even gave the name *"mutually assured destruction"* to let it sink deep into people's consciousness. This very notion, as well as the fact that governments – and evidently most of the public - universally accept the idea of nukes being real, means that all any of them need to do in order to be considered a "nuclear superpower" is to simply claim to have such a bomb in their possession and point at their facilities (thus preventing less significant, poorer countries from trying to become such superpowers) supposedly built to support its manufacture, and perhaps some of the supposed "nukes", which could very well just be conventional ones, if not empty metal casings. Therefore, even if the construction of nuclear weapons was possible, it would still make no sense for governments to actually build them, let alone to use them, in light of their perceived superiority in military power already being secured anyway.

Of course, this also goes the other way: if an authoritarian government that's looking to invade a foreign country needs to give their people a reason to present another as "hostile" or "dangerous", all they need to do is claim that the other country has a nuke – or any "weapon of mass destruction", for that matter. By the same token, and even just from a logical point of view, there would be no reason for any government to make the fact that they own such a bomb public, other than to instill fear into the masses instead of the governments that may actually pose a threat. It would only make sense for them to keep it a secret buried deep until the very last minute when it's being launched at the enemy, utilizing the element of surprise for a maximal effect. This is actually exactly what they initially did in the case of the Manhattan Project, which was kept a secret until after the two "atomic bombs" had already been dropped, but not so much in any other case since then. However, even this secrecy was likely just a façade to give credence to the implementation of new policies that made it possible for the same government to run any kind of clandestine project or operation without the knowledge of the public by way of "classification" from that point on, claiming that somehow "it's in the nation's best interest" to not even let the taxpayers know about it, who are meanwhile still forced to fund the whole endeavor.

Despite there being clearly no reason for us to – even when viewed from just a logical standpoint - assume that so-called "nukes" actually exist, the powers that be are - to this very day - trying really hard to convince us that we do in fact need to be deathly afraid of such weapons. For this reason, we shall now look deeper into their methods of deception and how they were built up.

On August 6 and 9, 1945, the United States dropped bombs – that were purportedly "atomic" - on the Japanese cities of Hiroshima and Nagasaki, leading to Japan's surrender and the end of World War II. These were the first and, to date, the only alleged instances of actual use of A-bombs in any warfare, while H-bombs are not even claimed to have ever been used anywhere outside of supposed tests. This is said to be due to their destructive power being – conveniently – "too great" and that it would therefore be "too dangerous"; as if that wouldn't be more the reason to use it as the most suitable weapon to quickly and effectively end a war...

At any rate, what made the bombing of the Japanese cities possible is said to be the culmination of the Manhattan Project: the Trinity test, which also marks the beginning of the "atomic age". This was the event where the successful detonation of the first A-bomb – which they named "Gadget" - is claimed to have taken place on July 16, 1945, conducted in a desert in New Mexico, USA. This one was purportedly an implosion-design plutonium bomb, similar in its principle of operation to the one nicknamed "Fat Man" that was later detonated over Nagasaki. Plutonium is not a chemical element that exists in nature, so in order to be able to build such a bomb, uranium first had to be turned into plutonium, which is a process of questionable feasibility to begin with. But even if we assumed that it was possible to create it, only trace amounts, not enough to allow for learning much about it were claimed to have been produced for a large part of the research phase.

Either way, about two months before this test, an officially non-nuclear (and little-known) test - using TNT (trinitrotoluene) – called the 100-Ton Test was carried out, allegedly to study the effects of the blast on various structures and materials to better calibrate the instrumentation for the supposed (nuclear) detonation of the Gadget itself. For the purpose of this test, hundreds of boxes of TNT were stacked on top of a 20 foot high wooden platform, overall weighing roughly 100 tons – hence the name. Tubes of "low-level nuclear material" were also scattered throughout the crates, allegedly to "simulate the radioactive products of a nuclear blast". Although, much more likely to provide a more palpable and measurable amount of radiation in the area after the Gadget itself went off. The explosion of this stack of TNT resulted in a 5-foot (1.52 m) deep and 30-foot (9.14 m) wide blast crater, with the moderately radioactive material dispersed in and around it. Following this test, they drove a lead-lined tank into the crater to collect soil samples as a rehearsal for the main event when, as they claimed, "radiation levels would be intense" at ground zero. The photos and the footage from the event show an explosion rather similar to those of so-called nuclear bombs we see in films, with an initial large ball of fire rising towards the sky to turn into a gigantic cloud of smoke, quite a bit like the "mushroom cloud" that is so characteristic of the – fictional - nukes. In fact, they look so much alike that directors have been caught using the 100-Ton Test footage as a depiction of a "nuclear" explosion on at least a couple occasions. This fact alone should, of course, already prompt every critical thinker to draw the conclusion that there is indeed absolutely no need for a weapon to have a nuclear core in order to be able to cause the expected phenomenon, making it even clearer just how easy the whole fakery is to pull off.

One way the Trinity (Gadget) test-deception itself could have been carried out, as many researchers of the topic suspect, is by two towers with hundreds of tons of TNT on each being built. They would have been far enough from one another so that the military personnel working on one would have had no way to communicate with those working on the other. This way they could be told that the one they're building will be used just for "purposes of comparison", while the other one has the actual "nuke" on it.

Meanwhile, the official story would have us believe that the Gadget bomb - a metal sphere with just a few tons of TNT in it to initiate the "implosion" of its supposed "plutonium core" weighing a few kilograms – was raised to the top of a 100-foot steel tower. The truth about what really went down that faithful day may never be determined with absolute certainty, as there seems to be no uncut footage of all the preparations leading to the detonation available anywhere.

At any rate, the bomb is claimed to have released somewhere between 16 and 25 kilotons of power depending on the source we look at, which tend to be – perhaps not too surprisingly – highly varying regarding the subject, even if only the official data from the different state-funded institutions' websites is considered. It also doesn't help that those who witnessed the explosion were, of course, watching it from a distance of many miles with nothing around it for comparison, and thus would have had a hard time discerning exactly how large it may have been, so they had no choice but to simply accept whatever they were told about it. Its initial flash is said to have been later "calculated" to be "brighter than a thousand Suns". But alas, lest the witnesses go blind from it, they were all ordered to lie face down on the floor with their eyes closed, facing away from the blast, and only allowed to look at the explosion seconds after the detonation - when the flash was already gone -, so none could have actually seen it.

Although the detonation had been originally scheduled for 4 a.m. when the time came it was raining, so the appointed hour was instead pushed to 5:30, which was right when the Sun was beginning to rise. This "coincidence" turned out to be extremely convenient, since the rising Sun's heat soon hit all of the observers at the Trinity site, which they were later told was "the heat coming from the explosion", to make it seem much stronger than it may have been. Moreover, the orange hue provided by the Sun's light, as well as the appearance of the Sun disk itself also likely helped to make this footage (as well as a few other ones), and the single color snapshot that was – accidentally - made of it, appear more ominous and therefore also more convincing.

The steel tower that held the Gadget is generally claimed to have been "vaporized", except for the twisted rods in its footing that can be seen on multiple photos, for some reason. The crater created by the explosion is uniformly said to be about 8 feet deep, however the alleged size of its diameter is just as dubious as the bomb's supposed power. Depending on the source one happens upon, it is either claimed to be one-half mile, 1,000 feet, or merely 330 feet across, while its full blast radius is generally set at roughly 1,000 feet. Although, the most widely used figure seems to be last and most modest one – perhaps not without a reason. If we consider that the fakery was most likely done using hundreds of tons of TNT, the blast couldn't have been more than a few times stronger than that of the 100-Ton Test indeed, despite it allegedly having the power that equals that of about 20,000 (using the most frequently propagated figure) tons of TNT.

Pieces of a green, glass-like - and purportedly mildly radioactive - mineral, later named "trinitite", were scattered in and around the crater, claimed to be made out of the sand of the area as it was heated up by the blast. Interestingly, not much of this mineral can be found at other test sites, not to mention that it looks suspiciously similar to tektite, which is a kind of mineral that can be found in nature. Not only that, but it is also quite easy to create fake "trinitite", as many have since done with the intention of selling it online. Despite allegedly having been created by a "nuclear blast", the radiation level of trinitite is admittedly so low that it can be safely handled without any protection. As for the radiation in the area near the detonation, by 1953 it was already deemed so insignificant that the first Trinity Site open house was held that year.

There were many other supposed "A-bomb" tests done along the following years, all of them with the same issues. During these tests, in the few cases where a recording was even claimed to have taken place, the camera generally didn't even shake when the supposed

"A-bomb" went off not too far away, and the houses, vehicles and trees - displayed as a way of demonstrating what the explosion would do to them - suspiciously look like mere desktop models.

Later on, once H-bombs were claimed to have been invented, there were tests allegedly done with them as well to see how big an explosive yield they can produce, however, all evidence points to that, similarly to the supposed "A-bomb" tests, these must have been conducted merely using large stacks of TNT, too. Not that it even makes a difference, since they never actually claimed to have used a single H-bomb anywhere in a war, nor are they planning on even pretending to do so, as of this day.

Perhaps an even more interesting event was the actual dropping of the first ever so-called "A-bomb", Little Boy. Or, most notably, the fact that it supposedly worked perfectly on the first try, despite its successful detonation relying on a purely experimental uranium gun-type assembly that was invented just for the sake of this particular device. A design which, in turn, relies on the principle of "uncontrolled nuclear fission", the creation of a "supercritical mass" of uranium-235. This was believed to be capable of initiating a kind of nuclear chain reaction that would end in an explosion with a yield similar to that of the Gadget. All of this, of course, was merely a conceptual technology that's never been, nor could it possibly have been, tested before - or even generally accepted by physicists as something feasible, for that matter. Akio Nakatani also made mention of this rather curious fact in his aforementioned book *Death Object* (p. 110.):

"(...) if we believe the official story, the Little Boy was in this (...) elite realm of weapons that are preternaturally "reliable, cheap, and easy to use". Just think: Little Boy, with no integration testing, relying on physics that had never been demonstrated, was shipped halfway around

the world with god knows what kind of manhandling along the way, in wartime, bounced all over in its delivery vehicle, and functioned under unpredictable and variable parameters of temperature, moisture, altitude, vibration, etc. – functioned perfectly to spec."

Indeed, such a belief would undoubtedly require one to have tremendous faith in the establishment. It is also worthy of noting that this particular bomb was only somewhat smaller than the BLU-82 bombs, nicknamed Daisy Cutter, known as the strongest non-nuclear bomb for a long time. These were often used for tasks like clearing dense vegetation, creating helicopter landing zones, or as an anti-personnel weapon first in the Vietnam War, then later also in other conflicts, such as the Gulf War and the early stages of the war in Afghanistan. Although this bomb is claimed to have a relatively low explosive yield compared to "nuclear" weapons, with its 5,700 kilograms of high-energy explosive made of ammonium nitrate and aluminum powder, it is in fact so powerful that it can have a blast radius as wide as 1,300 feet, which is about 300 feet larger than that of the Gadget's explosion.

Later on, starting from 2003, the U.S. Air Force has been utilizing a type of bomb called the GBU-43/B Massive Ordnance Air Blast, nicknamed the Mother of All Bombs (MOAB), the largest non-nuclear bomb in their arsenal, and the successor of Daisy Cutter. Despite having a yield equivalent to merely 11 tons of TNT, it has a blast radius of up to 1 mile, while its Russian counterpart, the Aviation Thermobaric Bomb of Increased Power, also known as the Father of All Bombs (FOAB), is said to be even stronger and is currently considered the most powerful non-nuclear weapon in the world.

Of course, seeing how successful the so-called "nuclear bombs" were said to be during war, it would have made no sense to use anything else in the future, especially since it's claimed that technology got so advanced along the following few decades that they managed to shrink such bombs to a small fraction of their original size while retaining their explosive yield. In fact, as the power of the bombs was claimed to get stronger with every upgrade, so did they allegedly shrink in size, supposedly making it possible to even fit them into intercontinental ballistic missiles – opening up a whole new level of fearmongering. No doubt, such significant technological advancements truly would have created weapons that are orders of magnitude more effective than any of the conventional ones, had they been real.

There was also a little story added to the deployment process of Little Boy to make the whole endeavor seem more plausible and interesting. They say that prior to its carrier taking off with the bomb, 4 other bomber planes have crashed upon takeoff in the past 24 hours, so Thomas Farrell (aka. "Deak Parsons"), a naval officer and an associate of J. Robert Oppenheimer, as well as the head of the Los Alamos Laboratory where the bomb's development was primarily carried out, wanted to make sure that if this happens to the bomber carrying Little Boy, it won't be armed, as *that would be catastrophic*. This meant he had to arm it mid-flight, which is something that has – similarly to the mechanism of the bomb itself - also never been tried before - with any kind of bomb, for that matter. Thus he is claimed to have practiced disarming and arming it again on the ground - to be able to do it better when in the air - for hours on end. Although this clearly made up detail certainly does add to the otherwise short and rather dull story of "taking off with a bomb and then dropping it", but alas, it also makes the whole endeavor seem that much more ridiculous and actually harder to believe for anyone with a critical mind of his own.

Nonetheless, let us also examine what exactly may, or may not have happened in the "A-bombed" cities of Hiroshima and Nagasaki. Perhaps the most striking thing we may notice when watching some of the footage of the mushroom clouds over the cities after the bombs were dropped on them is that they were filmed in such a way to make multiple smaller smoke clouds look like a single large one, most likely just to make the sight that much more dramatic.

Then there are also some oddities regarding the damage caused by the bombing according to not only video recording and photographs, but also personal reports. The explosion in both cities did not appear to have a single source, rather they were spread out uniformly, as if many smaller bombs had been dropped, or a large one that caused less of a blast and more of a conflagration. Official sources even mention many individual fires caused by the bombing, which then turned into a firestorm; a highly destructive event where a large, intense conflagration is formed and fueled by air currents and any nearby flammable material, occuring when the heat from individual fires creates its own wind system. Another proof of firebombing is that many of the buildings were barely damaged at all, while others just had their flammable parts burn down, with their structural integrity remaining fully intact. Telephone poles and trees can also be seen still standing upright in large numbers, while many buildings were reported to even have lightning rods, painted railings, flag poles, and other relatively fragile objects completely undamaged on them. These damage patterns are identical to how a city that was firebombed would look, such as in the case of Tokyo or Dresden that were bombed just a few months earlier. The more unique phenomenon that's claimed to have occurred in the two Japanese cities is the so-called "nuclear shadow", that would appear as a result of the "extreme thermal radiation" – which is supposed to include visible light, ultraviolet radiation, and infrared radiation, causing severe burns and starting fires over a considerable distance from the blast site – that is supposedly caused by A-bombs. Such shadows are claimed to be the outlines of humans and objects that blocked the "thermal radiation", the image of which was probably seen by many. Alas, oddly enough, some of these images clearly show that the "shadow" appears on a wooden surface which is not even damaged, proving the entire phenomenon to be nothing more than a hoax. Moreover, the idea of people or objects being instantly vaporized by the incredible heat of the blast of an A-bomb is also a part of this hoax, however, the more honest experts of the subject tend to admit that the notion is but a misunderstanding; the correct term, they say, is actually not *"vaporization"*, rather just *carbonization*. Which is exactly what happens to objects (or humans) that are burned by napalm bombs, for example.

Nevertheless, there was some radioactivity measurable at the detonation sites, but no more than in the case of any other kind of bombing, and even that had dissipated just as quickly as in all other cases. The Japanese actually begun rebuilding and repopulating both cities within a few weeks. Health issues claimed to be related to radiation poisoning were only ever diagnosed in a part of those that were either within a few kilometers of the hypocenters of the bombs; within 2 kilometers of the hypocenters within two weeks of the bombings; exposed to radiation from fallout; or not yet born but carried by pregnant women. Interestingly enough, nearly a quarter of those that belong to at least one of these categories are still alive today, almost 8 decades after the event. This is simply due to the fact that the so-called "nuclear radiation", or even the kind of radiation that's actually present after a firebombing, is much weaker and less persistent than all the official propaganda would have us believe. There is, of course, evidence showing that extreme amounts of the gamma radiation emitted by radioactive objects can have detrimental effects on human health and even lead to disorders in the embryo carried by a pregnant woman, however, there seems to be no conclusive proof of it being able to actually change one's genetic code and make birth defects hereditary as it's often claimed. It should also be noted that other kinds of radiations have also been shown to produce similar results in humans, in fact, in some cases the damage can be even more prominent. Therefore, it would be safe to conclude that the story of Little Boy and Fat Man being functional nuclear weapons is entirely fictional.

However, there are a number of other clues also pointing to the fact that nuclear radiation is nothing to be deathly afraid of. Perhaps the most shocking of them all is an admission that came from the establishment itself. During World War II and the early Cold War, the United States government produced a documentary film series called "The Big Picture". This series was created to inform the public and military personnel about various aspects of the war effort and the evolving geopolitical situation. It covered a wide range of topics, from military operations to post-war planning. In one episode, military personnel explain to us what we need to know about "atomic weapons" as follows:

*"To teach soldiers of the U.S. army exactly what atomic weapons can and cannot do and thereby alley any unreasonable fears of the A-bomb, a series of atomic experiments have been held on the barren lands of Nevada during the past several years. Today's Big Picture deals with the latest and most extensive of these experiments, Desert Rock VI. (...) Atomic weapons are truly powerful, but they don't mean the end of all life as so many people think. You **can** live through an atomic attack. And, by taking common sense precautions, live to fight another day. But at one mile, which is pretty close to one of these gadgets, ordinary clothing will protect you. Keep your sleeves rolled down and wear a hat. Of course, if you're in the shaded portion of a foxhole at the time of detonation, you are perfectly safe from the heat of the bomb. Anything that casts a shadow will protect you. And now we've come to what a*

lot of people consider the sixty-four-dollar question: radiation. This is the one new effect obtained by the use of an atomic weapon. Truthfully, it's the least important of the three effects as far as the soldier on the ground is concerned. Still, radiation affects the body much as an x-ray does. If enough is received, it 'can' be fatal. From an airburst, however, this fatal dose of radiation can be gotten only fairly close to ground zero, with distances practically never exceeding one mile. Since buildings are destroyed by blast out to a couple of miles, and burning occurs maybe three miles away, you can see the radius of fatal radiation is much less. Half of this airburst radiation occurs during the first second, the remaining half during the next 89 seconds. So the radiation hazard on the ground is over 90 seconds after the bomb goes off in the air."

The point of nuclear radiation being relatively harmless was later not only emphasized, but also demonstrated by Galen Winsor, an American chemist and nuclear physicist of renown who worked at, and helped design, nuclear power plants in towns such as Wimington, NJ; Hanford, WA; Oak Ridge, TN; San Jose, CA; Morris, IL. For the most part, he was in charge of controlling and measuring the nuclear fuel storage and inventory. He has spoken on national talk radio, traveled and lectured all over America, and made several videos exposing the greatly exaggerated fear campaign surrounding nuclear radiation.

One of his most famous works is a presentation filmed in 1986 which became known as *The Nuclear Scare Scam*. In this, he not only talks about how he used to drink and swim in radioactive coolant, but also consumes a piece of radioactive uranium live in front of the camera – a performance that he's also been doing frequently in his other lectures. Despite all of his escapades, he lived a long and fulfilling life until the day he died in 2008 at the remarkable age of 82. Perhaps the most important – and to some, dangerous - fact he revealed was that nuclear waste does not actually require costly storage, as it isn't nearly as harmful to the environment as they would have us believe, and that such propaganda is used to allow a handful of people to control the entire industry. Of course, it is not particularly hard to see why they like to use the radiation aspect of anything "nuclear" to try and scare us with it, considering that it – similarly to other kinds of radiation - cannot be seen or felt by humans, making it a perfect blank check for fearmongers. Needless to say, Winsor was never a darling of the establishment, and his work was constantly criticised for not conforming to the so-called "scientific consensus", despite all the empirical evidence he presented to prove his claims and debunk those of the mainstream pundits.

After the bombing of Japan and the ending of the war, another project called Operation Crossroads took place at Bikini Atoll in the Marshall Islands in the Pacific Ocean. This operation consisted of two tests - Able and Baker – in both of which an A-bomb was allegedly detonated, and is said to have been conducted with the purpose of studying the effects of "nuclear weapons" on naval ships and harbor facilities. Since the project took place not long after the end of World War II, in 1946, many researchers today suspect that the whole endeavor was actually just an excuse to get rid of military surplus after the war was done with. The explosions of the two tests – based on the available footage and information - were most likely simply caused by some of the larger bombs left over from the times of war. In fact, there had been many other similar "nuclear" tests carried out at Bikini Atoll over the next 12 years with a combined fission yield of 42.2 megatons of explosive power, and yet, reports from the 1990's were emphasizing that there are practically no signs of the devastation; there's only thriving marine life and healthy vegetation to be found at the detonation sites. Moreover, interestingly enough, no radioactive glass like the "trinitite" of the Trinity site was even claimed to have been found at the Atoll, further proving that it was all a hoax.

Now that we can rest assured that no nuclear bomb's detonation has ever been demonstrated, and established that it would have made little sense to even try to invent such complicated and risky weapons in the middle of a war, let us also examine the reason it would not be possible to do it even if someone actually tried.

The issue starts with the base idea, as even that is gravely faulty – and it is also the means by which the entire nuke-hoax ties in with the global deception. Which is, of course, quite unfortunate for all the terrorists (not including those who work in governments), seeing that they obviously wouldn't need to show any kind of restraint when it comes to causing destruction, since they would have no fragile public image to worry about. And that is yet another reason we can be sure that such weapons do not exist; if they did, we definitely would have seen at least one of the not-so-responsible extremist groups out there build and use it at least once since the bomb's supposed invention in 1945. Which is not the case, despite the fact that analytical power as well as relevant information far beyond that of the physicists involved in the Manhattan Project have been readily available to any average person at minimal cost.

However, the much more fundamental and manifest reason for the lack of proof is the fact that the existence of "atoms" in an object is merely a concept – one whose existence would be just as impossible to prove as that of the conceptual "space-time". This, of course, means that we wouldn't be able to manipulate atoms as we wish, just like we can't manipulate – or sense in any way - "space-time" either. Both of these theoretical inventions just serve as tools for building and maintaining their respective deceptions by allowing for the creation of equations that are based on them, which are then propagated as "proof" of the existence of the concepts themselves.

And, oddly enough, the key character is also the same one in the case of both hoaxes, as it is Einstein's theory of relativity, particularly his famous equation $E = mc^2$, that the entire notion of fission that could create nuclear energy was allegedly based upon – although some of the more honest physicists will admit that it wasn't actually required, or useful, at all. While Einstein's personal contribution in the development of any technology that had to do with nuclear fission consisted of nothing more than signing a letter composed by others, his role as "scientific icon" was – according to the story - needed to ensure that the attention of the War Department and the president could be captured. Of course, his fundamentally flawed equation was also made part of it clearly just to boost its acceptance by the public and make it more believable overall. Which is also likely the reason it was made the most famous equation in physics in the first place; so that more blind trust and fewer uncomfortable questions would arise about anything they happened to have associated it with.

Upon closer look, the equation itself is just as perplexing as it is immensely cherished and propagated by the establishment and their pseudoscientists. $E = mc^2$ basically states that the energy (E) of an object is equal to its mass (m) multiplied by the (two-way) speed of light (in a vacuum) (c) squared. This implies that a small amount of mass can be converted into a large amount of energy, and it's claimed to form the basis for understanding the relationship between mass and energy. This is also the principle according to which a single gram of uranium or plutonium in Little Boy or Fat Man could supposedly release enough energy for an explosive yield of up to 20 kilotons. However, the equation also brings up a question in the mind of every critical thinker: how would it be helpful to multiply the mass of something with the supposed two-way "speed of light" in a vacuum, knowing that the process has little to do with how light travels, not to mention it doesn't take place in a vacuum and definitely would be a two-way measurement? The answer is simple. Since the figure of c is inherently faulty to begin with, the equation could never have made any sense and therefore wasn't actually used for anything. In the case of the operating principle of a nuclear reactor, a different equation was used, which - needless to say -, did not include the light's assumed velocity, instead just the kind of variables that were actually workable.

The lukewarm Cold War

Shortly after the end of World War II, a fabricated charade predominantly involving the capitalist U.S. and the communist Soviet Union (S.U.) began, which was later dubbed the "Cold War" and lasted until the collapse of the S.U. in 1991. The development of the "A-bomb" and the execution of the Trinity test were actually claimed to have been an urgent endeavor not so much due to the already defeated Germans, but because of the "growing threat" the S.U. allegedly posed after World War II was over. The main purpose of this frivolous play was to gain more control over the common people of the world by essentially setting up a duality in it, while, of course, also pushing the usual lies and propaganda to further the anti-human agenda of both sides, including the starting of multiple dirty and – obviously - unnecessary proxy wars. All of this was easily achieved by feigning political, economic, and ideological opposition between the two largest powers (both clearly controlled by the same people from behind the scenes) of the time. This would then allow them to still be able to work together in certain ways to achieve their ultimate goal of deceiving, enslaving, and depopulating a large part of humanity.

The two most prominent achievements of the entire theater - regarding the relevant deceptions - were undoubtedly the efforts to solidify the nuclear weapon hoax by all sorts of disarmament treaties and by starting the so-called "Arms Race", and the establishment of the space exploration hoax by starting the ridiculous - and rather transparent - "Space Race".

One of the most atrocious examples of the two seemingly opposing sides working together actually happened some time before the end of World War II. A day after the Trinity test, a conference was started in Potsdam, Germany by the Allied leaders in order to decide the fate of the member countries of the Axis powers, as well as the entire Eastern block. During one session at the conference, president Harry S. Truman remarked to Soviet premier Joseph Stalin that the United States had built a "new weapon of unusual destructive force", to which Stalin replied that he would like to see the U.S. make "good use of it against the Japanese." Whether or not this was the main reason behind the bombing of the two Japanese cities would be hard to say, but regardless, it happened not long after the conversation of the two leaders.

As the story goes, after the bombings, Stalin felt so intimidated by the destruction caused by the supposed "A-bombs", that he immediately initiated the S.U.'s own version of the Manhattan Project, so that they may develop similar bombs of their own. And thus the "Arms Race" began, the taxpayers of both empires were further robbed by their governments to fund its endless expenses, and the reinforcement of the nuclear weapon hoax in the minds of the people advanced. It is said that the Soviets sent spies to the U.S. who managed to find out how an "A-bomb" is supposed to be built. However, even if this did happen, knowing that creating such a weapon is simply not possible, the endeavor likely served no other purpose than to add an extra bit of intrigue to the story in order to make the two supposed sides seem more hostile toward each other, and to make the A-bomb-hoax that much more believable.

Another example of presumable cooperation between the two empires is how the average number of neutrons supposedly produced per fission was said to be published simultaneously by the U.S. and the S.U. in 1955. Whether there really was some kind of research and the results were in fact correct, or it was all just a mockery of the people by the puppeteers pulling the strings, is anyone's guess, but it certainly is suspicious, to say the least.

In 1949 the Soviets – similarly to the Americans earlier - finally faked the creation of their first "A-bomb", initiating a "nuclear standoff"; the development and stockpiling of "nuclear weapons" creating a situation where both superpowers seemingly had the capacity to inflict catastrophic damage on each other. Of course, "the fear of mutual destruction" acted as a very convenient deterrent, leading to a "cautious approach" and avoidance of direct military conflict, letting the both the Cold War's and the A-bomb's deception go on indefinitely. And, from that point on, it would continue with both sides hand in hand, each playing their own part and taking their predetermined share of the swindle. Both the Americans and the Soviets were allegedly also "experimenting" with high-altitude "nuclear" explosions, but all of their footage seem to be equally fishy and not much can be proven by them.

Over the next few decades there have been a number of "nuclear weapon" testing moratoriums, as well as treaties and prohibitions preventing either their improvements or their use, which, of course, very well served the purpose of making the purported weapons seem like a huge threat to humanity. And, just as importantly, making the leaders involved seem like responsible, well-meaning humanitarians on the very top of the moral high ground. In fact, they even managed to turn the bombing of the two Japanese cities – and the killing of more than a hundred thousand civilians by it – into almost a sort of "good deed". This was done by making it one of the a central points of the anti-nuclear propaganda, emphasizing the terrible destruction caused in the cities as one of the main reasons why they should never be used again, implying and conveying the message to the public that the despicable deed was actually "useful" because it taught us all "what not to do". Despite the obvious fact that none but the sickest of minds would even think of ever doing such a thing in the first place.

THE GLOBAL DECEPTION

George Orwell, English novelist, essayist, and critic even wrote his take on this event, as well as the despicable nature of political propaganda in general in his 1946 essay *Politics and the English Language* (p. 10. 13.):

"In our time, political speech and writing are largely the defense of the indefensible. Things like the continuance of British rule in India, the Russian purges and deportations, the dropping of the atom bombs on Japan, can indeed be defended, but only by arguments which are too brutal for most people to face, and which do not square with the professed aims of the political parties. Thus political language has to consist largely of euphemism, question-begging and sheer cloudy vagueness. Defenseless villages are bombarded from the air, the inhabitants driven out into the countryside, the cattle machinegunned, the huts set on fire with incendiary bullets: this is called 'pacification'. Millions of peasants are robbed of their farms and sent trudging along the roads with no more than they can carry: this is called 'transfer of population' or 'rectification of frontiers'. People are imprisoned for years without trial, or shot in the back of the neck or sent to die of scurvy in Arctic lumber camps: this is called 'elimination of unreliable elements'. Such phraseology is needed if one wants to name things without calling up mental pictures of them.

Political language (...) is designed to make lies sound truthful and murder respectable, and to give an appearance of solidity to pure wind."

In his book *Nineteen Eighty-Four,* Orwell called this "newspeak"; a kind of propaganda that narrows citizens' range of thought, making it difficult for them to express, or even to consider, unorthodox ideas that do not align with the state's goals - in effect, preventing logical thinking. This is why fanatics of a given political party or ideology tend to defend even the most horrendous atrocities committed by those that they consider their allies, as long as they were done in the name of whatever they believe in. In other words, such people accept a false reality created in their minds by the state's distorted claims and propositions instead of the "ugly truth" that is obvious to most others. Today, the best way to see this in practice is asking an American nationalist what they think about their government interfering in the affairs of distant countries, invading them, or bombing purely civilian towns just to prove a point. Indeed, in the case of the bombing of Hiroshima and Nagasaki, whatever bombs the perpetrators of the inhuman wickedness actually used, they could have been simply dropped upon any uninhabited patch of land to demonstrate how much destruction they are capable of causing, getting the same results but without any human victims.

As it is known, there were claims made during the Cold War that the Soviets had an intercontinental ballistic missile (ICBM) posing a direct threat to everyone in the U.S. however, no credible evidence exists that there has ever been such a device, so it should be considered just another piece of fear propaganda. There were eventually also claims of an American ICBM being launched on one continent and arriving on another, but, needless to say no unedited film footage exists of this either.

Regardless, this lie of a Soviet ICBM significantly affected the everyday life of – mainly - the U.S. citizens during the height of the manufactured tensions in the 1950s and 1960s, as there was a heightened sense of fear and concern about the possibility of a nuclear conflict between the two superpowers. This fear led to various precautions and preparedness measures taken by the U.S. government, such as the following:

Civil Defense Programs: They were established to brainwash the public about the "dangers of nuclear weapons" and to provide guidance on what to do in the event of a "nuclear attack". This included the distribution of propaganda pamphlets, films, and public service announcements.

Air Raid Drills: Similar to drills conducted during World War II, schools and communities regularly conducted air raid drills, despite no real sign of danger ever actually having presented itself. These drills involved practicing seeking shelter quickly, often in designated fallout shelters.

Fallout Shelters: They were intended to protect people from the supposed "radioactive fallout" that would occur after a "nuclear explosion". Some were public shelters in schools or community buildings, while others were private shelters built in people's homes.

Emergency Kits: Citizens were encouraged to create emergency kits containing essential supplies such as non-perishable food, water, medical supplies, and other necessities that could sustain a family for an extended period in a fallout shelter.

Public Service Announcements: Governments and organizations ran this kind of regularly occuring propaganda on television and radio, advising people on what to do in the event of a "nuclear attack". This included information about evacuation routes, shelter locations, and emergency communication methods.

"Duck and Cover" Campaign: This famous piece of fear propaganda was perhaps the most ridiculous one of them all. It was promoted through educational films and posters, advising people, especially schoolchildren, to duck under desks or tables and cover their heads in the event of a nuclear explosion to reduce exposure to flying debris. After the "war", of course, some of the mainstream outlets pointed out that such an action would have been essentially pointless if a "nuclear attack" would have actually occurred nearby.

Cultural Impact: The fear of nuclear war permeated popular culture, influencing literature, movies, and television. This period of anxiety is reflected in the dystopian themes of many works produced during the Cold War era, further reinforcing the belief in people that they need to be deathly afraid at all times.

Needless to say, all this commotion greatly helped the development of the different anti-nuclear weapon treaties, as well as heavier government regulations regarding nuclear energy. This is how the Atomic Energy Act, the piece of legislation in the U.S. that governs the use of nuclear materials and technology, was conceived in 1946. It has gone through several revisions and amendments since its initial enactment, reflecting all the other regulations of nuclear energy that were since then implemented. The most significant version of the Act is that of 1954, which was, however, still amended in subsequent years. Its main goal was clearly to make everything "nuclear" seem extremely dangerous and detrimental to the environment by setting criteria for granting licenses and authorizations to those who would seek to utilize it in any way. This, of course, proved to serve very well in the brainwashing of the public, who would now be convinced that it really must be so strictly regulated that, not only would it become much more expensive to produce energy this way - which is otherwise very economical and efficient -, but it would also become virtually impossible for ordinary civilians to legally possess practically any radioactive material.

Later on, in order to further solidify the hoax and substantially boost the amount of fearmongering achievable by it, several arms limitation and anti-nuclear weapon treaties were negotiated as part of efforts to "manage the Arms Race" and "reduce the risk of nuclear conflict". Their progress was helped by a number of suspiciously convenient events, most significantly by 1962's ridiculous theater play called the "Cuban Missile Crisis", where the U.S. and the S.U. were claimed to have come to the brink of "nuclear war" over the placement of Soviet missiles in Cuba.

Some of the most significant treaties were the following:

Partial Test Ban Treaty (PTBT) - 1963: prohibited nuclear tests in the atmosphere, "outer space", and underwater, conveniently allowing only underground nuclear testing in the U.S. the U.K. and the S.U. - thus eliminating the need for the creation of more visual fakery.

Treaty on the Non-Proliferation of Nuclear Weapons (NPT) - 1968: having entered into force two years after being opened for signature - and still being in effect to this day -, it aims to prevent the spread of "nuclear weapons" and promote peaceful uses of nuclear energy. It recognizes five nuclear-armed states (the U.S. Russia, China, France, and the UK) and commits them to eventual nuclear disarmament. This treaty is perhaps one of the most prominent proofs of a world-wide conspiracy, as it involves 191 countries (as of 2023).

Strategic Arms Limitation Talks (SALT) - 1972: included the Anti-Ballistic Missile (ABM) Treaty and the Interim Agreement on the Limitation of Strategic Offensive Arms. Aimed at limiting the number of strategic ballistic missile launchers limited the deployment of anti-ballistic missile systems to protect against nuclear missile attacks by the U.S and the S.U.

Intermediate-Range Nuclear Forces Treaty (INF) - 1987: eliminated all supposed ground-launched ballistic and cruise missiles with ranges between 500 and 5,500 kilometers in the U.S and the S.U.

Strategic Arms Reduction Treaty (START) - 1991: mandated significant reductions in the number of deployed strategic "nuclear weapons" by the U.S and the S.U. both agreeing to destroy a third of their alleged "nuclear arsenal".

So once the nuke-hoax and the radiation scare were thus established and the fear instilled into not just the people of the West, but - to a certain extent - the whole of humanity, with all the regulations and treaties in place, there was no longer a need for further demonstrations of "nuclear explosions" – other than a number of supposed tests. This is also the reason there hasn't been one in such a long time, despite more and more countries claiming to own such weapons. In fact, it is alleged that there are currently over thirteen thousand nuclear weapons in the world, with the majority of them, of course, in the possession of the U.S. and Russia.

Regardless of the treaties, the supposed improvements and testings of "nuclear weapons" continues to this day – at least on paper. All of which, of course, also allows for immense amounts of the helpless taxpayers' money to be taken and artificially pumped into the economy continuously, with no end in sight. Thus monetizing the fear of the common people, who are made to believe they would be in constant grave danger if it weren't for those expensive projects "deterring the enemy". The "enemy", whose government does the exact same thing to their own subjects with the same reasoning.

Another endeavor that made good use of the manufactured tensions of the Cold War was the establishment of the CIA. It was done with the signing of the National Security Act of 1947 by Truman, allegedly as a response to the "changing geopolitical landscape" following World War II, the "emerging challenges of the Cold War" between the United States and the Soviet Union, and the spreading of Communism. In actuality, however, the organization would just go on to interfere with independent countries where the people have risen up against tyranny, claiming that "their independence movements might lead to Communism", and then install an unpopular dictator of the U.S. government's liking to rule over the citizens. Today, the organization is suspected by many to be involved in the systematic undermining of democracy, as well as the spreading of otherwise illegal – and especially harmful - "pharmaceutical products" mainly in, but not limited to, the U.S.

A similarly insidious use of the chaos - that the powers that be created - was the establishment of the North Atlantic Treaty Organization (NATO) in 1949, by the signing of the North Atlantic Treaty by twelve founding member countries. The organization was essentially supposed to be a mutual defense alliance, with members committing to consider an armed attack against one or more of them as an attack against all, and to respond with appropriate action. Its primary purpose was allegedly to "provide collective defense against the potential threat of aggression by the Soviet Union and its allies". Today it's being used to "address new security challenges", including "terrorism" and "cyber threats", or whatever the U.S. government deems a "problematic event". In effect, it is a wicked tool to centralize the control over otherwise independent countries' military forces, and if deemed necessary by the central leadership, pull any of the member countries into a war they would otherwise have nothing to do with.

In the middle of the Cold War, particularly in the 1950s and 1960s, the absolute peak of hilarity called the "Space Race" took place. It was claimed to be a period of "intense competition and rivalry" between the U.S. and the S.U. as if they were actual enemies. The mainstream pundits like to characterize this period as "a series of ambitious achievements and milestones in space exploration", with both superpowers vying for supremacy in "space".

Those who have already read the previous chapters of this book will likely need little explanation as to why it all could have been nothing more than a ludicrous, farcical hoax, but alas, it was where the whole of the "space exploration" swindle – an integral part of getting humanity to accept the models of deception as truth – was conceived. The first "great achievement" of the Space Race – which marked not only its beginning, but also that of the "Space Age" – was the supposed launching of Sputnik 1, the first artificial satellite, into "orbit" around the Earth by the Soviets in 1957. This was, of course, to be followed by an American satellite, Explorer 1, being claimed to be launched up in 1958 as a reply. This supposed deed is claimed to have been achieved by Wernher von Braun, German-born American engineer and his army group. Von Braun was a leading German aerospace engineer, playing a crucial role in the development of state-of-the-art rocket technology, and later becoming a key figure in the U.S.' space program. He and about 100 members of his group were allowed to immigrate to the U.S. after Germany was defeated, along with other former Nazis scientists, as part of Project Overcast and Project Paperclip. The official reason given for this is that *their expert knowledge was deemed critical to the defeat of Japan and, after the war, to the struggle against communism*. Von Braun essentially became a national and international focal point for the promotion of space flight during the 1950s, authoring or co-authoring a number of popular articles and books on the subject. Later, in 1975, he also founded the National Space Institute, whose objective was to generate public support and understanding of "space activities".

Still in 1958, the president of the time, Dwight D. Eisenhower signed a public order creating the National Aeronautics and Space Administration (NASA), a federal agency dedicated to so-called "space exploration". Von Braun and his organization were transferred from the army to this agency. As director of NASA's Marshall Space Flight Center in Huntsville, von Braun led the development of the so-called "large space launch vehicles". This also marked the beginning of an era of a whole new level of deceptions that are still going on strong today.

Then, in 1961, Soviet "cosmonaut" Yuri Gagarin was said to have become the first human to "orbit" the Earth - aboard a piece of wonky movie prop that they would refer to as a "spacecraft". This little propaganda-stunt was considered a "major milestone" in the Space Race. Needless to say, this was to be soon followed by the U.S.' program, which allegedly saw the first American in "space" in that same year, while also achieving "important milestones" in "orbital maneuvers" and "spacewalks".

The crowning of the entire "Space Race" was, of course, the so-called "Moon Race", which was essentially started at the beginning of the 1960s by president Kennedy, who set the ambitious goal of landing a man on the Moon and returning him safely to Earth before the end of the decade. The Apollo program supposedly achieved this goal with the historic Apollo 11 mission in 1969, when "astronauts" Neil Armstrong and Edwin "Buzz" Aldrin became the first and second humans to be believed to "walk on the Moon". It is said that they've spent about two hours there, during which the president of the time, Richard Nixon, somehow talked to them via a landline phone, then they headed back to Earth. All this was – miraculously - completed just a few months before the set deadline, on the very first try, with no significant issues or difficulties whatsoever, despite only supposed simulation training ever having been conducted, which would have clearly not prepared the "astronauts" for an environment and circumstances they could only have guessed about. Yet, the establishment was so confident in their success that they decided to broadcast the "first steps on the Moon" live to millions of people, even though the smallest mistake or issue could have had disastrous consequences, both in regards of the "astronauts'" health and the public image of the government – if the mission had been real.

The whole endeavor eerily resembles the case of the supposed building of the A-bomb. It was done just as hastily, out of the necessity of "beating the enemy to it", and, of course, just like the supposed "A-bomb", it worked perfectly on the first try during a high-pressure mission, with no real prior testing or meaningful, relevant training for the partakers. Moreover, just like in the case of the alleged A-bomb's explosion, we only have low quality, yet still clearly fake footage of the "monumental event" as "proof".

Although the clip of a few seconds of the "moon landing" that most people have certainly seen doesn't show much at all, those who seeked out the whole of the footage may have noticed a plethora of "oddities" in it. One of the most prominent things is how the "astronauts" are moving in a weird manner, sometimes falling over but being pulled back into an upright position by some unseen force, *as if* they were suspended on wires. Then there are other weirdnesses, such as multiple angles of shadows indicating multiple light sources (as if they were in a film studio), the flag waving just as if it wasn't actually in a vacuum, the letter *C* being visible on one of the "rocks" (which is what a prop on a film set would look like), as well as the "astronauts'" footprints looking different from what the soles of their uniformed boots - as seen in some museums – are supposed look like. Furthermore, the way the "Moon lander" with the passengers on it was filmed from the outside certainly should raise the question of who exactly was shooting such scenes – or the whole event, for that matter. There were also pieces of so-called "Moon rocks" acquired and given to different countries as gifts, but alas, when one of them was examined, it turned out to be nothing more than mere petrified wood. Of course, they've also made sure to "shoot a photo" of the Earth while they were up there, although, they seem to have forgotten where exactly they were supposed to have been on the Moon when they edited the so-called "photo", as the Earth appears near the Moon's horizon, even though it should have been above the heads of the "astronauts" from where they allegedly stood. Not to mention that the Earth's apparent size is about the same as the Moon's would be when viewed from Earth, despite the Earth being many times larger.

Luckily, even Aldrin himself made an admission – that might clear things up for those that might still have issues deciding whether the achievement of the "Moon landing" was real or not - a few years ago regarding the endeavor at a book festival, when an 8-year-old child asked him why nobody has been to the Moon in such a long time. His reply was as follows:

"That's not an 8-year-old's question, that's my question. I wanna know... but I think I know. Because we didn't go there, and that's the way it happened. And if it didn't happen, it's nice to know why it didn't happen, so in the future if we want to keep doing something, we need to know why something stopped in the past that we wanted to keep going. Money... is a good thing. If you want to buy new things, new rockets, instead to keep doing the same thing over, then it's gonna cost more money. And other things need more money, too, so having achieved what the president wanted us to do, and then what thousands, millions of people in America and millions of people around the world. You know, when we toured around the world after we came back, the most fascinating observation was signs that said: "We did it!". Not just us,

not just America, but "we", the world, different countries. They felt like they were part of what we were able to do. And that made us feel very good."

Unfortunately, no footage I've managed to find (even this short clip proved to be quite difficult – and increasingly so - to find) had any follow-up questions or a counter response to let us find out more about why he said what he said - especially the first few sentences -, but it certainly makes one think. Also, Aldrin points out a very interesting and important fact at the end of his monologue; that the people of the Earth all felt like they were part of the supposed "achievement". This was, indeed the whole point of the "mission"; involving as many in the process as possible, while keeping only a select few within the inner circles who actually take part in the faking itself. This select few perpetrators generally come from the military (as well as certain secret societies), thus being under oath of secrecy and unconditional loyalty to the government anyway, making it trivial to perform such "sensitive" operations with their help.

However, Aldrin's statement that there are insufficient funds is clearly incorrect, considering how much better technology has gotten since 1969, consequently making it much simpler and cheaper to accomplish the same goals. Not to mention that NASA's funding has increased dramatically since its inception, and that even when they were recently offered essentially unlimited funding for the task, NASA still couldn't rise to the challenge of (the faking of) putting humans on Mars – which has been one of their main announced goals for the "near future" for a long time anyway.

The Apollo-Soyuz Test Project of 1975 was yet another great example of the two so-called "enemies" actually – blatantly - working together to deceive, extort, and slowly enslave humanity. They called it a "symbol of détente" during the Cold War, as it purportedly involved a joint U.S.-Soviet mission with a "rendezvous and docking in space", showcasing international cooperation in "space exploration" while supposedly in the middle of a desperate - although bloodless - war with one another.

Later on, in 1983, when the people of the world have already seen plenty of movies and TV shows with "space" programming in it, the peak of the "Arms Race" known as the Strategic Defense Initiative (SDI), commonly known as "Star Wars", was initiated by U.S. president Ronald Reagen. It proposed the use of "advanced" (sci-fi) technologies, including space-based systems such as satellite-based lasers and kinetic energy weapons, to intercept and neutralize intercontinental ballistic missiles - including those carrying "nuclear warheads" - in various phases of their flight.

The idea was to not only solidify the space-hoax in the people's minds, but to also shift from the narrative of "mutual assured destruction" to a more sustainable - and believable - defensive strategy, in order to finally conclude the tedious pretense of war and move to a more passive and comfortable stage of the deception. Even at the time, many critics questioned the feasibility and scientific viability of the proposed technologies, but it was still attempted - its inevitable failure costing the nation's tax-slaves massive amounts of money. The program was admittedly "facing technical hurdles", so it eventually underwent some "changes", just as one would expect. Since, obviously, nothing that's "space-based" is actually possible to accomplish outside of sci-fi films, the focus of the program soon shifted to a more pragmatic and believable approach to missile defense, emphasizing ground-based interceptors instead, and eventually evolving into the Ballistic Missile Defense Organization in 1993, and becoming the Missile Defense Agency in 2002.

A world of fantasy imprisoning us

The so-called "scientific revolution" of the 16th and 17th centuries was supposed to end the "Dark Ages" by breaking with the old - mainly religious – dogmas, thus "liberating human thought" and "opening the way to a reinterpretation" of science, technology and philosophy. Although it did bring us such timeless innovations as the scientific method, but for the most part it was simply just a period in history when traditional values and real knowledge were replaced by pseudoscience, and the arbiters of what's right or true became the pseudoscientists - especially in regards of our cosmology.

As harmful and misleading as pseudoscientists can be, closely listening to what they say can sometimes still teach us useful things – as long as the necessary level of discernment is used. If nothing else, it can help us figure out what methods are being utilized in an attempt to make us believe that whatever the official narrative is, it fits our own experience, even when it clearly doesn't. Examining such methods can, in turn, make it possible for us to unpack and neutralize otherwise potentially harmful falsehoods and propagandas before they could exert their detrimental influence on us.

Perhaps one of the most insidious of these methods is the whole of the entertainment industry being used by the powers that be as a tool to blur the lines between sci-fi and real science. The most relevant example of this is, of course, the space- and globe-Earth-propaganda that so frequently appears in just about all branches of the industry. We may often experience this kind of brainwashing in films, television or radio programs and series, video games, print media, digital and online content, theme parks and attractions, and occasionally even in performing and visual arts.

However, the beginning of the era of the most prominent brainwashing may well have been actually marked by works of literature, especially certain works of prolific American writers Robert A. Heinlein and Isaac Asimov, as well as their English contemporary, Arthur C. Clarke. By the mid 1900s, their works have apparently greatly influenced the minds of the establishment's pundits, who saw an unparalleled opportunity in the world of fantasy that the three writers dreamed up. Many of their sci-fi novels and short stories were highly successful and quite a few of them were later also adapted into films - some of which became extremely famous and popular –, turning their writings into an increasingly more popular form of entertainment and perhaps the most effective way of programming the public's mind.

One of the first movies ever made, in fact, happened to be the 1902 space-film *A Trip to the Moon*, telling the story of a group of astronomers who go on an expedition to the Moon. It was directed by the French director Georges Méliès, who was – quite befittingly and perhaps not by chance – also an illusionist, a profession whose practitioners are defined as *"someone who performs tricks that deceive the eye"*. After this production, the space-programming became increasingly more frequent with each decade, and by the 1950s, on average, a new space-movie was released every year, to speed up to a rate of multiple films per year before the decade was over.

Of course, things like comics and radio shows were also pumped out used to push this kind of brainwashing by the early 20th century, so by the time NASA was founded in 1958, humanity was already used to the idea of one day traveling into "space", and especially to the Moon and to Mars. Nowadays, the entertainment industry has become so entrenched in the world of pseudoscience that we often hear even renowned astronomers shamelessly refer to popular science fiction films as "source material" for one of their ridiculous theories – which should clearly ever be regarded as mere sci-fi - in the hope of better promoting and propagating it via the visual programming that the people already know and love so much.

It should be mentioned, however, that fantasies of traveling into "outer space", and particularly to the Moon, presumably began to soar as early as 1608, when the novel *Somnium* (Latin for "Dream") was written by none other than one of the most famous of all science fiction writers and pseudoscientists, Johannes Kepler. This book that described the life of imagined inhabitants of the Moon also may well have been the first "modern" story of any kind of "space" travel overall. Although this is presumably his only published work that the mainstream pundits dare admit is nothing more than sci-fi, astonishingly, they still attribute "correct assertions" to this book regardless, such as the supposed "high temperature of the Moon's sunlit side" that was mentioned in it.

Needless to say, the novel was soon followed by an increasing number of others involving the same theme of "traveling to the Moon" by many different authors over then next decades and centuries.

In the modern times, a rather poignant proof of the entertainment industry and the media being actively used to do the bidding of the U.S. government was the 1950s collaboration between them and Walt Disney, who was already renowned for his ability to blend entertainment with education (or propaganda) at the time. He was tasked with creating three TV program series with the help of Wernher von Braun, who was working on the development of military rockets for the U.S. Army at the time. Their barrage of space-propaganda started in 1955 with the series called Man in Space, featuring animated and live-action sequences to explain the concept of "space travel" and the supposed "potential" for human exploration beyond Earth. This was soon to be followed by additional episodes of space-propaganda in the *Man and the Moon* and *Mars and Beyond* series, further brainwashing the public with the idea that "space exploration" is in fact possible, feasible, and should be expected to happen sometime in the near future. The last one of the three productions was likely inspired by Arthur C. Clarke's first novel about "space", *The Sands of Mars*, which was published in 1951. This sci-fi novel explores the experiences of the first human colonists on Mars and their struggles to adapt to life on the "Red Planet".

In 1959, Disney also teamed up with the U.S. Department of Defense (formerly War Department) to create a TV program called Eyes in Outer Space, using music and animation to speculate on the use of alleged "space satellite technology" which was claimed to be usable to modify weather. Although Disney himself died in 1966, the space (and other kind of) propaganda was continued under his brand name by those who inherited his enterprise, and it's being used in such ways even today.

The role of Arthur C. Clarke became similarly important to Disney's regarding the spreading of the deception when, in 1964, he was tasked to team up with famous American director Stanley Kubrick to create the iconic film *2001: A Space Odyssey*, which was released in 1968 – just a year before the supposed "Moon landing" took place. Just like Clarke, Kubrick also had a great interest in "space exploration", and collaborated with NASA - allegedly to "receive technical advice" - in order to let him make the movie "authentic and realistic", helping to create a visually stunning and technically convincing portrayal of what they called "space exploration". The film's plot is based on a 1951 short story by Clarke called *The Sentinel*, which he then turned into a movie script as the film itself was being directed by Kubrick, and is highly regarded for its groundbreaking visuals, not to mention that it is now widely considered one of the greatest science fiction films ever made. In fact, even the space-scenes in it looked so vivid and realistic in it that – in retrospect – it makes the low quality, grainy "Moon landing" footage of the following year - that was somehow passed off as "real" - look like an absolute joke.

Similarly to other space-propaganda productions, *2001: A Space Odyssey* also has a number of other establishment agendas featured in it as well. Other than simply showing "space" as a place we can travel to, it is also – most prominently - massively pushing the theory of evolution, as well as the existence of extraterrestrial life forms as things that should be taken for granted. Due to Kubrick's involvement in such a – clearly at least partially government-funded – propaganda-project, finishing right before the year of the supposed "Moon landing", many researchers today rightfully suspect that it was him who directed that piece of motion picture as well. This suspicion is further supported by the fact that some of his other films, such as *The Shining*, involves multiple references to the endeavor, with several hidden (and some not-so-hidden) messages hinting at fakery having been afoot. Aside from the countless - mostly decent - analysis videos of it, made by independent researchers that one can find online, the increasingly famous 2012 documentary *Room 237* also reveals and unpacks many of these messages.

However, Clarke's influence on the development of the space-hoax reached much further than just writing made up stories, not to mention that writing the script for *2001: A Space Odyssey* was not the only way he proved his talent for convincingly blurring the lines between science and fiction. In October 1945 he wrote an article titled *Extra-Terrestrial Relays: Can Rocket Stations Give Worldwide Radio Coverage?* for the famous British technical magazine The

Wireless World. In this article he envisioned a specific orbital height - about 36,000 miles above the Earth - which would allow an object to match the Earth's supposed "rotation period", making it appear stationary relative to a fixed point on the Earth's surface. This idea - based on nothing but Clarke' imagination – was so much to the liking of the powers that be that they soon started propagating it as actual science, and thus it became commonly known as a geostationary or Clarke Orbit, or the Clarke Belt. Moreover, his article also proposed a "communications satellite" system that would relay television and radio signals throughout the world. He suggested that with the help of just three "satellites" spaced equidistantly in his imaginary "orbit", 120 degrees apart, could provide continuous "global" coverage of such services.

Despite being based on essentially nothing but his imagination, this article was - unlike most of his other works - supposed to be non-fiction, so the establishment took the opportunity and made sure the world believes that this was indeed the case. To achieve this, they decided to pretend that Clarke's imaginary system is perfectly feasible, and thus it was claimed to be in operation within just two decades, with NASA allegedly successfully launching the first "communications satellite" into Clarke's made up "geostationary orbit" in 1964.

While it is officially admitted that Clarke's ideas detailed in the aforementioned article were "initially speculative", they were said to have "laid the conceptual foundations" for the supposed technology nonetheless, and thus the ideas that would normally belong in a sci-fi novel were taken over by the powers that be, soon to be presented to the public as "groundbreaking scientific discovery".

On one hand, it is – from the perspective of someone who knows the truth - quite fascinating that the satellite-hoax is still going strong today, with most of humanity believing it without question. On the other hand, however, it is the unfortunate but natural consequence of the programming we've all been put through by every manifestation of the establishment's media monopoly, just as it is with most other hoaxes. Most relevantly the space-hoax and the globe-hoax, which are, of course, fundamental prerequisites of the satellite-hoax.

One of the most prominent supposed "proofs" of the existence of "satellites" (other than CGI videos and images) is claimed to be the simple fact that we have cell phone and internet signal coverage "all around the world" (*Affirming the consequent*). Of course, that claim is clearly not even true, as anyone can tell who ever went too far from a cell tower only to find little to no reception signal on their cell phone due to a lack of network coverage or capacity in the area. Despite Clarke having written about 100% coverage everywhere being possible in 1945, nothing even close to that was achieved to this very day. Obviously, this is because the signal is sent out by the aforementioned ground-based towers, and not by imaginary tin cans flying 36,000 miles above our heads.

The fact is, cell towers have become so widespread over the past few decades that there are currently more than 300,000 of them in just the U.S. alone. Although they can often be easily spotted on tops of buildings, hills or even mountains, some cities require them to blend into the cityscape seamlessly, while certain rural areas even make a special effort to disguise them as a tree in an attempt to preserve the natural beauty of the place.

It should also be mentioned that, while the functionality of a GPS ("Global" Positioning System) is claimed to rely on "orbiting satellites", the signals supposedly coming from "space" are said to be traveling at the (two-way) speed of light – as per Einstein's thoroughly debunked theory -, which is then included in all of the calculations - meaning we can rest assured that they're all useless and pointless. Furthermore, the technology uses the Cartesian coordinate system, which is, of course, based on a two-dimensional plane geometry, also known as Earth's surface. Needless to say, a third dimension – altitude – was later added to the system, however, the GPS signals create circles on the ground level for the sake of positioning, which would therefore also only ever work on a flat plane. This means that the GPS would not only work better assuming a flat plane instead of a globe, but the fact that it's operational is actually another proof that the Earth simply cannot be spherical.

Although we are often told that if we look up at the sky at night we may be able to see one of the "thousands of satellites" flying through, however - even within the official narrative -, this is clearly impossible, as they're supposed to be about the size of a car and thousands of miles away.

Unfortunately, if one were to search for images online with the term *satellite in space*, he won't do any better either. He may get to feast his eyes upon countless images of what are claimed to be "photos" of satellites, however, upon closer look, it will - or *should* - quickly become very apparent to anyone that these are, in fact, nothing more than mere drawings or CGI. Not just *a few of them*, not even *most of them*, but each and every one of them, with no exception. And if we looked up the phrase *satellite on ground*, the ones among the resulting images that do look like they might actually be photographs will always be that of a regular satellite dish, which merely serve as antennae, receiving signals from another device. The devices sending the signals may be either cell towers, or one of those transmitters that are hanging from high-altitude helium balloons – which happen to look very similar to the more famous "orbiting satellites", with their bodies also covered with solar panels.

Not only would the notion of "orbiting" around the Earth be physically impossible, but every spacecraft in "orbit" would quickly get destroyed by all the debris that is claimed to be flying along that same path as well. Perhaps this is also the reason why not once can we see even (a fake) one in most supposedly "real" footage of the globe-Earth, despite the fact that there are allegedly thousands of satellites in orbit. In fact, they don't even bother to make them appear in movies around the ever-present CGI globes, presumably not only because it would be a lot of extra work, but also because they know well that most people either aren't aware or simply forget that all those satellites are supposed to be there anyway. After all, if they never show them anywhere, whether it be allegedly real or admittedly fake footage, the audience will learn to never expect it - at least until they specifically look into the matter and think about it long enough.

Revealing what the "satellites" actually built are used for is helped by the debris that occasionally crash into Earth's surface. These are generally claimed to be the remains of so-called "spacecrafts" left behind in previous "space missions". However, all available evidence shows that these are the same balloon-attached devices that we can see at the launch of a common high-altitude weather balloon, or the actual transmitter devices that, in fact, look exactly like what we've come to believe is a space-satellite – with the difference of a balloon being attached to it. Unfortunately - and understandably -, such crashed devices are quite a rare find, since the governments always try to make sure they get to the crash site first, so that they can get the "cleaning process" done and dispose of the evidence before the average citizen sees it and starts to figure out that he's been fooled his whole life.

Even the engineers that work on the parts of supposed "spacecrafts" are – similarly to those working on parts of a "A-bomb" - compartmentalized and thus left in the dark as to what *really* happens to the final product once they're finished. This serves the purpose of not only lending them plausible deniability when asked about the hoax, but also that of making them believe – and spread the word – that they were indeed involved in a "space-project" – thus unwittingly further propagating the hoax.

Furthermore, the launching process of the rockets that are supposed to carry a "satellite" (or anything else) into "space" is no less fishy either. As anyone who watched one of these events must have noticed, the trajectory of the rockets is not exactly that of one that's going straight up into the sky, or "space", but rather one that goes upwards for no more than maybe a few kilometers before making an arc towards the ground. And that is precisely the moment the authorities will try and gaslight us by telling us that *"it only appears to curve downwards, but it is in fact already in outer space"*. The reason this deception works so well is because the average onlooker will clearly have no way to verify how high the rocket has actually reached, since at this point it is simply too far away to tell. As for those not watching it live but rather on a screen, the deceivers always make sure to switch the actual footage to a very obvious CGI animation right before the rocket is about to start turning sideways.

Another problem with the notion of things going to "space" is one that the deceivers created for themselves for some reason, namely the so-called "escape velocity", which is the minimum speed an object is claimed to need to break free from the "gravitational attraction" of a massive body, without further propulsion, and enter into "space". Needless to say, its formula includes a number of obviously fallacious, unknowable and asinine things, such as the mass of the "massive body" (e.g. "planet", moon), the distance from the center of that body to the object's center, and, of course, the unmissable "gravitational constant". Since all of these data are based on the same logical fallacies that the globe-hoax itself was built upon, there is clearly no reason to even consider the validity of the formula, and therefore also the notion of rockets going anywhere near a supposed sky-vacuum. This is especially true knowing that Earth's "escape velocity" is claimed to be 11.2 km/s (not counting air resistance), which is many times faster than most rockets have ever even been made to appear to be moving.

Although no recording of the rockets intended for "space" crashing into the ground can ever be seen, one can get a fairly good idea what's likely happening to them by simply examining their direction and trajectory. Upon analyzing multiple launches, it becomes quite obvious that most, if not all, rockets eventually end up crashing into the ocean to hide the evidence of it never reaching "space", which, of course, also explains why they always seem to do the launches on or near a coast.

Although some people still refer to so-called "spacewalks", or the "astronauts" seemingly floating in a "zero-gravity space station" as a "proof" of something, these are actually some of the easiest parts of the hoax to debunk, even without mentioning the (to us) obvious fact that even the very idea of "outer space" is an impossibility.

First of all, let it be noted that even if it was possible to do all of the above, it would still make absolutely no sense to actually carry it out, since there is really no benefit to doing so, and it's incredibly easy and cheap to fake it anyway. In fact, anyone who knows a little bit about filmmaking can fairly simply make a rather convincing video of himself seemingly floating in what appears to be a "space station" with the help of an augmented reality software, having to spend no more than a few dollars. Of course, there are some cases where a higher grade of trickery takes place, and an even more realistic display of weightlessness is required. In such cases the "space agencies" utilize what's known as a "zero-gravity plane"; an aircraft that is used to create periods of weightlessness or "microgravity" for its occupants. These specially modified airplanes follow a specific trajectory called a parabolic flight path during which they alternately climb and descend in a steep, roller-coaster-like maneuver. As the they climb, the occupants experience a period of "free fall", simulating the feeling (and appearance) of weightlessness for about 20-30 seconds per parabola. These planes are officially used for scientific research, filming scenes for motion pictures with simulated weightlessness, as well as "astronaut training". Although this is certainly much more costly than simply conducting the deception with the help of a software alone, it still clearly wouldn't even make a dent on a "space agency's" budget, even if it was being done all day long every single day.

Another way the "training of the astronauts", is claimed to be done is by placing them underwater in "training pools", along with the "spacecraft" they'll have to pretend to do maintenance work on (while being filmed, for some reason). Needless to say, this kind of training wouldn't make much sense, considering that being in a vacuum would feel as different from being underwater as it possibly can. However, it does make "spacewalks" extremely easy to fake with the help of some CGI, since the necessary appearance of "floating" is provided by the water, and every detail that would be telling of the hoax will be – ideally - invisible to the viewers anyway.

Naturally, there are some cases when things don't work out exactly as planned, and certain "oddities" get revealed to the viewers. One of such mishaps is when we can see air bubbles escape from the "astronauts'" helmets during their so-called spacewalks. When a NASA worker was asked about it in an interview, he said that the bubbles were probably just "sweat", or coming from the cooling garment, or perhaps they're just "flakes of paint" flying off of it due to the "harsh conditions" in "space". Why he needed to – incriminatingly - mention any kind of water or wetness only to then immediately abandon that argument and try to blame it on chipping paint instead, is anyone's guess. Unfortunately for them, however, unedited underwater "training" footages are also published, and the air bubbles clearly visible in them look exactly the same as these "unknown objects" seen during the "spacewalks", so there is really no room for doubt regarding the method of this fakery.

The insides of "space stations" also have a number of serious red flags in them, such as the messy jungle of cables and all the fragile equipment hanging out far from every wall of the extremely tight, crowded cabins. It may be that such a disorderly, chaotic system provides an interesting display for the viewers, and perhaps even make them believe that something quite complicated, expensive and important is being conducted there, but it would certainly be hard to operate it even in a perfectly stable ground building. Indeed, it is a good thing that the whole endeavor is merely a deception, as all of the cables and devices would inevitably keep getting accidentally ripped out and destroyed by the personnel floating and stumbling around on the station – which would be moving at a mind-boggling speed - if everything were truly as claimed.

Yet another obvious sign of the space-fakery was the series of public admissions of the extremely limited capabilities of "space exploration", made by then U.S. president Barack Obama, as well as a number of different NASA employees over the past decade. In these, they detailed how it's a shame that *we've never been able to get past "low Earth orbit"* (LEO), which is supposed to be an altitude between 160 km and 1,000 km above Earth's surface, essentially openly admitting the faking of the "Moon landing". At one point, a "newly built space module" was introduced by one of them as the "innovation" that will finally allow us to "explore space" beyond that height, further confirming the awkward but inescapable truth. Naturally, all of this means that either those who made these statements, or the astronauts who claim to have been beyond the altitude of LEO are lying.

Over the past few decades, the art of conflating reality with computer-generated imagery (CGI) has become the bread and butter of the professional deceivers. Perhaps one of the most enfuriating examples showing us just how blatantly it's being done is the deeds of Elon Musk, South African-born American entrepreneur (and currently – officially - the richest person on Earth) who formed the aerospace company SpaceX in 2002. It was the first private company to allegedly successfully launch and return a "spacecraft" from "Earth orbit" and claimed to be the first to launch a crewed "spacecraft" and dock it with what they call the "International Space Station" (ISS). With this enterprise, Musk is said to have helped usher in the "era of commercial spaceflight", although it should be noted that the U.S. government also funded SpaceX with many billions of dollars, so technically nothing that was supposedly achieved through it should be considered Musk's own merit.

Regardless, an almost unparalleled cult of personality has been built around him in the recent years through multiple publicist activities, making him one of the most popular people of our time, and somewhat of a symbol of resistance against the tyrannical globalist elite. In fact, their followers are often so obsessed with his person that they don't even seem to care that he's actually often pushing certain agendas that are very much to the liking of the aforementioned elite, the obvious space-propaganda only being one of them.

It also seems to be overlooked by them that he sometimes just about admits being a fraud. The most prominent one of such cases was undoubtedly in a Q & A that was held at a conference after supposedly launching a car - made by one of his other companies - into "Earth orbit" in 2018. In this, one of the attendees asked him – among others – what amounted to "how it felt to see his car "orbiting the Earth"", to which he replied the following:

"Well, I think it looks so ridiculous and impossible, and you can tell it's real because it looks so fake, honestly. We have way better CGI if it was fake... And, you know, the colors all look kinda weird in space, there's no atmospheric occlusion, you know, like, everything looks too crisp (...)."

Of course, those that have seen the aforementioned footage will understand why he said all this; the whole thing indeed looks very fake (and it also shows a glitch, as it often happens with CGI), but not because it is so "real", rather because it clearly isn't.

In 2019, Musk also started another venture within SpaceX called Starlink, a so-called "megaconstellation" consisting of "satellites" which are supposed to provide internet service. As of 2023, it is claimed that Starlink had 3,660 active satellites, about half of all the currently "active" ones purportedly in "orbit". While dots of light claimed to be representing these can indeed be seen moving through the night sky, they may as well just be large helium balloons (or even drones) flying anywhere between a few and a few dozen kilometers high. The internet provided by them could also be explained by the helium balloon method, as there have already been other companies working on such solutions to solve the problem of many regions on Earth being left with no internet connection - which is actually another clear proof of the fact that artificial satellites don't exist. One of such companies was Google/Alphabet, who started Project Loon, by which they aimed to use such balloons - essentially flying cell towers - to beam high-speed cellular service from the sky to low-connectivity areas. Although this particular project was eventually grounded by that corporation, the idea was later salvaged by other enterprises.

Further proof that Musk is essentially just being used as a tool and being pushed into the front by the powers that be appears in the 1948 sci-fi novel *Mars Project: A Technical Tale*, written by none other than Wernher von Braun himself. In this book he details calculations and arguments to "show" practicality of a mission to Mars and the establishment of a colony there, supplemented with colour illustrations and a technical appendix. What's even more interesting is that the book says that the highest leader on Mars will be known as the "Elon". This is especially peculiar in sight of the fact that Musk is well-known for having big plans regarding a – first ever - manned trip to Mars in the following years (although, I would urge everyone to not hold their breaths, but also keep their eyes peeled for another possible dose of CGI fakery). Naturally, the official standpoint is that the matching of Musk's first name and that of the position of the ruler of Mars in von Braun's book is merely a coincidence, but if we're honest, one would have to be exceptionally naïve to think that this is the case, while the implications of the apparent conspiracy and the message that it sends us may be up for contemplation.

Another big player in the game of deception was Carl Sagan, American astrophysicist, cosmologist, author, and "science communicator". He played a significant role in popularizing pseudoscience, particularly in the field of astronomy and space exploration, brainwashing the public with not only the mainstream lies and hoaxes, but also adding concepts of his own. It is said that his "research" as an astronomer contributed to all sorts of "great" (nonsensical) things, such as "learning" about the atmospheres of various "planets", the "greenhouse effect" on Venus, and the seasonal changes on Mars. One of his most well-known books is *Cosmos* (1980), which accompanied the television series of the same name and became one of the best-selling "science" books of all time. In his works, he often emphasized the importance of a "cosmic perspective" - a view that recognizes the Earth as merely a small and interconnected part of the "vast cosmos". The following lines are from the aforementioned book *Cosmos*, which perhaps best reflect this dark view of the world he had (p. 190):

"For as long as there been humans we have searched for our place in the cosmos. Where are we? Who are we? We find that we live on an insignificant planet of a hum-drum star lost in a galaxy tucked away in some forgotten corner of a universe in which there are far more galaxies than people. This perspective is a courageous continuation of our penchant for constructing and testing mental models of the skies; the Sun as a red-hot stone, the stars as a celestial flame, the Galaxy as the backbone of night."

This kind of worldview is, of course, something that the powers that be are trying their hardest to have us all adopt, as the beliefs included in it make a man fragile and easy to control.

Due to this kind of message Sagan was sending the people, he was, in fact, so highly esteemed by the establishment that they even involved him in several government-funded "space missions", as well as the development of the ridiculous Search for Extraterrestrial Intelligence (SETI) program, where he also served as an institute board trustee. SETI was founded in 1984 as a "scientific" effort aimed at detecting signals from "extraterrestrial civilizations" - of which they've yet to find any to this day. Regardless, Sagan seemed to have been fully convinced of their existence, as he often included discussions about the search for extraterrestrial life in his popular "science" works and television series and frequently advocated for the "scientific exploration" of this possibility. In his 1996 book *The Demon-Haunted World: Science as a Candle in the Dark*, he detailed the circumstances that eventually turned him into the person that could serve as an instrument of deception as follows (p. 58.):

"The phrase 'flying saucer' was coined when I was entering high school. The newspapers were full of stories about ships from beyond in the skies of Earth. It seemed pretty believable to me. There were lots of other stars, at least some of which probably had planetary systems like ours. Many stars were as old or older than the Sun, so there was plenty of time for intelligent life to evolve. Caltech's Jet Propulsion Laboratory had just flown a two-stage rocket high above the Earth. Clearly we were on our way to the Moon and the planets. Why shouldn't other, older, wiser beings be able to travel from their star to ours? Why not? This was only a few years after the bombing of Hiroshima and Nagasaki. Maybe the UFO occupants were worried about us, and sought to help us. Or maybe they wanted to make sure that we and our nuclear weapons didn't come and bother them. Many people seemed to see flying saucers - sober pillars of the community, police officers, commercial airplane pilots, military personnel."

So, it would seem that even Sagan himself was merely a victim of all the space-hoax (and nuke-hoax) propaganda that humanity was already being showered with during his younger years. Be that as it may, he certainly does a good job of pushing the belief in "billions of planets", which, of course, automatically necessitates the belief in "alien lifeforms" as well, simply because of the mathematical probability provided by the notion. As for people seeing "flying saucers", it can be quite easily explained. While "aliens" clearly don't exist, UFOs are very much real, but they are likely just man-made aircrafts that are either nothing more that weather balloons, or possibly secret government-made ones used for the sole purpose of deceiving the public into believing in aliens, as well as a potential "alien threat".

Moreover, interestingly enough, later in the same book Sagan makes a pretty convincing case for not believing what he and others like him say (p. 193):

"One of the saddest lessons of history is this: if we've been bamboozled long enough, we tend to reject any evidence of the bamboozle. We're no longer interested in finding out the truth. The bamboozle has captured us. It's simply too painful to acknowledge, even to ourselves, that we've been taken. Once you give a charlatan power over you, you almost never get it back. So the old bamboozles tend to persist as the new ones rise"

Remarks to a similar point - of precarious origins - have also been attributed to him, such as the following:

"The dangers of not thinking clearly are much greater now than ever before. It's not that there's something new in our way of thinking – it's that credulous and confused thinking can be much more lethal in ways it was never before."

"We have also arranged things so that almost no one understands science and technology. This is a prescription for disaster. We might get away with it for a while, but sooner or later this combustible mixture of ignorance and power is going to blow up in our faces."

"Today, we're still loaded down – and, to some extent, embarrassed - by ancient myths, but we respect them as part of the same impulse that has led to the modern, scientific kind of myth.

THE GLOBAL DECEPTION

In a sharp contrast to those quotes, however, the following is also attributed to him – which is perhaps the most revealing of his true nature:

"I didn't know what other worlds looked like until I saw Bonestell's paintings."

The person he refers to is Chesley Bonestell, who was an American painter, designer, and illustrator, best known for his work in the field of "space art". He played a significant role in popularizing the visual depiction of "space" and "astronomical scenes", especially during the mid 20th century. He also collaborated with astronomers and science fiction writers (such as von Braun) to paint celestial bodies and "scenes of space exploration" for them. His paintings are generally labeled by pseudoscientists as "detailed" and "accurate", and they had a significant impact on popularizing "space exploration concepts" and inspiring both the public and so-called "professionals" to be even more enthusiastic about all things related to "space".

In fact, his impact on the world of pseudoscience seemed to have been so immense that Joseph Chamberlain, director of the famous Adler Planetarium in Chicago, went even further and made the following statement:

"It might even be suggested that without Bonestell and his early space age artistry, the NASA era might have been delayed for many years, or it might not have happened at all."

This notion was further confirmed by the following remark from Arthur C. Clarke himself:

"Chesley is the original - he's been there ahead of them all. Neil Armstrong? Well, Tranquility Base [the name given to the supposed "Moon landing site"] *was established over Bonestell's tracks and*

discarded squeezed-out paint tubes. The man not only moves across space, but also across time. He was present at our world's birth and has also set up his easel to paint its death..."

With Bonestell, a mere painter, being regarded as essentially one of the pioneers of "space exploration" even by so-called "experts", it's not hard to see why many today consider the whole concept to be nothing more than fairy-tale for adults.

Bonestell was even involved in the film industry, contributing to the visual effects of several classic movies, such as *Citizen Kane* (1941) and *Destination Moon* (1950). Naturally, he wasn't the only artist of the 20th century to be employed as a faker of "space" - he was simply the most famous. Nonetheless, the knowledge of such methods is important, as they are able to explain how the public could have been deceived so effectively even before the existence of digital editing and CGI, simply using paintings and – in some cases - models.

It is also important to mention that the space-hoax, and especially the alien-hoax also had other goals beside simply scaring the public with the possibility of an outside threat. In the 1980s, president Ronald Reagen gave a series of speeches, in which he said that the people of the Earth would "unite" if faced and extraterrestrial alien threat from "another planet". This didn't seem to mean much at the time, other than pointless ramblings and wishful thinking, but then, in the 1990s George H. W. Bush brought into the public conciousness the notion of creating a "new world order" (NWO) in a number of his speeches. In these, he talked about how this NWO would "unite" us all under a centralized government, "eliminating" many of the world's currently existing problems. Of course, he may have forgotten to mention that it would create new, much greater problems instead, although, those would be problems for us, not for them, so in their eyes they obviously don't count anyway.

THE GLOBAL DECEPTION

Nonetheless, these speeches finally made it clear for everyone (that has a mind of his own) what Reagen actually referred to when he wanted the world to be "united", especially if we consider that H. W. Bush was the vice president during his reign, as well as his immediate successor. Not only did the two politicians' speeches cover the same point of uniting the world under a centralized control for "the greater good", but these speeches were also coming regularly in turns. This was likely done this way in order to conflate their two seemingly different topics in the public's minds, letting them believe that the NWO is just as much of a benign agenda as the notion of uniting our forces against hostile invaders to defend ourselves.

Later on, in the mid 2010s, the alien/UFO-agenda escalated further when leading politicians, such as Bill Clinton, Barack Obama, and Hillary Clinton - at least one of them every year for a few years - were invited to talk on either one of the country's most popular late night talk shows. On these shows, they were asked about "alien lifeforms", UFOs, and whether they know of any secret files about them. As one would expect, they didn't openly reveal anything definitive – as to not make the trickery too obvious -, but they all made sure to covertly hint at either the fact that they're very much convinced of the existence of extra-terrestrial lifeforms, or that "they are instructed to say there are no secrets", but in fact, "there might be some things that they just can't talk about". Perhaps not too surprisingly, even one of the most famous sci-fi movies about an alien invasion, *Independence Day*, was mentioned as a reference to the subjects of "secret government research" in Area 51, and how the invading aliens might eventually "hopefully not" behave, planting more seeds of the alien- and the NWO-agendas by way of subtle fearmongering.

Then there are also the so-called "educational programmes" where astronomers are interviewed on similar topics. One of the more prominent shows included none other than Michio Kaku, who has been frequently asked about all sorts of space-nonsense over the past decade. His main purpose in these shows seems to have been pushing the idea that there are in fact "billions of planets" in existence, with at least a part of them being habitable, meaning that – mathematically speaking - there simply must be some among them with intelligent life on it. Another frequently – also not just by him - repeated claim was, naturally, that the universe is "billions of years old", implying that many of those alien lifeforms would be much older and therefore more advanced than humans, thus potentially posing a great threat to us. Needless to say, this aligns perfectly with the agenda we've so frequently seen many leading politicians push. They also made sure to frequently bring up the claim that if we were invaded by them, we would quickly need to decide who to organize Earth's defense, clearly hinting at – and once again planting the seed of - the notion that we "need" a centralized, totalitarian one-world government to "lead" and "protect" us all.

Contrary to popular belief, as even one of the presidential pundits admitted during one of the aforementioned talk show interviews, it is not the examination of UFOs or aliens that is being conducted at Area 51, but rather just secret military research. And, clearly, if there is one facility that's admittedly used in such a way, there could be many others that are not quite as well-known. In fact, today it's often considered common knowledge that the more advanced armies are actually at least 25 years ahead of the civilian world when it comes to technology. Therefore, it would be safe to assume that all the reports and – somehow always very grainy - recordings of "flying saucers / triangles" or "mysterious glowing objects" in the night sky could be nothing more than man-made experimental aircraft. Of course, in many cases it can be explained even simpler with weather phenomena, weather balloons, drones, rockets, or aerial explosions. It is also interesting that whenever one of these objects crash into the ground, the crash site tends to be sealed off by armed soldiers, even when the object is known to be nothing more than a plastic crash dummy. Then, if civilians ask the "wrong" questions or saw what they weren't supposed to, they would get in trouble for it. In fact, even military careers can be destroyed if an individual among them refuses to keep his mouth shut about the truth.

Needless to say, those who desperately want to believe in aliens will try to spin this and claim that all the secrecy is due to the fact that the government is hiding them from us, but knowing what we now know, that seems out of the question. Even if one were to assume that aliens do exist, it would make no sense for the government to constantly feed us all the alien-propaganda in an attempt to make us believe in them, only to then do everything in their power to hide their existence from us when it's finally revealed as "truth". What's much more likely is that their secrecy merely serves the purpose of making it seem like there is "something to see" where there is in fact nothing, further reinforcing the belief in aliens in the minds of the more gullible.

Indeed, the whole deception and the fearmongering could never work if all of humanity knew that Earth is a closed system, as a belief in aliens would be practically non-existent to begin with.

The space exploration scam

After the first "Moon landing" supposedly took place, it is claimed that the Apollo project has seen five more successful crewed missions – naturally, with no major errors or issues - to the Moon in the following years, with the last one allegedly happening in December 1972. For some reason, that was the last purported manned mission to anywhere beyond low Earth orbit, and, as it's been mentioned in an earlier chapter, we have since then *lost the technology, and it's a painful process to build it back*. Moreover, the telemetry data tapes from the first supposed trip are claimed to have been recorded over by someone either by accident or due to being "repurposed" because of "budget constraints", as such a thing apparently just happens with the most important historical relic ever to be produced. Needless to say, the data tapes of later missions suffered a similar fate, claimed to have been either erased and reused or conveniently stored in suboptimal conditions – despite huge government funding -, leading to degradation.

There's no doubt that even without realizing that all of the "Moon missions" must have been mere fakeries, let alone the fact that "outer space" can't possibly be real to begin with, it should still be quite astonishing and frustrating for any layman to see just how little all the so-called "space agencies" managed to achieve since the last supposed "Moon landing". No doubt, we may often hear people who were born in the mid 1900s say that they all thought we would have colonies on the Moon and make regular trips there and back on our flying cars before the century was over – as the propaganda they grew up with had them believe. Yet, in stark contrast to such hopes, most missions since 1972 have been focused on nothing more than purportedly "conducting research" aboard different "space stations", but mainly on the International Space Station (ISS). Although it is claimed that these endeavors resulted in "advancements" in technology and science, there is obviously no evidence that any of them would have required any research to take place in a flying tin can.

Of course, regardless of the lack of evidence, maintaining the public's belief in that claim is crucial for governments who wish to extort more money out of their helpless subjects in the name of "progress". While all of humanity has every right to feel affronted by the deception, the outcry should be particularly strong from those individuals whose government runs a taxpayer-funded "space agency", as they are directly affected financially by the pointless spending. In fact, the "space exploration" scam has been turned into such a deep money-suck over the past decades that it is now a multi-hundred-billion dollar industry, most of it funded, of course, by the tax-slaves unfortunate enough to have an agency set up in their homeland.

Although there are now dozens of "space agencies" in existence, all of which are unfortunately robbing their respective taxpayers blind with the promise of maybe eventually achieving something of use, it is quite obvious that all proverbial roads lead back to NASA. All of the other agencies seem to use the same methods of fakery as them, utilizing the same low-effort CGI animations and repeating the same well-established buzz-words in a desperate attempt to convince the public that they are in fact carrying out something of importance and value. There are, naturally, also frequent official inter-agency collaborations, again to make everyone think that something "big" is happening thanks to the ridiculous amounts of money they were forced to pay in taxes to their overlords. They also serve the purpose of maintaining the belief that governments are generally prioritizing and working hard on "space exploration" and the supposed "technological developments" that would come with it. Nonetheless, NASA are still clearly the leaders of the pack, and the ones that decide which direction the narrative has to go.

It seems that the way the deceivers among the U.S. political elite plan to keep the charade going indefinitely is by regularly making promises of incredible achievements "in the near future", and then, when the years come and pass and still none of it has happened, they blame it either on "low funding" or clearly fabricated political reasons. This is significantly helped by the unfortunate fact that the average voter apparently does not have a very good memory and tends to forget not only the promises of politicians, but often even major scandals, after only a few months. Of course, it is also supported by the whole of the political system, which is designed to allow the deposed politicians to absolve themselves from all responsibility by claiming that the four-year cycle – not to mention if they don't get to complete it - was just too short to carry out all the great deeds they had planned for the country. Although, to be fair, this kind of issue is – unfortunately - not something that would be unique to the U.S. at all.

NASA, just like all other space agencies, operate under the authority of the national government, which establishes the legal framework, allocates funding, and sets the overall goals and priorities for "space exploration". So when it comes to deciding which direction to take, ultimately the president will have the power to do so. This is why we predominantly hear them making the promises of such wondrous deeds as building a colony on the Moon and Mars, landing on and mining asteroids, collecting and returning samples from a number of "planets" and their "moons", establishing commercial "space" tourism, and so on. Although these promises have been ongoing since the founding of NASA with very little in terms of actual – supposed - achievements, none of the presidents seemed to have any trouble telling the public just how "close" they are to actually fulfilling one of their promises, and that they'll definitely get there one day as long as the taxpayers give them more time and, of course, money. Another important role of NASA was to serve as a tool for artificially creating a large amount of jobs, as well as so-called "inspiration" for the common folk who, sadly, wholeheartedly believed in the feasibility of "space exploration".

It is hard to say whether the presidents themselves even know about "space exploration" being a deception, or any of the other hoaxes and psyops for that matter; after all, they are – similarly to most politicians – merely the puppets of those who create them. For all we know, every one of the presidents and even most of their colleagues may wholeheartedly believe that it's all real, and had the best of intentions when trying to decide about new projects. However, it should be noted that not knowing about something does not absolve one of his responsibilities, especially when he assumes the role of president of a superpower.

The first president who had a role in the charade of "space exploration" was Dwight D. Eisenhower, who was also the one that signed the legislation that started NASA itself. He specifically wanted it to be under the Department of Defense rather than a private company, and to only employ people from the army as staff members, however, his colleagues convinced him otherwise, so it ended up being a (seemingly) civilian organization.

One of Eisenhower's first deeds after NASA was founded was to use the establishment media to propagate a recording of his voice, which was allegedly playing from a tape recorder on the freshly launched satellite that's flying around Earth in its "orbit", making it the first human voice to be claimed to be broadcast from "space". We have no way of knowing exactly how many actually believed this farce to be true, but the endeavor may well have been the first act of the endless theater play that is "space exploration".

Then came Kennedy's turn, who became the second president to have a role in maintaining the "space exploration" scam, though he was most likely unaware of it being just that, not to mention that he himself may well have ended up falling victim to it eventually. While he wasn't much of a "space"-enthusiast, he still wanted to achieve something big that's "space"-related for a possible re-election and to beat the Soviets in the supposed "Space Race". To this request, his vice president Lyndon B. Johnson, a lover of "space" who helped establish NASA, suggested that a trip to the Moon should be possible as early as 1967.

Kennedy jumped on this promise and increased NASA's budget massively right away to make sure the mission was well-funded, then made a passionate public speech about what's to come. His goal with this speech seemed to have been to convince everyone just how incredible an achievement the supposed Moon landing will be, so he mentioned all the details involving its technical features as well as the difficulties to overcome. Whoever wrote the speech for him, made the process of the endeavor seem so unbelievable and unrealistic that anyone who knows the truth may think the purpose of the speech was actually to make people realize just how ridiculous and far-fetched the whole idea of the "Moon landing" was, and that there was simply no way it could ever be done.

At that point, however, it is possible that almost everyone involved - including Johnson and most NASA employees - still wholeheartedly believed that it was possible to pull off such a thing, and seemed to have worked hard on figuring out a way to do it. It is likely that one of the most shocking of all disappointments hit Kennedy when he talked with NASA administrator James Webb in a meeting in 1962, nearly 20 months after his big speech that sparked up the public's interest with its monumental promises. Webb spoke grimly about the Moon-project's situation, letting Kennedy know that it is not their first priority at all, then continued to explain – in barely coherent sentences – that it's mainly because they've found that sending rockets outside of Earth's "atmosphere" has proven to be "much more difficult" than they first thought. Kennedy then pressed on, urging Webb to make the project the agency's top priority, emphasizing how crucially important it is for political reasons. Webb then continued to detail all the other factors which convinced him that the Moon landing would be a very tough if not impossible task, including the fact that they don't even know if humans can survive in "weightlessness", and that they know exactly nothing about the properties of the Moon's surface, so the mission could easily end in disaster.

10 months later Kennedy seemed to have accepted the disappointing fact that the U.S. is unlikely to be the first to (pretend to) get to the Moon, so he changed his strategy and instead suggested that they should join forces with the Soviets and go there together, ending the "Space Race" and likely decreasing NASA's budget significantly. He talked about this in his last address to the United Nations, but alas, his idea wasn't exactly popular with the perpetrators of the "space exploration" scam and he was killed roughly a month later under questionable circumstances.

With Kennedy's death, his vice president, Johnson became the new president, and as one might expect, the "Space Race" was promptly back on once again and NASA's previously increased funding remained in place.

Johnson's name has been associated with multiple – to say the least – dishonest endeavors, such as the establishment of the Warren Commission (officially the President's Commission on the Assassination of President Kennedy), which supposedly aimed to investigate his predecessor's murder. Although this may seem like a rather noble deed, even some of the more honest mainstream sources admit that it is a subject of great controversy, since many details and evidence were ignored and in the end a supposed lone gunman with a petty motive was chosen as the killer. Of course, they have no other choice than to admit that something was quite off with the investigation, due to the fact that in 1976 a new congressional committee, the House Select Committee on Assassinations was established with the purpose of reopening the cases and continuing the earlier investigations of not only Kennedy's assassination, but also the 1968 murder of civil rights leader Martin Luther King Jr. The committee found that the original investigations into both Kennedy and King assassinations were deficient, and the final report concluded that Kennedy was likely assassinated as a result of a conspiracy, but unfortunately it did not identify specific individuals or groups involved.

After Johnson's term ended, Richard Nixon was next in the line of presidents. As it was already mentioned in an earlier chapter, it is claimed that he spoke to "astronauts on the Moon" from a landline phone in the White House in 1969 during the first ever so-called "Moon landing". He was determined to keep the ball rolling with the Apollo "Moon missions", as they proved to be the perfect distraction for the U.S. citizens from the highly unpopular Vietnam war that was raging on at the time. In the meantime, he was also "working on ending the war", which, along with the "successful space programs", made him so popular that he managed to win the next election as well. During his time in office, Skylab, the United States' first so-called "space station" was claimed to have been launched up into the imaginary sky-vacuum and continued to "orbit the Earth" until 1979. It was said to have hosted three manned missions overall, supposedly providing "valuable data for scientific research in microgravity".

Following mounting pressure and the threat of impeachment in the wake of the Watergate scandal, Nixon announced his resignation in 1974, and left office the next day, making him the first (and currently the only) U.S. president to resign.

Nixon's vice president, Gerald Ford then assumed the presidency (unelected) and later pardoned him for any crimes he might have committed while in office. A year later the Viking Missions were supposedly carried out, where two "spacecrafts" were claimed to have been sent to Mars, allegedly conducting "experiments" to search for signs of life and provide "valuable data" about the Martian surface. Perhaps it is better not to think about how they managed to convince anyone that they could pull off such a feat, considering that Mars is supposed to be about 34 million miles away from us, while just a decade ago NASA was admittedly having trouble even getting a rocket out of Earth's "atmosphere". Nonetheless, that same year the Apollo-Soyuz Test Project, a joint "space docking" mission between the U.S. and the S.U. was also claimed to have taken place, symbolizing the end of the "Space Race" with a joint hoax.

The so-called Space Shuttle program was also initiated during the presidency of Gerald Ford. This is claimed to have been integral to the construction of the International Space Station (ISS) and is said to have carried out numerous "scientific missions". The first so-called "orbiter" in the program was initially to be named Constitution in honor of the U.S. Constitution's bicentennial, however, due to the letter-writing campaign by fans of *Star Trek* (an extremely popular American sci-fi TV series about adventures in "space"), urging the name to be changed to Enterprise, which was the name of the show's protagonists' spaceship, NASA promptly complied and made the change. Which is, of course, not at all surprising if we consider that the same group of people whose ancestors and contemporaries created and solidified the premise for all the sci-fi space-propaganda films and TV shows were also the ones who established NASA. With this little publicity stunt, they aimed to not only pay homage to their loyal fans as well as the industry that keeps the masses under hypnosis, but also bring the idea of "space exploration" closer to the common folk and, naturally, give them another reason to believe in it. Not only that, but it clearly served as a great tool to distract the public from the fact that they haven't been – even just allegedly - back to the Moon in years at that point with no plans to travel to Mars either, the reason for which obviously getting harder for the establishment to explain as time was passing by.

The next president was Jimmy Carter, who was not particularly enthusiastic about "space", in fact, in 1979 he even considered shutting down the Space Shuttle program due to the many "issues" it had encountered, however, since an immeasurable amount of money has already been sunk into it, he had no choice but to keep it going and hope that eventually it will achieve something worthy of mention. Nonetheless, Carter did perhaps his most important part in contributing to the hoax when he made a televised public service announcement together with Gerald Ford, which was, of course, allegedly done via a "communication satellite" in real time, despite clearly looking like pre-edited footage and sounding like a low-effort TV commercial. Not to mention that it also had the very same purpose as one, since it was simply them going on about how "useful" and helpful all the "space missions" have been to humanity. The whole recording makes one feel as if such missions were all just a mediocre product they're trying desperately to get people to purchase, or to keep agreeing to fund it - practically trying to make them believe that just about everything good that has recently been or is about to be invented or discovered is somehow the "spin-off of space technology".

Next in the line of presidents was former Hollywood actor Ronald Reagen, who was quite a big fan of "space". Despite his enthusiasm, he still didn't feel necessary to start any missions of actual "exploration", as the public still seemed to be satisfied enough with the distraction provided by the bottomless money pit that was the Space Shuttle program. Although, even this program was suspended for more than two years after the supposed disaster where the "space shuttle" Challenger fell apart shortly after its launch, allegedly killing its seven crew members. While this may have seemed like a tragic accident indeed, evidence shows that it was nothing more than another staged event, since all of the crew members were found to be alive and well even three decades later at different workplaces, with some of them even using their original names. This rather insidious psyop of an "accident" was likely done for the sake of providing the public with further distractions from the fact that still nothing of substance has been achieved by NASA. Of course, it also served as the perfect PR stunt for the establishment to gain more sympathy and support from the taxpayers and get them on board for further funding of NASA to "make things safer", as well as to remind them of the so-called "challenges and risks" associated with human "spaceflight", thus also winning more respect for the industry.

Utilizing his skills as an ex-actor, Reagen liked to give passionate public speeches. In some of these, he made mention of how "great" of an investment the nation makes when pouring money into the industry, and how it inspired the people's imagination - this latter statement being something that one would have a hard time debating. At any rate, he certainly did a good job milking the previous missions that were perceived as "successes", further popularizing "space exploration", keeping taxpayers hopeful about its future, and, naturally, making more promises of actual explorations eventually happening.

Once Reagen's second term was over, his vice president, George H. W. Bush, a former director of the CIA took his place as the new president. Similarly to Reagen, Bush was also very much into "space exploration", and thus one of his first deeds was, of course, to increase NASA's budget significantly. A proposal for a project called Space Exploration Initiative (SEI) was also introduced by him in his first year in office. The primary goal of this project was to send humans "back to the Moon" and eventually to Mars, although Bush offered no estimate of the cost of these ventures and no timetable for carrying them out. The proposal included the establishment of a permanent human presence on the Moon by constructing a lunar base, which was also intended to serve as a stepping stone for future crewed missions to Mars. Moreover, it also detailed plans for the retirement of the "space shuttles" and the development a new "spacecraft" and launch system capable of supporting lunar and Mars missions.

Bush outlined this vision in a speech at the National Air and Space Museum on the 20th anniversary of the Apollo 11 "Moon landing", but the SEI's goals seemed so far-fetched and were deemed so expensive that even some of his own party's politicians, as well as professionals of the industry criticized it and advised him not to go through with it.

Al Gore, a Democrat of Tennessee and chairman of the Committee on Space, Science and Technology, and a senator at the time said the following about the idea:

THE GLOBAL DECEPTION

"By proposing a return to the Moon and a manned base on Mars, with no money, no timetable, and no plan, President Bush offers the country not a challenge to inspire us, but a daydream to briefly entertain us, a daydream about as splashy as a George Lucas movie, with about as much connection to reality."

Although Gore has been consistently wrong on a number of matters over the past decades, he certainly hit the nail on the head with these remarks.

Due to all the criticism, Bush then made an announcement the following year, in which he proudly presented a timeline. He thought it should be possible to send humans to Mars before the 50th anniversary of the "Moon landing", and he boldly referred to these plans as a "new age of exploration". To make sure this would be considered feasible, he even asked a NASA expert for advice, who calculated that with about half a trillion dollars they should be able to make it happen by 2020. Needless to say, none of the plans detailed in the SEI were ever achieved or even attempted to be faked, likely because faking anything "permanent" - such as a base on the Moon - would be impossible, as they'd be found out by everyone sooner or later. Perhaps an exception to this rule is the Hubble "Space Telescope", which they did claim to deploy into low Earth "orbit", although its role more or less meaningless, since it merely allows them to bombard us with computer-generated illustrations claimed to be "photographs" of supposed objects in "space" somewhat more frequently than before.

The next president was Bill Clinton with none other than Gore himself as the vice president. To the great disappointment of all space-lovers - but quite understandably -, one of Clinton's first actions was to shut down the SEI project. While the so-called "International Space Station", a successor of the Russian "Mir Space

Station" was claimed to be built (way over budget and well behind schedule, naturally) and put into operation during his presidency, he had no plans of sending humans further out into "space", only robots to explore Mars. These unmanned "expeditions" allegedly provided detailed mapping of the Martian surface, and even rumors of discovery of signs of life were brought up, however, these were – likely due to caution – not so widely propagated and aroused little public interest anyway.

Clinton was succeeded as president by George W. Bush, the son of former president George H. W. Bush. Although W. Bush did set the goal of getting "back to the Moon" by 2020 - which was supposed to be a stepping stone to Mars -, we now all know how this plan worked out - or rather, how it did not. In all likelihood, the only reason he even proposed this goal was because of the pressure he was placed under after the Columbia disaster in 2003, when the "Space Shuttle" Columbia allegedly disintegrated during its "re-entry" into Earth's "atmosphere", for which the national leadership was blamed; namely for "not replacing old spacecraft" and "not providing a vision for NASA".

Of course, the event itself is rather questionable, as the only kind of footage that is claimed to show the shuttle's disintegration actually shows not much more than a dot of bright light that descends rapidly from the sky, leaving a trail of smoke, while slowly falling apart into multiple, smaller dots of lights. It all looks quite similar to the so-called "meteorites" that later always turn out to have been just devices shot out of planes for the sole purpose of mass-deception. While this is the most likely explanation, naturally, one cannot rule out the possibility that there really could have been some sort of an aircraft that was destroyed mid-air, and that the entire crew of "astronauts" was indeed killed (sacrificed) as it was reported. However, the details of the investigations at the crash sites also arouse suspicion, such as the claim that they managed to recover every crew member's remains, and so much of the supposed "shuttle's" debris that it could have been just about fully rebuilt from them. This is all very unlikely to be true, since in the case of other, similar aircraft-disasters, the reports generally show that not much is found or even left of the planes, and the bodies of the casualties are also rarely found.

At any rate, the event certainly came in handy for the government, as they got to suspend the entire shuttle program for multiple years due to the "investigations", while NASA – obviously – still continued to receive its massive funding while having to do even less for it than usual – if such a thing is possible. Although the program was later resumed and plans of sending robots to the Moon in a series of missions in preparation for manned lunar missions – named Constellation program - were made, naturally, nothing noteworthy was achieved despite the now "much clearer" vision provided by the younger Bush.

The next president in line, Barack Obama, almost immediately killed the Constellation program as he had a chance, and instead of focusing on lunar missions, he made plans for manned missions to land on an asteroid by 2025, and to build rovers that would be sent out to explore Mars by 2030. To "ensure" NASA's success, their budget was once again increased significantly, however, it seemed to have little effect, considering that not much more was achieved during the Obama administration regarding "space exploration" as any of the others before.

In fact, private companies, such as SpaceX, Northrop Grumman and Boeing were even selected to team up with NASA to either develop crewed "space" transportation systems to let "astronauts" (pretend to) travel to and from the ISS, or to conduct regular resupply missions and "scientific experiments" in support of it. The supposed development of the Orion "spacecraft", part of NASA's previously killed Constellation program also continued, with the goal of "deep space exploration", letting "astronauts" go beyond low Earth "orbit", but alas, nothing came of it in the end. Another purported development, the Space Launch System was also started, designed to be the most powerful rocket ever built and intended for similar "deep space missions", including crewed missions to the Moon and Mars, but apparently not achieving anything significant either.

The one supposed "success" of the industry during this period would have been provided by a "spacecraft" that was launched much earlier by a previous leadership, which allegedly conducted a "historic flyby" of Pluto in 2015, making the first close-up images of it. However, upon closer look, one might notice an odd shape on the so-called "planet", namely that of the head of Disney's famous cartoon dog, Pluto. Therefore, it would be quite hard to consider the image – and hence the whole endeavor - anything other than the mockery of the taxpayers.

Then it was Donald Trump's turn to become the nation's leader, and he didn't mess around much, offering NASA essentially unlimited funds and just asking in turn for what would have been already expected: manned missions to the Moon and Mars. He made passionate speeches about how it's important to *"think big and dream even bigger"*, and how *"we will no longer accept politicians who are all talk and no action"*, and uttered many more inspiring words as such. Unfortunately, however, even the greatest of passions, commitments, encouragements, limitless funding and an open timeframe seemed to not be sufficient to achieve even just as much as what 1969's technology allegedly made possible in a heartbeat.

And so, still nothing of value was even perceived as achievable by the whole of the "space industry", nor was it about to be anytime soon. Not long after the grim realization of this disappointing fact hit the leaders of the nation, it was announced that they are no longer interested in sending anyone to Mars, and instead just want focus on "returning" to the Moon for the time being.

This was the beginning of NASA's – currently ongoing - Artemis program, which envisions establishing "sustainable lunar exploration" and "returning" humans to the Moon by the end of 2024, using it as a stepping stone to hopefully later also travel to the dot of light on the sky called Mars. If these goals seem familiar, there's a good reason; they are exactly the same as those that H.W. Bush's Space Exploration Initiative (SEI) had decades earlier. What would have made the leaders think that this time the same plan will be more feasible and won't be killed like the previous one was is anyone's guess, seeing how technology was already so much more advanced at the time of SEI than in 1969.

Upon visiting NASA's Artemis webpage, as it is so characteristic of our zeitgeist, their description of the program makes sure to let us know that they will be filling the mandatory "diversity" quotas in the very first sentence. Indeed, their top priority is apparently not to achieve the highest possible safety, cost-effectiveness, speed, or durability for the mission, but rather to include the first woman and the first "person of color" in it, so that they, too, can (pretend to) go to the Moon. And this is exactly why the mission would be just about guaranteed to fail even if it were something that would actually be doable.

Quite possibly Trump's most interesting speech was also about "space exploration", and it's very telling of its entire history. Likely the most intriguing line from it is as follows:

"For almost six decades, NASA's work has inspired millions and millions of Americans to imagine distant worlds and a better future right here on Earth."

Without a doubt, these words perfectly and eloquently describe the whole of the industry; it's simply a factory of dreams and illusions that fuel not only a monumental hoax, but also a significant part of the economy. This notion also explains the reason that the many tens of millions of dollars wasted daily on NASA's budget don't seem to bother most American taxpayers. It is because they were made to believe that it is not only an honor to have the agency "do its work for them", but also that it is their own "patriotic duty" to keep it going by funding it.

Perhaps one of the most farcical acts of the Trump administration was the signing of the National Defense Authorization Act for the fiscal year of 2020, which officially established the United States Space Force as the sixth branch of the U.S. military. The "Space Force" is supposed to be tasked with organizing, training, and equipping military personnel and so-called *"space professionals"*. They are claimed to be focused on "space operations", such as activities related to "satellite operations", missile warning systems, "space-based communications", and "space situational awareness" – whatever these might mean. Of course, in reality this new department is just a clever trick to reinforce the public's belief in "space" itself, as well as to have more of them join the military and possibly become cannon fodder in the vain hope of maybe one day going on a "space mission".

This brings us to the current times, when the president is Joe Biden and it's starting to become painfully obvious to everyone that the position of "president" itself is essentially just a meaningless formality, as even one that can hardly finish a sentence and barely knows where he is can fill it and be regarded as no less than the "leader of the free world".

Nonetheless, a promise was made in 2019 that America will "return" to the Moon within 5 years, meaning it should happen before the year 2024 is over, and this administration seems to be just as serious about it - and thus the Artemis program is still on track, at least for now. No doubt, though, that if they do decide to finally end the decades-long procrastination and go through with faking another "Moon landing" at last, we shall either see one of the lowest quality deceptions we've ever had the misfortune to be mocked by, or an exceptionally high quality, cutting-edge CGI production done with some of the most modern equipments.

One of the few supposed "achievements" of this administration so far was the alleged deployment of the James Webb "Space Telescope" in 2021, although even this should be considered a massive failure, since it was originally planned to be launched in 2007 – not to mention that all it got us were a bunch more of the usual so-called "photos" that a NASA employee clearly put together on his computer. Although there have been many other fakeries in the past years, such as the rover and the helicopter that were purportedly both "successfully deployed on Mars" - which were claimed to be "historic moments" -, these were not nearly convincing enough for anyone with a functioning eye and an awake mind. So there certainly is room for improvement in this area for the powers that be – especially if they want to fake something permanent, such as a "Moon base".

The religion of evolution

Even though the theory of (Darwinist) evolution, also known as "evolution by natural selection", is clearly not something that could be put through the scientific method, and therefore cannot be considered a scientific theory, the majority of so-called "scholars" in today's world take it as seriously as if it were. In fact, many even dare to call it "scientific", since, unfortunately, the general understanding of most of humanity seems to be that adherence to it just means that one shall *observe and declare* – which is what theoretical "sciences" are essentially all about. Of course, the theory of evolution is even worse than some of the theories from other pseudoscientific branches, such as astronomy, cosmology, or astrophysics, as those at least usually have something to observe – even if not much else.

In order to still somehow make it seem like a plausible theory, its pundits came up with the idea that the use of the scientific method is *"not more valuable than other types of knowledge"*, but simply just *"more reliable in uncovering natural laws"*. Which clearly makes no sense, knowing that adherence to it *absolutely is* the requirement for any claim to be rightfully called scientifically validated, not to mention that natural laws don't need to go through the method. They must also know this well, which is proven by the fact that just about every major source of Darwinist propaganda makes sure to emphasize just how "scientifically validated" their theory is – which would obviously not be necessary if it truly were. Just like it wouldn't be necessary to do an incredible amount of marketing, which is what Darwinism received not long after its birth, with magazines and newspapers writing praises about it on a regular basis for a long time.

Another rather telling sign is that some of the most prominent sources even refer to it as *"a fact and theory"*. Again, if a theory has adhered to the scientific method and became validated by it, it is considered a *scientific theory*. Therefore, none would feel the need to specifically call it a "fact" at that point, as this would be completely trivial to all and thus naming it such would be redundant – not to mention suspicious.

The game of trying to skid the wheels by claiming "science" in the case of such theories has gotten to the point where even the criteria for it to be defined as "scientific". On the website of the National Library of Medicine, ncbi.nlm.nih.gov, there's a highly relevant part of an article written by Claudia A.M. Russo, professor of genetics,and Thiago André, evolutionary biologist. The "enlightening" words go as follows:

"One should regard science as a process in which scientists formulate hypotheses to explain certain facts and to test their predictive models by confronting their predictions with new facts ([Steven W.] Gilbert, 1991). A fact is something that we observe. For instance, when we drop an object, it falls to the ground. This is a fact. The scientific theory that explains why objects fall is the theory of gravity. A valid scientific theory can never become a fact ([Stephen Jay] Gould, 1981), as there is always the possibility that a future explanation will better match newly discovered facts."

Clearly, it is ridiculous to suggest that merely "testing models" (which they hardly even do) will somehow make them "scientific", or that one can just modify a "scientific theory" later on if it should become invalidated, and still keep it – although, it's quite obvious why they want to include this allowance. Not to mention that they decided to rename "phenomena" to "facts" to better fit their needs, but at this point it likely won't surprise anyone just how much the truth is being distorted by the proponents of pseudoscience. As for the "*scientific* theory of gravity", we all know that dropping something doesn't "prove it", as "spacetime" is only conceptual, not to mention that not everything will even fall down if dropped, but at least it's a perfect example of how one deception is being used to reinforce and make arguments for another.

Naturally, there's a very good reason why the pundits of the theory want to feign scientific validity for it at all costs. Make no mistake; despite the idea of the Big Bang and Darwinist evolution being - sometimes admittedly - just theoretical creations conjured up as "possible explanations", they are also something that the modern heliocentric model simply requires in order to maintain its perceived functionality. This is also clearly one of the main reasons they are taught in schools as scientific theories, or facts, though even many of those who teach them have a very shaky belief in them – or a complete lack thereof.

Indeed, even if we allowed for these theories to have "moving parts" that can be modified at will in any given second – which is, of course, done frequently and proudly -, they also have crucial parts that just can't be gotten rid of no matter what, assuming a solar centred worldview and a globular Earth. Such examples of necessity are the presumption of an evolution of the world that lasted billions of years, the presupposition of many celestial bodies – including the Earth - having been formed into a sphere over such an extended period of time, and, of course, the idea that there's an incomprehensibly vast void surrounding us with countless "other planets" in it – many of them too far to even see.

THE GLOBAL DECEPTION

To expose all of the lies included in the two theories that go hand in hand, it is important to look at what knowledge in our world we can actually trust. To find out what these fundamental facts are, we have to start the examination from the beginning of it all; the creation of the universe itself.

There are only two possible ways to explain this process, which are called the *ontological primitives*. They are as follows:

- **Natural creation:** a godless universe created itself and life from nothing by an explosion, taking a very long time.

- **Intelligent design:** a kind of intelligent consciousness carefully designed and then created the universe with all its living beings within a relatively short time in a supernatural way.

Of course, some would say that there's a third option, namely the idea that, while a god set things into motion, it stopped the work there and just let a – no longer godly – evolution take its course *(Theistic evolution)*. However, this can easily be disregarded, as it is really just a weaselly version of the concept of natural creation, with the Big Bang element of it simply replaced with something that obviously makes more sense.

No doubt, both of the above scenarios would seem quite astonishing at first glance to the average, uninitiated person, as they can certainly be hard even for some of the more seasoned researchers to wrap their minds around.

On one hand, there is a world that creates itself out of nothing, whose existence suggests no intelligence, and thus can only be the work of chance, and therefore has no purpose, utility, or meaning. Everything that has happened since its creation is also just an inexplicable series of coincidences, always completely devoid of any purpose or meaning. Life could only come into being in it if inanimate objects were somehow transformed into living organisms – strictly by accident.

On the other hand is a world created by an intellect perhaps utterly beyond human comprehension, with a thoroughness, detail and precision that a mere earthly consciousness could clearly never hope to achieve or even fully understand, yet, we can constantly feel how it's filled with emotions, reason and motivation.

Even Einstein, perhaps the most famous of all pseudo-scientists and the idol of many Atheists, expressed his – surprisingly judicious - views in this regard in a 1930 interview when asked if he considered himself a Pantheist - someone who identifies the universe with a divine power – as follows:

"Your question is the most difficult in the world. It is not a question I can answer simply with yes or no. I am not an Atheist. I do not know if I can define myself as a Pantheist. The problem involved is too vast for our limited minds. May I not reply with a parable? The human mind, no matter how highly trained, cannot grasp the universe. We are in the position of a little child, entering a huge library whose walls are covered to the ceiling with books in many different tongues. The child knows that someone must have written those books. It does not know who or how. It does not understand the languages in which they are written. The child notes a definite plan in the arrangement of the books, a mysterious order, which it does not comprehend, but only dimly suspects. That, it seems to me, is the attitude of the human mind, even the greatest and most cultured, toward God. We see a universe marvelously arranged, obeying certain laws, but we understand the laws only dimly. Our limited minds cannot grasp the mysterious force that sways the constellations. I am fascinated by Spinoza's Pantheism. I

admire even more his contributions to modern thought. Spinoza is the greatest of modern philosophers, because he is the first philosopher who deals with the soul and the body as one, not as two separate things."

Of course, despite these wise words and his leaning towards either Pantheism or Deism, Einstein still accepted the idea of Darwinist evolution as something plausible, not to mention that his work had an important role in maintaining this deception - just like so many others. Not only does the Big Bang theory require his "gravity" to grant it the ability to create "spheres", "orbits" and "galaxies", but his equations are being used to make the supporting disciplines of Darwinist evolution, such as geology, archeology, paleontology and astronomy (and all its branches), seem more plausible. This also helped create a synergy between them, where each can be used build upon and "prove" the others in an endless loop of circular reasoning.

Pantheism and Deism seem to be the obvious choices for those that want to keep clinging onto Darwinist evolution but realize that the Big Bang theory makes no sense in light of the natural laws, therefore such people can usually be reasoned with. While, as it should be now needless to say, the kind of people that are generally the most unreasonable in this regard, and would undoubtedly find the creation of the world the hardest to explain are the Atheists.

An Atheist has no choice but to believe the following according to the current state of so-called "science": at the beginning of the beginning, there was nothing. "Nothing" happened with all this nothingness, so it turned into a "point of infinite density", which, for no reason at all, detonated itself. This explosion somehow created debris in the form of massive balls of either gases or rocks, then, without any reason, a part of the universe thus created magically came to life and spontaneously reorganized itself to also be able to reproduce itself, with which it had no purpose whatsoever.

Although none of these assumptions can be proven in any way and it goes against all natural laws, human experience and logic, however, in the absence of a supernatural creative power, one would unfortunately only be left with such a comical story as an "explanation" for the whole of existence. Therefore, one could confidently say that it takes significantly more faith to believe that a supernatural power did not create the universe than it does to believe that it did. And that is precisely the reason why Darwinist evolution is just another religion, in fact, one of the most dishonest of them all. That is because, while other religions at least tend to admit that they require faith, the religion of evolution is claimed to be based on scientifically proven facts. Of course, that could not be further from the truth, and we shall examine in detail why it is so.

The main concepts of the Darwinism include the idea that species change over time, and those that are better adapted to their environment are more likely to survive and reproduce, passing on their advantageous traits to future generations. So far, there is nothing far-fetched about it, since we can actually observe slight changes in individual species over the span of a few generations – which is likely why this is generally how the theory of evolution is described.

The problems will, of course, begin when one goes further into it and meets the claim that, given enough time, one species can, in fact, turn into another, and thus all of them – including us, humans - are interconnected through "common ancestry". Similarly to the cases of heliocentrism and globe-Earthism, most of the so-called "evidence" we get for this theory, naturally, consists of drawings based on speculations.

Moreover, even the most "devout" pundits of the concept have no choice but to admit the widely known fact that there's a so-called "missing link", referring to a "transitional fossil" that would bridge the "evolutionary gap" between two closely related species, as such a gap is too blatantly obvious to everyone to be denied – as much as the believers of the theory would love to. However, it is important to realize that even this notion is merely a parlor trick carefully designed to deceive the masses, since there's actually not "one missing link", but innumerable of them.

Indeed, we should see countless intermediary versions of every species, in fact, there should be no specific, clearly distinguishable species at all, since all of them would be changing constantly. It would all be extremely easy to observe for anyone, and additional proof wouldn't even be necessary, as the reality of the concept would be simply so obvious that none would even feel the need to question it for a second. Naturally, those who subscribe to the theory try to defend their faith in it by claiming that the fossil record is "incomplete" only due to the – conveniently - rare and selective conditions required for fossilization to occur *(Baseless assertion, Confirmation bias)*.

There has been eventually a new concept invented and inserted into the original Darwinist fairy-tale to try and fix the "difficulty" caused by the lack of probative geological records, namely the theory of "punctuated equilibrium", proposed by paleontologists Stephen Jay Gould and, to a lesser extent, Niles Eldredge in the early 1970s. It suggests that "evolutionary change" is characterized by long periods of stability (equilibrium) punctuated by brief episodes of rapid change instead of a slow, gradual process – thus hoping to explain why there's no evidence of any transitional stages anywhere *(Moving the goalposts, Baseless assertion)*. No doubt, if it wasn't so important for the establishment to make humanity believe that their ancestors were in fact monkeys, maybe they could have had some humility and admitted defeat when Darwinism was clearly debunked, discarding it entirely. But alas, it was deemed too imperative for their deceptions to be fully functional, so, once again, they chose the path of (further) dishonesty instead. Of course, this new invention would reduce the problem slightly, since the number of fossils required as proof would be somewhat reduced. However, even if we assumed that punctuated equilibrium is a plausible hypothesis, there should still be a very large number of them available, as well as countless "hybrid" species all around us, so ultimately this invention still provides no real help to Darwinism. Regardless, as one might expect, this useless, stillborn invention made the two pseudoscientists who came up with it, but especially Gould, a huge favorite of the establishment, advertising and celebrating them and their theory in major media outlets, and even declaring Gould a "living legend".

Another little trick the pundits of Darwinism have come up with to help them skid the wheels of their pseudoscience was the propagation of the notion that if any living organism develops resistance to any kind of chemical substance and passes it on to its offsprings, that's a "shining proof" of "evolution". While they may have been able to fool a large part of the laymen and even most of the academics, it should be obvious to anyone capable of critical thinking just how faulty this assumption is. The problem with their claim is, of course, that even if a certain kind of change occurs in the creature's system and certain genetic traits are lost, it can never result in new traits being gained. In other words, if a species becomes immune to the effects of a certain substance over a few generation, it will still remain the same species, no matter what.

One of the most frequently repeated arguments for Darwinism, which is also considered one of the "greatest", is that the fact that human DNA is 98% similar to chimpanzee DNA is evidence of common descent. Unfortunately for its pundits, this is clearly another faulty claim, and one that can actually help us debunk the whole of Darwinism.

One of the main issues with it is that it's very misleading, since the complex-coded genome is so huge that a 2% difference is actually very significant, as it amounts to DNA with a count in the range of millions of differing base pairs. Furthermore, a major obstacle for the whole theory is the fact that while chimps have 24 pairs of chromosomes, humans only have 23; and in order for a species to be able to reproduce, these numbers *must* match. Not only that, but even in the rare cases when different but very similar species whose chromosome count matches, such as a horse and a zebra, give birth to a hybrid offspring, it cannot reproduce, since – just like all hybrid breeds – it is born sterile.

Therefore, it can be concluded that nature inherently abhors fundamental changes in the genomes of individual species, and in fact it does everything in its power to prevent the inheritance of mutations. This is why the pundits' supposed "great" argument for Darwinism actually provides one of the best arguments against it.

Then there's the unavoidable hardship caused by the dilemma: if the theory holds true and every species was originally a single celled being, did the eyeball or the eye socket evolved first? This is a big issue, because there is nothing to hold the eyeballs in place if the eye sockets are not already present for them. On the other hand, if the eyeballs only evolved later on, why would the eye sockets even develop in the first place? This massive contradiction remains unresolved to this day, to the greatest shame of all the pundits of Darwinism.

In fact, it has been – along with some other uncomfortable questions - such a bothersome, gaping hole in their story that the prestigious U.K. newspaper, *The Guardian* even published an article with the title *Do we need a new theory of evolution?* on June 28, 2022, because of such problems. It was written by science writer Stephen Buranyi, and the following are its most relevant lines:

"Strange as it sounds, scientists still do not know the answers to some of the most basic questions about how life on Earth evolved. Take eyes, for instance. Where do they come from, exactly? The usual explanation of how we got these stupendously complex organs rests upon the theory of natural selection.

For one thing, it starts midway through the story, taking for granted the existence of light-sensitive cells, lenses and irises, without explaining where they came from in the first place. Nor does it adequately explain how such delicate and easily disrupted components meshed together to form a single organ. And it isn't just eyes that the traditional theory struggles with. "The first eye, the first wing, the first placenta. How they emerge. Explaining these is the foundational motivation of evolutionary biology," says Armin Moczek, a biologist at Indiana University. "And yet, we still do not have a good answer. This classic idea of gradual change, one happy accident at a time, has so far fallen flat."

(...) at the turn of the 20th century, four decades after the publication of On the Origin of Species and two after his death, Darwin's ideas were in decline. Scientific collections at the time carried titles such as The Death-bed of Darwinism. Scientists had not lost interest in evolution, but many found Darwin's account of it unsatisfying. One major problem was that it lacked an explanation of heredity. Darwin had observed that, over time, living things seemed to change to better fit their environment. But he did not understand how these minute changes were passed from one generation to the next.

At the start of the 20th century, the rediscovery of the work of the 19th-century friar and father of genetics, Gregor Mendel, started to provide the answers. Scientists working in the new field of genetics discovered rules that governed the quirks of heredity. But rather than confirm Darwin's theory, they complicated it. Reproduction appeared to remix genes - the mysterious units that programme the physical traits we end up seeing – in surprising ways. Think of the way a grandfather's red hair, absent in his son, might reappear in his granddaughter. How was natural selection meant to function when its tiny variations might not even reliably pass from parent to offspring every time?"

Indeed, the theory is so glaringly irredeemable that even the pundits themselves have no choice but to admit that no matter what they come up with in an attempt to fix its original "difficulties", these "solutions" will only create more problems.

Needless to say, the few alleged physical proofs of the supposed "trans-species evolution" presented to us in the form of what may, or may not be actual fossils are all very problematic as well.

Eldredge, the aforementioned co-creator of the theory of "punctuated equilibrium", even admitted this problem in his 1985 book *Time Frames: The Rethinking of Darwinian Evolution and the Theory of Punctuated Equilibria* as follows (p. 52.):

"Paleontologists cannot operate this way. There is no way simply to look at a fossil and say how old it is unless you know the age of the rocks it comes from. And this poses something of a problem: if we date the rocks by their fossils, how can we then turn around and talk about patterns of evolutionary change through time in the fossil record?"

So, in a nutshell, rocks can only be dated by the fossils inside of them, while the fossils are dated by the rocks they were found in. If we're going to be honest, this fact alone should be considered the end of not only Darwinism, but also the disciplines of geology and paleontology, as they are clearly all fraudulent, since they all build on each other's baseless assertions to reinforce their own in a hellish loop of sneaky deceit. It is actually nothing short of a miracle that they even managed to survive this far without (almost) anyone calling out the obvious – and admitted - fraud and putting a stop to it.

What they've come up with as a "solution" for this monumental issue is the claim that the depth of sediment relates to the age of rocks found in it. Of course, as promised, this gives rise to a number of new problems; such as not knowing the rate at which the sediment would have accumulated and eroded at any given location, or how many years have passed between periods of deposits, or how long of an interval a layer of sediment represents.

Perhaps the above "difficulty" is the reason that all of the alleged paleontological "evidence" of so-called "early humans" eventually turned out to be either much younger than first claimed (at most a few hundred years old), or straight up fabrications. One of the most prominent – and least known - cases of this kind was the Piltdown Man hoax that involved the "discovery" of the supposed remains of an "apelike human ancestor" in England in 1912. This "great find" included a human-like skull and an ape-like jawbone which, if genuine, would have represented the much-needed and crucial transitional form between apes and humans.

Needless to say, the "scientific community" and the world press took the bait right away and widely celebrated the "discovery" of the coveted – and thus far extremely elusive - "missing link". Although the hoax was hugely successful, after 41 years of deceit it was exposed as a man-made combination of a human skull, orangutan jawbone, and chimpanzee teeth. The culprit who forged it was - conveniently

- never discovered, or at least never revealed, even though it may have been quite easy to find out who did it even before the finding of the "fossil", since a human skull would have gone missing, not to mention the presence of monkey bones in England. Of course, the only reason such a flimsy hoax could be so successful is because the whole of the establishment, as well as their pseudoscientist punits clearly wanted to believe more than anything that there is finally a shred of evidence of Darwinism.

Whether it was merely cognitive bias and wishful thinking on their part, or their higher echelons were actually involved in carrying out the "prank" itself, is anyone's guess. Only one thing is certain: thanks to the deception, the spread of not only Darwinism but also Atheism was massively accelerated during its run. Not to mention, that, as it should be now obvious, the revelation of it being nothing more than a dirty hoax received nowhere near as big a media coverage as its praise and celebration as a "great discovery" did 41 years earlier.

What is especially interesting about Darwinism is how much it was welcomed and loved by Marxists and communists. Friedrich Engels even regarded Darwin's work to be *the* ideology that would be "perfect for their movement", while his friend and co-conspirator, Karl Marx referred to it as "most important", and one that suits their purpose in that it "provides a natural scientific basis for the historical class struggle". Later on, he even mentioned that he thinks that Communism is "a form of evolutionary development", then eventually went on to send Darwin an autographed copy of his book *Das Kapital*, with accompanying words that could only be described as something a love letter would have - with Darwin then thanking him and praising his work in a letter of reply. In other words, Marx and Engels both thought that Darwinism would serve as an invaluable tool for the brainwashing of the public who will, in turn, become much easier to control in their communist "utopia".

Just like those that praise Communism do it (often despite knowing how impracticable and utopistic its base concept is) because it seemingly offers a "quick and easy" solution for very complex issues, the two crooks obviously also didn't favor Darwinism because of how flawless of a concept it was. They rather did it due to its power to convince the – in big part freshly atheist – masses by providing them a seemingly "clever" and simple alternative. Since Darwinism was something that could help them destroy traditions and religions, especially Christianity, which the communists desperately wanted to do, it made perfect sense for them to adopt it.

Make no mistake, Darwinism, just like communism, was never meant to be taken seriously – at least not by those who were tasked to propagate them; both concepts are merely weapons in the hands of darkness in the eternal war against a free and prosperous society. A clear sign of this fact is how communist icon Vladimir Lenin used to refer to the people gullible enough to buy into his views as "useful idiots". In today's world, most of these people can be found among the so-called "progressives" or "liberals", who are, of course, anything but progressive or liberal, and their hopeless naïvety just helps the oppressors of humanity further their age-old insidious agenda.

Furthermore, as it logically follows, all of the "inventors" of such harmful theoretical contraptions as Darwinism or communism should be considered mere puppets that are controlled and used by other, much more powerful figures from behind the scenes.

Nonetheless, after having read *On the Origin of Species*, the two lunatic puppets, Marx and Engels, were not only promoting their own insane and logically flawed ideologies anymore, but also that of Darwin. It wasn't long before Marx's close friend and collaborator, a German socialist politician who was one of the most prominent figures in the early socialist movement in Germany, Wilhelm

Liebknecht, has also read the book, and, just like the other two communists, promptly fell in love with the concept described in it. According to the memoir-book *Reminiscences of Marx and Engels*, Liebknecht later confessed about his and other communists' almost manic obsession with Darwin's work as follows (p. 106.):

"When Darwin drew the conclusions from his research work and brought them to the knowledge of the public, we spoke of nothing else for months but Darwin and the enormous significance of his scientific discoveries."

Moreover, the addition of the farcical Primordial Soup theory to the Big Bang theory as one of many "possible explanations" for an atheistic "creation" of life was carried out by Soviet biochemist Alexander Oparin, just months after Joseph Stalin, one of the greatest mass-murderers in history, came to power and took charge of the so-called "scientific community" of his country. Oparin's concept suggests that life on Earth originated from a combination of "simple organic molecules" present in the "early" oceans, lakes, or other bodies of water, all of which somehow came into being about 10 billion years after the supposed Big Bang. Eventually, more complex molecules (polymers), and ultimately life itself, supposed to have managed to somehow develop spontaneously in all the "soup" in the form of single-cell organisms, which are now said to be our "Last Universal Ancestors" (LUA).

Since it would be hard to give a coherent explanation as to where the chemical compounds that could supposedly do all this came from within the framework of an atheistic narrative, it is now said that they have – conveniently - arrived with meteorites. Which are, naturally, now claimed to have supplied us with not only these ingredients, but all sorts of things that may be required for any atheistic theory to maintain the appearance of plausibility.

Regardless of its obvious fundamental issues, the concept of the Primordial Soup gained prominence in the 1950s following the famous Miller-Urey "experiment" conducted by (the politically strongly left-leaning) American chemists Stanley Miller and Harold Urey. In this endeavor, they simulated what they thought the conditions of the "early Earth" were by creating an "atmosphere" containing gases believed to be present at that time, such as methane, ammonia, and water vapor, and subjected it to electrical discharges to simulate lightning. The so-called "experiment" produced amino acids, the building blocks of proteins, which, of course, is claimed to be supporting the idea that the conditions on "early Earth" could have led to the formation of organic molecules (*Confirmation bias, Experimenter effect, Baseless assertion*). Needless to say, this is not the case at all, although that certainly did not stop the establishment from putting the so-called "scientists" on a pedestal and showering them with praises and awards for seemingly furthering the Darwinist narrative.

The first problem with the endeavor is that there is simply no way to actually know what kinds of gases and chemicals may have been present at the time of the supposed Soup-event 3.8 billion years ago. Or whether the Soup even existed, or that any lightning was present, or that it could indeed provide the same results as their energy source. So the whole premise was clearly based on nothing but guesswork. Not only that, but the conclusions from the result are also very much flawed.

Since the amino acids which they managed to produce are not even close to being an actual protein, only some of its building blocks - with proteins also being just one of four kinds of building blocks of a living cell -, what they did was in fact very far from "creating life". Moreover, even if they would have somehow created all of the 100 amino acids of 20 varieties that are required to form an actual protein, these acids still would have had to spontaneously come together to form one on their own. Not to mention that even if such a thing could somehow happen, the protein would still need to combine with the other three building blocks to construct a cell, which would need to possess a cell structure with an intricately embedded genetic code and DNA composition.

What's also quite interesting is how those who claimed to have been fighting so adamantly against Communism after World War II have since become the biggest proponents and promoters of some of their most important doctrines, such as Darwinism, Atheism and the supporting theoretical "sciences". No doubt, this is another glaring proof of just how insincere the alleged "war" against them truly was.

The dinosaur hoax

As it now may be suspected by many, the notion that "dinosaurs", also known as "dragon lizards", once lived on the Earth is, similarly to Darwinism, actually based on nothing but speculations. Of course, Darwinism is often referred to as the "theory of evolution", giving away the fact that it is merely a "possible concept" – at least to those who understand that it's not meant in a scientific, but rather just a colloquial way – while it is very different in the case of the dinosaur hoax.

Not only is it claimed that dinosaurs "provably" existed, but the supposed "proof" is seemingly all around us in museums and exhibitions, while the belief in their authenticity is constantly being reinforced by so-called "scientific" papers, magazines, and, naturally, all of pop culture. Therefore, hardly anyone would even think about questioning their existence today, and those that dare say that they are but a hoax tend to be ridiculed almost as much as those who try to let others know that the Earth is in fact not a sphere and doesn't move.

The way dinosaurs are imagined and presented to us undoubtedly makes them seem cool and fascinating, their appearance massive, menacing and awesome. This is why they rightfully become the favorites of so many children from a very young age, with many retaining their love for them even in their adult years, often not willing to give it up even when facing the fact that their existence lacks real evidence.

The fully formed concept of these supposed "prehistoric creatures" was invented in 1842 by British anatomist and paleontologist Richard Owen, marking the point when the recognition of "dinosaurs" as a distinct group of "extinct reptiles" began. Owen classified them in a group he called *Dinosauria*, a word created by combining – and slightly modifying - the Greek words "deinos", meaning "terrible", and "sauros", meaning "lizard". His newly coined term was meant to describe some of his supposed "fossil discoveries" from the early 19th century that he thought he had successfully identified as specimens of ancient, long extinct reptiles. However, each of these supposed specimens only had fragments of bones as "proof". The pundits of the hoax actually didn't have much to show to the public in regards of what they think dinosaurs might look like until alleged "discoveries" in the middle of the 19th century in North America – despite having written and talked about them in detail more than a decade earlier in "scientific" reports and lectures.

Regardless, Owen was praised and celebrated by the powers that be for the concept he invented. Over the next decades he became superintendent of the natural history collections at the British Museum and was even allowed to live in a cottage of the British royal family, who greatly adored and eventually even knighted him. He frequently gave lectures on his supposed researches, attended by many prominent people, including Darwin himself. The two of them were initially friends, however, this changed once Darwin's *On the Origin of Species* was published, as Owen disagreed with some aspects of the idea detailed in it, rather subscribing to an evolutionary concept similar to that of punctuated equilibrium. Although, many suspect that he was merely jealous of Darwin's success, as Owen did have a history of trying to undermine the work of others and even take credit for their achievements whenever he had the chance.

Once Darwin's famous book was starting to gain popularity, a wild search allegedly began for fossils that would be able to support the concept of evolution. As one would expect, just two years after the book was published, a "historical discovery" was claimed to have been made when a "fossil" of a so-called "transitional species", an Archaeopteryx, or "ancient wing", was allegedly found in a limestone quarry in Germany. This supposed "fossil" was said to be about 150 million years old (based on speculation), and, since it seemed to have the feathery body of a bird and the head of a reptile, it is claimed to be "the missing link between dinosaurs and birds" – although, it would be more accurate to call it "one of the billions of missing links" *(Biased data collection, Complexity bias, Confirmation bias)*. Since this alleged "discovery" seemed to fit well with Darwin's theory, it was, naturally, hyped up by the establishment and celebrated as "empirical evidence" of one species transitioning into another.

Although the Archaeopteryx is regarded as "one of the most important fossils", and fans of Darwinism frequently bring it up as one of their "best proofs" to this day, unfortunately, as it should be obvious, there are major issues with it. Firstly, there were suspiciously only a few supposed fossils ever found of this species - somehow all of them in the same area. However, this suspiciousness is still dwarfed by the fact that evidence produced in the early 1980s showed that someone took the skeleton of a small reptile, put cement on it, and pressed a modern feather into the cement to create a forgery. Fred Hoyle even wrote an entire book on the topic in 1986, titled *Archaeopteryx, the Primordial Bird: a case of fossil forgery*. The reason such forgeries are abundant and easy to get away with is that most so-called "ancient fossils" are – to this day - dated by the age of the rocks near where they are found. So, if the skeletal remains of a modern-day animal were to be found in the same location with a rock that's claimed to be "ancient", the remains would be deemed "ancient" as well, without further ado. This method is, of course, completely arbitrary, as they use radiometric dating to "determine" the ages of rocks, which is admittedly very unreliable and essentially can be used as an excuse to come up with any number that the given "expert" wants to – or is required to.

Since the other supposedly "discovered" specimens of the "ancient bird" were claimed to have been all "found" in the same region, it seems obvious that they must be no more real either.

Nonetheless, Owen bought the alleged "fossil" for a rather hefty sum, then put it on display in the museum he worked in, starting the world-wide trend of supposed "fossils" being made available for public viewing instead of just locked away for the "experts" to examine.

Although, this is quite deceiving in light of the fact that - even today - all museums (unless they're dishonest about it) admittedly only put plaster or resin replicas on display, while the alleged "fossils" that are actually claimed to be real remain locked away from the public, restricted to "trained researchers". This is claimed to be necessary due to the actual fossil specimens being delicate and able to be easily damaged or degraded by exposure to light, humidity, temperature variations, and handling, and therefore need to be "carefully stored and preserved". While this is suspicious enough - not to mention convenient for those that might wish to pull off a hoax -, it may even seem like a somewhat reasonable excuse. At least it would be, if it weren't for the fact that the "fossils" on display usually look nothing like the ones hidden from the public.

In some cases, the supposed finders of "dinosaur fossils" even claimed that they are radioactive, so they painted them with lead to make them safer to handle – with which they also managed to push two different hoaxes at once. Of course, the claim that such fossils are not safe to be around, or that they are not safe from the visitors, can also give one an excuse to lock away the allegedly real bones or teeth, while putting admittedly fake art pieces – generally much larger, fully formed skeletons - on display.

Indeed, in most cases it is not even claimed that an entire fossilized skeleton was found, even when the whole museum is full of what look like "authentic dinosaur skeletons", but admitted that merely just a single bone (or its fragment) or tooth was discovered. This "great find" is then usually simply locked away in a dark room to be "carefully stored and preserved", while the paleoartists (artists that depict "prehistoric" life or environments based on "fossil evidence"), sculptors, model makers, and technicians get to work on the forgery that is to be displayed instead. Even when a real fossil is to be exhibited, it's generally significantly modified to enhance its appearance in a way that better supports the narrative of "ancient animals". Those doing the preparations work closely with paleontologists to ensure that the deception goes precisely the way they want it to.

It starts with the paleoartists and sculptors creating a "lifelike representation" of what the authorities imagine the animal to which the bone or tooth supposedly belonged looked like in their full form – based on nothing but assumptions. Then it's the model makers' turn to take the paleoartists' drawings and bring them to life in three dimensions. They use a variety of materials such as plaster, resin, or fiberglass to craft the physical substitutes. Next, a technician will apply mold materials to the original fossil or the sculptural model to capture its form into a mold, which is then used to produce multiple replicas. Once the mold is ready, the casting process begins by the chosen material being poured or injected into the mold to create a replica. The replicas are then meticulously painted to match the colors and textures of the original fossils, then details such as skin patterns, scales, or feathers are added to enhance "realism". Lastly, the completed forgery may be mounted on armatures or supports for display in museum exhibits, ready make the unsuspecting visitors believe whatever the perpetrators of the hoax want them to.

As it may be obvious to many by now, the real reason for all this hassle has nothing to do with concern for the well-being of a piece of bone or tooth someone found in the dirt. For one thing, those pulling the strings of the dinosaur hoax know very well that a few bones and teeth - something that one might accidentally dig up in his backyard - would not be considered a particularly interesting or meaningful discovery by the public, and thus they won't make their way to a museum just to look at them.

In fact, the perpetrators of the deceit make sure that as few people as possible realize that they are actually hardly going to see any real fossils, or that if they do realize it, at least have them believe that all the replicas and sculptures presented to them instead are "accurate depictions" of the original fossils. This is because the perpetrators clearly understand that most people would be even less likely to ever attend an exhibition if they knew that not only are the real fossils they might see generally small, plain and boring, but a large part of what they'll see is but a collection of modern forgeries.

Needless to say, once Owen started the trend of putting "fossils" on display in a museum, people started flocking to such exhibitions for a chance to take a look at the supposedly fascinating and unique finds. This essentially gave birth to the industry of fossil collection, as well as a new motive to create fake ones - apart from "just" deceit. He and everyone else who planned to enter the fledgling industry were now greatly invested in acquiring supposed "ancient fossils", as they could expect to profit massively when exhibiting them in a museum.

Knowing this, as well as the deception-aspect of the industry, it is perhaps not too surprising that just about all alleged "dinosaur fossils" ever "discovered" were found by someone who had significant vested interest in it, as opposed to people everywhere finding them randomly, all around, as it is with all other kinds of fossils. Moreover, there have been examples of authorities being caught having planted fake fossils at locations where they knew "non-initiated" laymen would go digging in hopes of finding some. It is also more than suspicious that there are only a few locations in the world known for allegedly containing "ancient fossils", with a single excavation site often providing a plethora of them, while the rest of the whole region seems to have none of it.

Although there has never been a single mention of "dinosaurs" or anything similar in any culture over our thousands of years of recorded human history, as one would expect, the establishment made sure to try and patch up this plothole in their story. The way they are hoping to do this is by telling us that some of the mythological beasts, such as dragons and other reptile-like creatures, are actually referring to dinosaurs – which is, of course, just as much of a baseless and unprovable assertion as most of the others they came up with in support of their hoax. They've also decided to change the conclusions of old finds retroactively, claiming that they were "cryptic fossils", meaning that they are thought to have actually belonged to dinosaurs but were "misidentified" at the time because researchers didn't yet know what exactly they were looking at.

The most famous of such examples is what's said to be the "first scientific account" of a "dinosaur fossil", which was the femur of an animal described by the British naturalist Robert Plot in 1677. The fossil's size led him to suggest that the bone had come from an elephant brought to Britain by the Romans some centuries earlier – which is what it most likely was indeed. However, in the 19th century, by looking back to illustrations of the bone - conveniently claimed to have been "lost a long time ago" – paleontologists started claiming that the femur fragment was in fact the lower end of a thighbone of a so-called "Megalosaurus" *(Biased data collection, Complexity bias, Confirmation bias)*. This supposed species was "coincidentally" also the one mentioned in 1824 in the first ever "scientific description" of a purported "ancient reptile", which was based on the front half of a lower jawbone. One that could have just as well been from an existing large reptile - or just a plain forgery, like so many other finds turned out to be.

The first alleged dinosaur skeletons were supposedly found – in suspicious abundance – in 1877 in Wyoming and Colorado states in the U.S. although, even these were not claimed to be full skeletons - nor were any other finds to this day. Nonetheless, the supposed discovery of these specimens is claimed to have initiated the "Bone Wars", also known as the "Great Dinosaur Rush". It was driven largely by the efforts of American palaeontologists Othniel Marsh and Edward Drinker Cope, ending in 1897 when one of them died. Needless to say, they both had a seemingly endless budget for this endeavor, since they both had either a wealthy family member or relative with ties to the deep state – the ones pulling the strings of history – funding them.

It is claimed that they quickly became extremely competitive and ruthless in their supposed race for the proverbial title of "best paleontologist", which, of course, - very conveniently -, resulted in them ostensibly discovering at least 136 "new dinosaur species". With this, they have clearly done a huge favor for the Darwinist establishment that craved such finds like a morsel of bread. Unfortunately, the authenticity of these – similarly to all other supposed "dinosaur fossils" – is very much questionable, seeing how the two of them were not even present at the excavations most of the time, and that they also paid for a number of laymen to send any fossils they find to them, making their origins even harder to verify. Not to mention that their personal credibility has also been demolished, as their endeavors were referred to as "some of the most underhanded shenanigans in the history of science".

The two paleontologists were said to have been financially and socially ruined by the end of the "Bone Wars", however, this would make little sense in light of the fact that they've "discovered" so many "new dinosaur species" and countless fossils altogether. This would undoubtedly bring them great fame and fortune, not to mention that most of their funding was provided by other members of their families to begin with.

One may say what he wants about the financial elite, but if there's one thing we have to admit, it's that they certainly aren't known for being stupid. Therefore, it seems obvious that they wouldn't go ahead and exhaust their resources and ruin their reputation just to prove an ultimately meaningless point to one another. A much more likely explanation for Marsh and Cope's apparent "rivalry" is that the wealthy relatives who funded them were in fact also the ones who tasked them with going on explorations and excavations, and faking a conflict to make the whole story more believable and give it more plausibility. The appearance of a rivalry and the drama between them also served the purpose of distracting the public and preventing them from thinking "too much" about their finds or wanting to examine them more thoroughly. Not to mention that it made it possible for them to bring forward a large amount of so-called "discoveries" and "fossils", thus giving the hoax a huge push without raising suspicion.

THE GLOBAL DECEPTION

Another interesting case of suspicious finds was that of a team led by Argentine paleontologist Luis Chiappe and his American colleague Lowell Dingus in 1997, both of whom worked for the American Museum of Natural History in New York at the time. They were exploring a remote corner of northwestern Patagonia for evidence of fossil birds, and, perhaps not too surprisingly, during their second day in the field they've already spotted a "promising" rock face in the distance that – for some reason - they thought might contain fossils - or so the story goes. They've allegedly found about 195 clusters of eggs at that spot, with each cluster containing at least a half-dozen eggs. Purportedly all of these eggs had a pitted pattern that's claimed to had been seen before in what were said to be "dinosaur eggs". Although "dinosaur eggs" are even claimed to be one of the rarest fossil discoveries, apparently they just happened to stumble upon thousands of them at a single spot. Not only that, but this already astonishing find also included fossilized embryos and fossilized skin, which are even more rare. This was indeed a major discovery of a plethora of supposedly ancient fossils amounting to a historical milestone for the profession of paleontology, found essentially by accident, coincidentally by two people who happened to work for a museum and therefore could benefit more than anyone from such a find. Certainly a wondrous occurrence fitting for a fairy-tale, in fact, one might say that it seems simply far too good to be true.

Indeed, such an incredible eventuality is so unlikely that even some of the mainstream pundits of the dinosaur hoax had doubts about its authenticity at the time. The problem is not only that the law of probability would hardly allow it, but also the fact that if dinosaurs had been real, they would have been scattered across the world, thus providing many smaller fossil finds. It would have made no sense for the supposed animals to all gather up to die together in an area that's the size of a quarry or a tar pit. This argument can't even be countered by saying that "fossilization has some very specific requirements", because there have been at least a few cases where "dinosaur fossils" were allegedly found just lying in the dirt with seemingly no special conditions present to help fossilization. The fact that most of the allegedly "ancient" fossils are claimed to be found in small clusters – practically always by highly invested individuals - is therefore a strong indication of either that they were deliberately planted there by the perpetrators of the hoax to advance their agenda, or that the "finders" were simply lying and made forgeries themselves.

Whether all of the paleontologists are in on it can be up for debate, however, it should be noted that, since there is no truly reliable dating method for bones with no soft tissues on them, let alone for rocks, they can be quite easy to deceive as well when it comes to the age of a find. It should also be noted that the process of fossilization in nature, and whether eggs (or bones) can even be fossilized at all is still a matter of debate, and even students of paleontology are often disappointed to realize that what they're told is a "fossilized egg" looks exactly like a round stone piece, and therefore practically indistinguishable from that. Not to mention that anyone can bury an egg anywhere and find that not only will it not turn into anything resembling a piece of stone, but it will in fact soon start to rot from the inside.

Furthermore, assuming that fossilization of bones and eggs in nature is actually possible, it is quite odd that none of the species known to have been killed in masses for certain, such as American buffaloes, left a significant amount of remains in the ground, despite their death also being much more recent than that of the supposed dinosaurs.

The dinosaur hoax is a multi-faceted one, as it aims to have us believe not only the farcical lies of Darwinism, but also the notion that hydrocarbons, primarily coal, oil (petroleum) and natural gas should be thought of as so-called "fossil fuels". According to this wild supposition, these crucially important energy carriers formed from the remains of dead plants and animals by undergoing geological processes over millions of years. Although this is obviously a completely unprovable theory based solely on speculation, it is extremely useful for the perpetrators of all the deceptions to have as many people believe in it as possible. By telling us that it takes this long for such fuels to form, they are also able to rightfully make the claim that we will eventually run out of it, while also using it as a "proof" that the "prehistoric times" – and therefore dinosaurs and cavemen, or "early humans" – really existed.

To achieve widespread propagation and acceptance of this belief, they made sure that most Western schools only teach the religion of evolution, Big Bang, and mainstream astronomy to students, generally not even mentioning the many issues with them, let alone bringing up any alternative theories or worldviews. In numerous cases, there are "educational" (propaganda) videos shown in schools to children in order to brainwash them, first depicting dinosaurs, and then their remains being processed into petroleum. They may also be shown charts of how much oil is supposedly left in the world - according to the older versions of which, it already should have run out a long time ago.

Unfortunately, even if one were to entertain the idea of both Darwinism and dinosaurs as something plausible, plenty of questions would still remain. For example, why would evolution create mostly just reptiles in the "prehistoric times", but then all kinds of animals instead, as well as humans, after the dinosaurs were gone? Shouldn't life have been more diverse in the time period when the dinosaurs lived, which is claimed to have lasted nearly 200 million years, as opposed to ours, which we've allegedly been in just for a fraction of that? Why would this time period produce much smaller animals? Also, why and how would anything else survive an event that purportedly wiped out most, if not all dinosaurs, seeing how they were the dominant creatures at the time?

There are also other problems with the concept of dinosaurs that's presented to us, such as the fact that there is simply no way they could have consumed enough nutrients to power their oversized bodies, especially with the plants having been the same size they are today. Over the decades, even bio-mechanical analysis has been performed on their supposed skeletons, which concluded that many of their species would have also been far too heavy for their skeletons to support them. This would have been the case even if they had moved at the pace of a snail, let alone if running at high speeds, which is what would have been required for many of them to be based on their comparison to modern animals. Such issues and paradoxes – or plotholes - have been bothering the pseudoscientists for quite some time. Stephen W. Hurrell, British science author and former engineering designer writes about this in his 2020 book *From dinosaurs to Earth expansion* as follows (p. 8.):

"Dinosaurs in particular appeared to follow a lifestyle much too active for their size. Calculations indicated their bones were too weak, blood pressure too high and they would be unable to run even if they looked like they should. The problems concerning their large size, high blood pressure, weak bones, ligaments and muscles had generated a large number of ad hoc theories totally unrelated to one another. The trouble with these theories is that they have no predictive power since they are only formulated to explain a restricted set of facts."

One should not worry, however, as a "solution" to universally circumvent all such problems was eventually conjured up in the form of yet another version of the incessantly overused, arbitrary glue of so many theoretical models; gravity. This new concept is called "palaeogravity", meaning *the force of the Earth's surface gravity in the past* – which is claimed to have been significantly weaker, thus "fixing" the above discrepancies within the dinosaur hoax.

Clearly, this theory has just as little "predictive power" as any other guesswork the powers behing the scenes have come up with in order to try and explain away some of the more noticable issues with their concepts, but with this argument they can at least once again use two different deceptions of their own to reinforce one another.

Unfortunately, though, their problems don't end with this, as there are still issues that even the assumption of an imaginary pseudo-force can't solve within their own narrative.

As a matter of fact, dinosaurs' mating and reproduction would have been also physically impossible for many if not all species due to either their short, stubby legs, or the fact that the huge tail of the mate they would be mounting would completely block all access from behind. Moreover, there would have been also the issue of getting up onto those species that allegedly had spikes or a bone blade on their back, as well as the fact that even with the presupposed "weaker gravity", likely none of them would have been able to bear the weight of not only its own body, but also that of another, possibly even bigger specimen.

Not to mention that many of them, such as the famous T-rex, would have had such disproportionate bodies – with their front half being multiple times heavier than their tail - that there is simply no way they could have even stood up at all.

Finally, the series of convenient patch-theories within the narrative of the dinosaur hoax culminates in the supposition that what's known as the "Cretaceous-Paleogene (K-Pg) extinction event" has somehow wiped out the majority of the dinosaurs, along with many other species.

This event is believed to have consisted of two main occurrences. One of them would have been a gigantic "asteroid" hitting the Earth, causing massive fires, a "nuclear winter" effect with debris blocking sunlight, and tsunamis. The other one would have been immense, prolonged volcanic activity during the same time period, releasing large amounts of lava and gases into the air, leading to acid rain and contributing to the so-called "greenhouse effect", supposedly altering the Earth's climate.

The convenience of this explanation as to why there is no evidence of the existence of dinosaurs other than a relatively low amount of supposed fossils cannot be overstated. Not only does it reinforce the idea of "outer space", devastating "asteroid impacts", life possibly originating from another world, as well as a so-called *nuclear winter*, but, as an added bonus, also the belief in what has become known as "climate change".

Global warming without a globe?

In the chapter *Fearmongering cranked up*, it was mentioned how some state powers like to frequently manufacture the illusion of their own usefulness and efficiency in order to give themselves the legitimacy for existing in the first instance. As mentioned, they achieve this by "protecting the public" from fictitious - or self-made – disasters, thus earning the public's trust (at least until they're found out) while also gaining more control over their lives. These facts are going to be important to remember moving forward, as they provide the sole reason for the invention of anthropogenic (human-induced), "global warming" and "climate change" (GW and CC).

First of all, let us examine what these two terms mean according to Webster's dictionary:

- **Global warming:** *"an increase in the earth's atmospheric and oceanic temperatures widely predicted to occur due to an increase in the greenhouse effect resulting especially from pollution."* - (*Greenhouse effect: warming of the surface and lower atmosphere of a planet that is caused by conversion of solar radiation into heat in a process involving selective transmission of short wave solar radiation by the atmosphere, its absorption by the planet's surface, and reradiation as infrared which is absorbed and partly reradiated back to the surface by atmospheric gases)*

- **Climate change:** *"significant and long-lasting change in the Earth's climate and weather patterns."*

Needless to say, the premise of both concepts is riddled with the usual logical fallacies, such as baseless assertion, affirming the consequent, appeal to consensus, and cherry-picking – just to name a few of the most significant ones. Not to mention that they, naturally, can't possibly be put through the scientific method – since one cannot do tests on all of Earth's air or water at once -, despite being claimed to be "based on science", automatically making them pseudoscience. Moreover, as the more adept may have realized it right away, there is one big issue with their definitions: they are hopelessly vague.

In the case of "global warming" (GW), what is the required increase in temperature for it to qualify as such? Where should the measurements be conducted for them to be able to credibly validate the concept? Who is allowed to make predictions and how will he be held accountable if they should fail to come true? Who will pay the hefty price – often measured in human lives - for his blunder?

Unfortunately, things are even worse in the case of "climate change" (CC), as it's a much shorter and more ambiguous definition. Critically important questions are left open by it, such as: what counts as a "significant" change? How long should a "long-lasting" change last? How do we know when it begins and when it ends? Also, is the Earth's climate even supposed to stay the same forever?

The fact that these crucial matters are not part of the definition should raise a huge red flag for everyone. Of course, its obscurity is by design; it needs to be this way so that it can eventually entirely replace the notion of GW, which has been debunked and invalidated so many times over the past few decades that it's likely starting to become embarrassing even for the almost entirely shameless pseudoscientific community and their handlers. Since there are many places in the world that are not only not getting warmer, but in fact have been getting significantly cooler over the past decades and centuries, this change of the terms must happen if they wish to continue the hoax. The vagueness of CC provides a universal, blank check-like solution, as it can mean anything they want at any given moment. It can be used as an explanation for the slightest bit of apparent warming, or extreme cold, or too much / not enough precipitation, or too strong / too weak winds - as well as anything in between. And if the weather happens to be boring, then it is, of course, just *weather*, and not the *climate*.

What's worse is that this doesn't even stop at the different weather events anymore. If someone suffers – or dies - from a serious disease that an establishment-prescribed drug had caused, then they will now tell us it was actually caused by CC. If people are stressed out and have a hard time getting enough rest, it's due to CC. If a plot of land becomes barren after chemical were dumped on it by a large corporation, CC is to blame. There is really no limit to the ways this brilliantly versatile psyop can be applied for the purpose of gaslighting the public, as long as it furthers the agenda of the powers that be.

As a predecessor, and later an integral part of the GW-narrative, the concept of a "greenhouse effect" (GE) that's caused by "greenhouse gases" is crucial to the success of the hoax. Its name refers to the way it supposedly operates, as if the Earth was essentially placed inside of a glass ball, or a "greenhouse" made of gases which lets sunlight in, but only lets out a part of the heat generated by it near the Earth's surface, reflecting back or absorbing the rest. According to official sources, the GE is actually essential for life on Earth, as it helps maintain a temperature range suitable for living organisms, but human activities, particularly the burning of fossil fuels and deforestation, have significantly increased the concentration of "greenhouse gases" in the atmosphere, and therefore also the effect's intensity. Of course, this very concept is just as ridiculous as it sounds. Not only because the Earth is not a globe and thus can't have a ball of gas surrounding it (not that gases would ever behave like that anyway), but also because floating gas molecules would clearly not be able to act as a physical barrier that could trap heat energy. Not to mention that there is, naturally, not a single shred of evidence of such a layer of gas' existence, as the whole concept is based on models that are based on conjectures.

The methods used to brainwash the population into believing in the GW/CC hoax are eerily similar to those that are employed in the case of most other deceptions mentioned in this book. Children are shown cartoons on TV and so-called "educational videos" in schools that tell them the entire world's climate is changing rapidly and dangerously, and that they are the ones to blame. The entertainment industry is also continuously pumping out endless streams of propaganda of this kind, including it in films, TV shows, magazines and books.

Some of the most prominent pundits of this hoax are also the same ones that can be found pushing the Copernican globe-Earth narrative, such as Stephen Hawking, Bill Nye, Neil DeGrasse Tyson, and, of course, in a large part, NASA itself.

Make no mistake, certain human activities can indeed be very detrimental to the environment, such as severe air and water pollution or deforestation or oil spills, however, these are predominantly caused by large corporations, whose owners - more often than not – happen to be friends with the same politicians who seemingly endorse the protection of the environment. This, in turn, means that there is actually very little that the average tax-slave can do about the whole issue, although he is the one that has to take most of the responsibility according to the establishment's propaganda.

Perhaps the first major milestone for the GW/CC hoax was the establishment of Earth Day in 1970 in the U.S. It was exceptionally hyped up by the state's media conglomerate, which clearly indicates that the powers that be wanted it to be a huge event which can eventually be turned into a worldwide tradition. It was – and still is – very appealing to most, since its purported goal was to "save the planet" by raising awareness of banal and obviously terrible occurrences, such as air and water pollution, and oil spills.

This resulted a favorable public opinion of all so-called "environment protection efforts", making it possible for those pulling the strings to push through legislations that otherwise would have been difficult to do. It also led to the establishment of the EPA (Environmental Protection Agency) less than 8 months after the event. In an exceptionally hideous example of government overreach, the Supreme Court ruled in the case of Massachusetts v. EPA in 2007 that the EPA had the authority to regulate "greenhouse gases" under the Clean Air Act.

This ruling proved to be incredibly destructive, as two years later the EPA declared CO_2 a "pollutant", claiming that it "contributes to CC and poses a threat to public health and welfare", despite the well-known fact that it's essential for the growth of plants. In fact, even an excessive amount of it is so beneficial to them that those operating greenhouses often install machines in them whose sole purpose is creating more CO_2, which makes the plants inside grow faster and bigger as they absorb it. This fact also proves that not only is there not "too much" CO_2 in the "atmosphere", but more of it would be favorable for all living beings on Earth.

Nonetheless, this declaration by the EPA paved the way for them to regulate and set standards for so-called "greenhouse gas" emissions from various sources, including vehicles and power plants, to address the supposed "risks" associated with "climate change".

Since it was somewhat colder than usual in America in the 1970s, at that time the elite's tool for fearmongering was not yet GW, but rather an "impending ice age", or "global cooling". By the early 1980s, as it was starting to get warmer again and it became painfully obvious to everyone that this widely predicted "ice age" is not coming, the "experts" decided that the focus of their propaganda should no longer be "too much cold", since obviously no one would buy that anymore, but instead "too much heat". So they gave up on the decade-long ice age scare completely and made great efforts to invent and propagate the notion that there is a connection between human activities, such as the burning of fossil fuels, and the allegedly "observed" increase in "global" temperatures – thus coming up with the concept of the GE. Not long after this, discussions about GW also started to enter public discourse and policy conversations, slowly morphing the GE-hoax into something bigger. It was around this time that one of the more well-known doomsday-predictions for the year 2000 was announced, namely that the Earth will become almost completely uninhabitable due to the effects of GW. Even in spite of the countless previous blunders and failed predictions of the so-called "experts", a large part of humanity fell for the trickery and GW became widely accepted as a "fact" throughout the 1980s.

However, the powers that seek to control the world soon realized that just GW alone will not be sufficient to fool the world for long, as it is simply too transparent and limiting. After all, even the most gullible would sooner or later notice that there's clearly no observable worldwide increase of temperature, even if some localities may experience occasional heatwaves, just like they have countless times throughout history as part of a natural process. So, in order to prepare the ground for something more "flexible", the United Nations has established the Intergovernmental Panel on Climate Change (IPCC) in 1988, officially introducing the idea of the much more versatile CC (as well as an arbitrary authority that can impose the fraud upon the world), which would soon largely replace the played-out concept of GW.

Nonetheless, GW as a tool of fearmongering still wasn't entirely abandoned, simply due to the fact that it undoubtedly sounds much scarier than its updated version. In essence, whenever it is hotter than usual anywhere in the world, it's brought up again to scare the public, but when it is colder, wetter, or windier than usual, CC is automatically blamed instead – basically reserving GW just for the hotter-than-average days.

Seeing the concept's decline, in 2023 the UN even started pushing the idea that GW should be upgraded to "global boiling" – clearly to make it sound even scarier. Their reason for doing so was that July of that year has reportedly set a new heat record at some places (although there is absolutely no proof that this was actually the case) – while they, naturally, ignored the many localities where the entire summer was in fact exceptionally cold. Of course, all that such an alleged "heat record" would mean anyway is that the highest measured temperatures may have risen at certain places, usually over a whole century and only by a centigrade or less, but this would apparently be a "great cause for concern" – at least according to the alarmists.

Indeed, they do like to claim that even a single centigrade of rise in temperature is somehow able to melt glaciers, even though such a miniscule change would clearly not be sufficient to actually make a significant difference in almost any way anywhere in the environment. Nonetheless, they still have to cling onto this notion, as this is what allows them to also blame CC (and GW, to a lesser extent) for just about every single flood, tsunami, forest fire, and storm that occurs anywhere in the world, regardless of their actual cause. News programs regularly tell us how CC causes all of these things, but when it turns out that the real cause was in fact something else, this discovery gets little to no coverage by the same pundits.

Perhaps the most enfuriating examples of such distortion of the truth are the reports of forest fires, which are almost always claimed to have been caused by CC, while in most cases turn out to have been in fact caused by arsons. Not too surprisingly, such culprits usually tend to be so-called "climate activists" – if not government agents - themselves, trying to strike fear into the hearts of the public and hoodwink them into adopting their belief in GW/CC.

To make things seem even scarier for the people, some of the mainstream "news" programs also started using warmer colors for their weather forecasts' maps recently, so that areas that used to be shown in green to represent a heat of over 30°C were turned into an alarming red even when only representing a temperature of around 20°C.

By 1989, information supposedly coming from so-called "satellite images" – or, more accurately, a computer-generated animation of a colorful spinning globe – is claimed to have convinced most "scientists" that the average temperature of the Earth will rise by 2 to 5 degrees celsius over the next 100 years. Professor Richard Lindzen, American atmospheric physicist has warned us about trusting any climate models in the 1990 documentary *The Greenhouse Conspiracy* as follows:

"I don't think we could speak of the models as being accurate at this point, they're experimental tools. We're trying to forge these tools. To use them in a forecast mode for delicate things like this warming is calling on an accuracy these models simply do not have."

Regardless of his and many other actual (contrarian) experts' warnings, however, this model of deception became an integral part of what's been fueling the GW/CC hoax, although, like all other pseudoscientific models, it has been slightly modified throughout the years to better fit reality and thus remain at least somewhat believable to the masses. Needless to say, in order to achieve widespread support for it, the pseudoscientific elite still had to make sure that no views that oppose the official narrative can be heard by the public on any of the major TV networks – from which documentaries like *The Greenhouse Conspiracy* were, of course, all banned - or read in any of the prominent newspapers or "science magazines". Similarly to the other hoaxes, the actual scientists who try to speak out against it and reveal its lies are also generally denied funding and their careers can be expected to be stifled or even ruined.

Another fact that's been helping the case of the perpetrators of the hoax tremendously is that weather stations are placed very unevenly across the Earth; for example, there is only one of them representing about one third of the entire Atlantic Ocean. Moreover, what's even more concerning is that many of them are placed next to airport runways with acres of tarmac surrounding them, where the measurements will obviously yield much higher results than they normally would out in nature. The same goes for the temperatures recorded by the many stations placed in what are known as *urban heat islands*, which are localized areas within urban environments that experience higher temperatures compared to their surrounding rural areas.

As one might expect, as cities grow and these heat islands expand with them, so will the measured values also increase over the years and decades as more and more of the natural vegetation is replaced by concrete and tarmac. This can result in a temperature increase of

2-3 degrees at such locations, which, of course, happens to coincide with the climate models' predictions – while the rural areas may show no change at all. So what's actually being detected in many regions of the world is not "global warming", but merely urban warming. However, while even today only a small part of the world is urbanized, most of the weather stations are, naturally, placed in such areas. This is precisely why presenting all the "rising" temperatures from these erroneous measurements may seem like a compelling argument for GW to the average layman who lives in a city, making this a perfect tool for the perpetrators of the deception to successfully pull it off. To make things even harder to see through, the purveyors of the hoax, including high-level institutions such as NASA, have been caugh falsifying data on multiple occasions to make charts where the annual average temperatures seemed significantly higher than they actually were, especially throughout the past few decades, which is where GW needed the biggest "push" to sell its lie. Of course, most people have never actually looked into the supposed "science" behind the hoax - just as it is with most others -, which is why they have no way of knowing just how faulty all the data is that it's based on.

Nonetheless, even if one were to buy it all, there are still further issues with the concept of a "warming trend" on Earth, as it largely depends on the time period examined. For example, if one were to look at the average temperatures from the mid 1930s to the mid 1970s, he will notice a sharp drop - despite the continuously rising CO_2 levels in the air. *This proves that not only is there no cause-effect relationship between the two values, but there is not even a correlation!*

There is also evidence that there have been extended periods during the medieval times when it was in fact warmer - even in the regions that are considered to be currently "warming" - than it is these days - despite much lower human population and no industry back then.

This is proven by the records of plants and insects being present in areas where they couldn't possibly live today due to the significantly lower temperatures. Indeed, this is a clear proof that even if the climate of any given region does in fact change over multiple centuries – or perhaps even just decades -, it is simply a natural process which man has absolutely nothing to do with.

The claim of continuously and permanently melting ice caps, glaciers, and ice sheets is also an interesting one, as there has never been a shred of evidence shown for it, and yet, a large part of humanity takes it for granted. To achieve this, the powers that be have been using a number of different methods to wage psychological warfare against the people. One of these is cherry-picking data by presenting photos of snow-covered locations shot during winter and ones shot during summer - rightfully with no snow - to the public as "proof of GW/CC", without, of course, telling them when they were taken. Another one of their favorite tricks is presenting photos of sad looking polar bears that appear to be stranded on a small sheet of ice seemingly floating lonely in the middle of the sea - as if they are hoping to imply that that piece of ice is all that's left of the entire Arctic Circle, which serves as the animal's only natural habitat. This is then supplemented with the - undoubtedly frightening - notion that seals in the region are also losing much of their natural habitat due to GW, and thus the poor polar bears are starving and slowly going extinct. However, all of these assertions are contradicted – and debunked - not only by the fact that there is simply no evidence of Arctic shrinkage, but also by the fact that polar bear populations have actually increased over the past few decades.

Given that there are hardly any permanent inhabitants in the interiors of Antarctica, Greenland, or just about any other one of the locations claimed to be "melting", the public has no choice but to rely on the words of "scientists" who are greatly invested in telling us that the polar ice is in fact gradually shrinking. With this, the pseudoscientific elite essentially utilizes the fallacy of special pleading to have us believe that these remote, unpopulated locations are in fact being affected by GW/CC incomparably more than any place we are likely to ever visit, which, of course, poses a great danger to us.

All of this is not to say that ice or snow anywhere - even in the polar regions - will never melt or even disappear for extended periods of time, however, these can all be easily explained by natural causes, such as the different types of geothermal activities.

Luckily, the climate alarmists themselves often provide some of the best evidence against their own claims. Two of such cases were in 2013 and 2016, when teams of gullible pseudoscientists went on an expedition to the Antarctic in hopes of proving to the world just how "melted" the ice was there. Ironically, they managed to prove the exact opposite, and had to find out the hard way just how wrong they've been when they had to be rescued after their ships got stuck in the thick sheets of ice that are covering the region where they thought there would be none. Such blunders are, of course, the results of the fact that the very notion of "globally" melting ice was based on cherry-picked data. In many cases, the ice that is actually melting at any location - that we're being told about the most frequently - have been in fact retreating since before the industrial revolution, while many that are not being advertised anywhere near as much are constantly expanding.

In order to patch up this devastating plothole in their story, climate alarmists invented the concept of "paradoxical shift"; water melting from beneath the Antarctic ice shelves and refreezing back on the surface – which is yet another claim that, naturally, lacks any evidence – and logic – to support it.

The claim that "sea levels are rising" is, unfortunately, also one that is lacking of evidence, which is not too surprising, seeing how it relies on the notion of melting polar ice being a reality. However, even without knowing how faulty that notion is, it'd still be a very easy claim to debunk, as numerous measurements are being done frequently all across the world, and, while some may show a slight rise, many others instead show a dropping sea level. Furthermore, the landmasses which are supposed to be "endangered" by this concept are, at the same time, also rising and subsiding; and doing so at different rates depending on their location. This often makes the proper measurement of the supposed "sea level rise" impossible, since there may be no way to determine whether it really was the sea rising or the land dropping.

Of course, once again, tricks can be and are being played by the powers that be even in this regard, as they like to just cherry-pick data from a period when the average results show rising, while ignoring the data that would either indicate dropping or no change. Or the fact that even the Netherlands, a country partly below sea level, is still doing just fine after all this time.

Meanwhile, to add insult to injury, the more affluent pundits of the hoax are buying up coastwise properties and entire islands left and right, with no concern about the obvious fact that if they were right about what they preach, their expensive acquisitions would soon be – or already would have been - devoured by the sea. An especially bold and outspoken pundit of the hoax is American actor Leonardo

DiCaprio, who is held in high esteem by the alarmist elite that even grant him opportunities to give sanctimonious speeches at top level institutions and organize street marches that are widely covered by the mainstream media. One of his most memorable speeches was given at the UN, where he used every acting skill he could muster to tell the world what essentially amounted to *"I may not be a scientist, but I fully trust them to tell me the truth, therefore I must be right when I parrot back what they told me".* In 2016, he even made an alarmist propaganda film – needless to say, filled with lies and fallacies - titled *Before the Flood,* which was, of course, heavily hyped up by the establishment and made available for everyone to watch for free on a number of different platforms. Unfortunately for him, it does not help his case that he purchased multiple coastline mansions worth tens of millions of dollars over the last few decades, and even had an entire hotel complex built on his private island in Belize - despite apparently believing that all of these will soon be washed away by the sea.

It should also be noted – as it is clear as daylight - that no financial institution would ever give out loans for the construction of any building anywhere the alarmists say will be underwater within a few years if they trusted their words, as getting into such endeavors would be far too risky from an investor's standpoint.

As many must already know, most Western government policies favor large corporations that can afford to either meet their ridiculous "environment protection" standards or simply pay the hefty fines for not living up to them, while small businesses are being crushed left and right by these same regulations. Furthermore, to make things even worse, they also often like to limit the usage of readily available and affordable methods of energy production, as well as heating, creating artificial blackouts and letting countless citizens freeze to death every winter in the name of "environmental consciousness".

One of the most worrying knock-on effects of alarmist environmentalism and all the fearmongering it entails is that young, impressionable people develop mental disorders, thinking that the world is about to end and it's collectively all of humanity's fault, often driving them to escape into drug and alcohol abuse, or even to commit suicide in desperation. Moreover, many in the West decide to either have fewer, or no children at all in "consideration" of how bad humans are said to be for the health of the Earth, which is an integral part of the GW/CC propaganda. Of course, such effects can generally not be seen anywhere else in the world, only in countries with a predominantly white population, where the hoax – along with the alarmist notion that fewer children is better for the environment - is propagated the most relentlessly - *by far.*

Despite the fact that the careless – or deliberately exaggerated - predictions made by the establishment's pseudoscientists and politicians can have such devastating effects on humanity, they hardly ever get called out - let alone punished. At the end of their workday, they just leave their workplaces as if they had done a good job, getting into their expensive, gas-guzzling cars to drive home to their well-heated – or air-conditioned – mansions to their half dozen children without a care in the world. That is, if they don't take a private jet to one of their laughably hypocritical, luxurious climate-conferences, or worse yet, one of their private islands where some of them often do unspeakable things to other humans.

Of course, the pundits and their power-hungry masters keep telling us that all they do mainly serves the purpose of "saving humanity", even when the measures taken to achieve this supposed goal is actually making it much harder for a large part of humanity to survive. They tell us that we must cut our CO_2 emissions - and eventually reduce it to zero -, all the while they tend to have orders of magnitude greater "carbon footprint" than the average tax-slave, with clearly no intention of reducing it one iota. Indeed, their hypocrisy seems to know no bounds, seeing that if they were actually serious about their claims regarding the "dangers" CO_2 (plant food) poses to the environment, they would have already shut down everything non-essential, such as the whole of the entertainment industry, including all the sports events – with special regards to motorsports. In addition, it is obvious that launching any kinds of rockets would be a thing of the past, since they waste an immeasurable amount of "fossil fuel" and provide absolutely nothing of worth – other than, of course, despicable propaganda. And yet, none of the above is ever even mentioned by the official alarmists as something that should be dealt with, since they clearly have great vested interest in all of it, not to mention they know very well that CO_2 is not a pollutant.

All of this should make one wonder: how many more times do the so-called "climate scientists" and their politician cronies have to show their two-facedness, get things horribly wrong and make entirely faulty predictions before humanity stops listening to them?

As it was briefly mentioned before, the GW/CC hoax has a significant part of its foundation built upon the idea of so-called "fossil fuels", which, of course, relies upon the dinosaur hoax and the concept of a billions of years old Earth. Needless to say, the notion that *"fossil fuels are bad for the Earth and therefore must not be used"* (at least not by the average tax-slave) is extremely convenient for the oppressive powers that wish to rule over us, as it allows them to convince the people to give up their motorized vehicles and utilize either much slower, or much more centralized ways of transportation. This, naturally, grants the elite significantly more control over our lives, as they will have a much easier time observing and following our every movement, not to mention that, in the case of public transportation or driverless cars, they can even regulate how often and how far we can travel.

Not only that, but, since the above hoaxes were built upon the modern, mainstream cosmology and cosmogony of the world, which, as we know, also tie in with Darwinism and the Big Bang theory – and therefore the concept of a heliocentric globe-Earth as well -, they also serve the purpose of reinforcing the public's belief in these frauds. And that is how all these deceptions form a full circle of masterfully crafted lies that exist in synergy.

Seeing just how intertwined all these hoaxes have become, it is perhaps not too surprising that one of the most important organizations tasked with providing climate-related information and data purportedly to "help understand, monitor, and adapt to climate change" is called the Copernicus Climate Change Service (C3S), one of the six thematic services provided by the European Union's Copernicus Earth Observation Program. This unfortunately-named, tyrannical institution also happens to be the one that is responsible for propagating the "global boiling" nonsense.

Another prime example of the molding of two major deceptions is a recently propagated claim that *"Venus used to be more Earth-like, but climate change made it uninhabitable"*, with which the pseudoscientists clearly attempt to once again utilize the fallacy of special pleading in order to further brainwash the more gullible. While this method has the potential to make one claim strengthen the other in the eyes of those who believe the former, fortunately, it also holds the possibility of making someone realize just how ridiculous one is if he's already doubtful of the other.

What's perhaps the most overwhelming to even think about when it comes to the GW/CC hoax is the amount of brainwashing it required to make a large part of humanity believe that a regular farm with animals on it is actually more harmful to the environment than solar and wind farms, or the factories where the solar panels and wind turbines themselves are produced. And yet, this is exactly what they are trying to have us believe when they tell us that we need to not only reduce the human population drastically – to save humanity, of course, -, but also that those who are deemed worthy of being let live will have to give up eating meat entirely in favor of processed plant- and insect-based proteins.

Such so-called "sustainable practices" will, naturally, only be enforced upon the average tax-slaves, and not the billionaire string-pullers and their cronies who themselves tend to already own vast farmlands that will, no doubt, still be allowed to produce for them whatever their hearts could possibly desire – which quite likely won't be insects. Interestingly, just as it is with most major deceptions, and especially Darwinism, the most prominent advocates of GW/CC can generally be found on the far left of the political spectrum. These crooks will often use the guise of environmentalism to gain popularity, and, as soon as they come to power, try to take as much control as possible over their subjects' lives in the name of "saving the planet".

The dark side of the deception

As the saying goes, *"the devil is in the details"*, and in the case of the deceptions unpacked throughout this book, it is literally like that. So, now that we have the Copernican globe model and all its appendages completely dismantled, we shall further explore their backgrounds to gain full understanding of the reasons behind their existence. It was already mentioned how these concepts were all built up on philosophical grounds as opposed to provable facts, however, we only got to take a short glimpse at the actual ideologies that ultimately resulted in their birth - and there were indeed plenty of those involved in the process.

At first glance, it may seem that the doctrines of globe-Earth heliocentrism, Big Bang, Darwinism, GW/CC, etc. are entirely secular and only serve an atheistic agenda. Indeed, erasing Theism is one of their primary goals, as it was - regarding heliocentrism - very poignantly pointed out by the German philosopher Friedrich Nietzsche in his 1974 book *The gay science; with a prelude in rhymes and an appendix of songs* (p. 181.):

"Where is God? (...) I will tell you. We have killed him - you and I. All of us are his murderers. But how did we do this? How could we drink up the sea? Who gave us the sponge to wipe away the entire horizon? What were we doing when we unchained this earth from its sun? Where is it moving now? Where are we moving? Away from all suns? Are we not plunging continually? Backward, sideward, forward, in all directions? Is there still any up or down? Are we not straying as through an infinite nothing? Do we not feel the breath of empty space? Has it not become colder? Is not night continually closing in on us? Do we not need to light lanterns in the morning? Do we hear nothing as yet of the noise of the gravediggers who are burying God? Do we smell nothing as yet

of the divine decomposition? Gods, too, decompose. God is dead. God remains dead. And we have killed him. How shall we, murderers of all murderers, console ourselves?"

However, despite all appearances, there is actually a deeply religious, occult agenda also embedded into all deceptions such as heliocentrism. These are, in fact, the fundamental underlying belief systems that drive the creation and shape every aspect of every major deception – and they are as dark as can be. Not only that, but there is also proof of the involvement of certain religious groups and secret societies, especially the Jesuit Order (aka. Society of Jesus) and Freemasonry, in the invention, endorsement and propagation of these sinistrous concepts. In fact, many of the most famous pseudoscientists and political figures were – and still are - well-known Jesuits and Masons. In regards of their role in the major deceptions and hoaxes, they are indeed so prevalent that if one were to randomly point at any one of the historical figures or modern deceivers mentioned in this book and claimed that that person was either a Jesuit or a Mason, he would be right much more often than not.

It is also interesting to note that the majority of Masons (especially at the higher ranks) seem to be of Jewish origin, although it is less surprising in light of the fact that Freemasonry has many roots in the Hebrew cultural circle. In fact, one of their most well-known symbols, the letter "G" refers to the unraveling of spiritual mystery which is termed "Gnosis" in Hebrew (while some also consider it to be depicting the omnipotence for (the Masonic) God, Lucifer as the supreme being). Masonic lodges in general can be perceived as modern-day Solomon Temples due to the pattern and order after which they are fashioned – with things like Moses' Ark of the Covenant and the Star of David also often appearing in them as favored symbols. Another one of the Masonic symbols that has its roots in the Hebrew scriptures is Acacia, describing a sacred wood commonly called "shittah", which is used to make furniture, especially pieces put together for the Ark of Covenant and the Sacred Tabernacle of God, while also depicting the "immortality of the soul". Not to mention the fact that the 16th rank ("degree") in Masonry is called the "Prince of Jerusalem".

In addition, ancient Egyptian symbols such as the frequently seen "Eye of Providence", also known as the "All-seeing Eye", depicting the "Architect of the Universe" who "sees all and knows all about the human deeds, thoughts, and actions", as well as symbols related to ancient Egyptian deities. One of such is the two-headed eagle Mammon-Ra (Mammon being the demon of Avarice and one of the ruling princes of hell in Abrahamic mythology), which is perhaps their most beloved deity. Naturally, pyramids, whether intact or missing the capstone, are also among the most frequently used symbols in Freemasonry. Kabbalistic symbolism such as the Tree of Life – whose name was later adopted by the Darwinist "phylogenetic tree of life" - and numerology also play an important role in Masonry, while the usage of sun disks or sun rays – usually coupled with another symbol - clearly attests to their sun-worshipping traditions. Although, in their case the Sun represents more than just the heavenly body that gives us warmth; to them it means the "Bringer of Light", or "Light-Bearer", also known as Lucifer, or the Morning Star (the Sun), who is, needless to say, the Biblical fallen angel opposing God, Jesus and his teachings.

It is also often associated with Horus, the Egyptian falcon-headed deity, the son of Osiris and Isis, who had the Sun and the Moon for eyes and is often referred to as a sun god, sometimes even just depicted as a winged sun disk. According to his mythology, one of his eyes was damaged in a fight with his uncle Seth - god of the sky, desert and storm -, but was healed by the god Thoth. The figure of the restored eye then became a powerful amulet known as the "Wadjet Eye", or "Eye of Horus" which is, of course, where the Masonic "Eye of Providence" actually originates from. Horus was later identified by the Greeks with Apollo who, as a sun god, was also called "Phoebus", or "bright" – also providing the namesake for the missions of the Moon landing hoax. In turn, Apollo was previously referred to as Helios, or "Sun" in Greek, who was their original sun god, to eventually - under the Roman Empire - be replaced by the Sun itself, which came to be worshipped as the Unconquered Sun. The celebration of the Unconquered Sun, also known as Sol Invictus, was a Roman festival held on December 25th, known today as Christmas. The date of December 25th was chosen to coincide with the winter solstice when the daylight begins to lengthen again.

Moreover, one of the two names used for the 28th degree in Masonry is "Knight of the Sun" (the other one being "Prince Adept"). The movie *A Trip to the Moon*, which can be considered the first space-propaganda film in history, has a poster artwork depicting the Moon with a human face with a giant bullet in one of its eyes. One eye of a person being shut or covered is one of the most obvious and frequently used signs that the establishment puts out there for the public to covertly convey their occult message and Satanic allegiance to the public. Thus, the poster for *A Trip to the Moon* was one of the first Eye of Horus symbolisms that we so often see all around us in the entertainment and advertising industries nowadays, giving us a clear sign as to who is behind the narrative of space travel and exploration – and, of course, the mainstream part of the industries altogether. Such covert messaging is highly favored by them because they hold the belief that if they tell us about their dark ways, even if in a coded manner, it would be considered a warning for the people, and therefore they, as the perpetrators, are absolved from all responsibility for their dark deeds that may follow.

In light of all this, it is not hard to see just how intertwined Freemasonry – and therefore everything connected to it - is with ancient sun-worshipping religions and their deities. This undoubtedly shows a clear picture as to why their historical "scientists", most notably, of course, Copernicus, felt it so important to put the Sun in the center of our world and make sure that as many people consider their concept the truth as possible.

Moreover, Manly Palmer Hall, a highly esteemed Canadian author, lecturer, astrologer, mystic and 33rd degree (highest rank) Freemason wrote about the goals of Masonry in his 1923 book *The Lost Keys Of Masonry* as follows (p. 20-21.):

"Man is climbing an endless flight of steps, with his eyes turned toward the goal at the top. Many cannot see the goal, and only one or two steps are visible before them. He has learned, however, one great lesson, and that is, that as he builds his own character he is given strength to climb the steps. Hence a Mason is a builder of the temple of character. He is the architect of a sublime mystery - the gleaming, glowing temple of his own soul. He realizes that he best serves God when he joins with the Great Architect in building more noble structures in the universe below."

Whether the *"universe below"* is supposed to be our own world or another one beneath it may be left ambiguous, but Hall's words certainly make it clear that the so-called "Great Architect" they worship is in fact a separate being from the Christian God, as opposed to what some mainstream sources might have us believe.

Unfortunately, even the average Mason tends to have no clue about any of this, since a new member is simply promised a "path to the light" and isn't being told - until he reaches the highest rank - that this "light" is in fact Lucifer. Nonetheless, the Luciferians don't consider him an evil figure, but rather an "angel" that rebels against an oppressive power; a benevolent "God of Light". Albert Pike, 33°

Mason and former Grand Commander of the Supreme Council - which used to govern the Scottish Rite Freemasonry in the U.S. – wrote a book of great importance in 1871, which was then traditionally given to all candidate Masons upon their receipt of the 14th degree of the Scottish Rite. This book goes by the name of *Morals and Dogma of the Ancient and Accepted Scottish Rite of Freemasonry*, and it says the following about Lucifer and the way he is called (p. 210.):

"The Apocalypse is, to those who receive the nineteenth Degree, the Apothesis of that Sublime Faith which aspires to God alone, and despises all the pomps and works of Lucifer. Lucifer, the Light-bearer! Strange and mysterious name to give to the Spirit of Darknesss! Lucifer, the Son of the Morning! Is it he who bears the Light, and with its splendors intolerable blinds feeble, sensual or selfish Souls ? Doubt it not!"

Of course, symbolism implying sun-worship and pagan traditions is just as prominent with the Jesuits, whose main symbol is an emblem depicting a sun disk with the letters "IHS" in its center, which is an acronym for the Latin phrase "Iesus Hominum Salvator", which translates to "Jesus, Savior of Mankind" – thus also seemingly mixing paganism with Christianity.

Needless to say, the Jesuit Order contributed significantly to the creation and propagation of heliocentrism as well. When the Order was founded in 1540, the Earth was still accepted to be in the center of the universe, but merely 3 years later Copernicus' historical book detailing his heliocentric theory was published. Then, just a century and a quarter later, one of the first comprehensive depictions of the supposed globe-Earth, along with its interior, was presented – in a rather esoteric way - by Jesuit scholar Athanasius Kircher in his book *Mundus Subterraneus (Underground World)*, which played an important role in the early development of the discipline of geology. The Jesuits also made sure to secure the full support of the Catholic Church for heliocentrism, with the help of historical figures such as Christopher Clavius, German Jesuit mathematician and astronomer. He was a strong advocate of heliocentrism, and his work played a crucial role in the development of the now widely used Gregorian calendar, a reform of the Julian calendar introduced by Pope Gregory XIII in 1582. The Gregorian calendar is solar in nature, meaning it is based on the Earth's supposed revolutions around the Sun. Its primary purpose was to reform the Julian calendar to bring the date of the spring equinox closer to March 21 and to better align with the "solar year".

However, there is yet another, even darker layer to the world-wide deceptions with similar roots. To understand how it functions, it should be noted that certain numbers, signs and symbols are very important to the world's deceivers, as they are the way they can openly communicate with each other without alarming the general public of their presence, and they also see them as holders of inherent power. As a famous quote often attributed to Confucius says:

"Signs and symbols rule the world, not words nor laws."

Although it is true that even words and letters are often used for the same purpose. They have an especially great significance for religions such as Judaism, since each Hebrew letter also has a numeric value, and thus the language can be used to convey hidden or coded messages. In Judaism, the *Torah* is the written law, and there are two different interpretations for it: the *Talmud* provides a Rabbinical interpretation of the scripture, while the *Kabbalah* provides a mystical interpretation of it.

This leads us back to Freemasonry, where Kabbalism is the most prominent. Albert Pike wrote about this in his aforementioned book *Morals and Dogma* as follows (p. 474-475.):

"Masonry is a search after Light. That search leads us directly back, as you see, to the Kabbalah. In that ancient and little understood medley of absurdity and philosophy, the Initiate will find the source of many doctrines; and may in time come to understand the Hermetic philosophers, the Alchemists, all the Anti-papal Thinkers of the Middle Ages, and Emanuel Swedenborg."

It is important to note that, while the followers of the Torah and the Talmud are awaiting a messiah, Kabbalists believe (although rarely admit) that they themselves are the chosen ones destined to rule the world. Of course, this fact is buried quite deep in their exceptionally verbose scriptures, which were, in turn, originally written in a coded language as a way of keeping it away from the masses and only let a select group of scholars understand the true meaning of its words – and even they were only allowed to study it from the age of 40. The teachings of Kabbalism are also inextricably intertwined with the tenets of Alchemy, Rosicrucianism, Hermeticism and, of course, Freemasonry.

According to numerology, which has many different languages serving as code systems, each number has a unique vibration that can influence our personality, relationships and overall life. Some numbers are more powerful than others, and in Kaballah, these are called "master numbers", considered to be carrying great spiritual force. The number 33 is one of the most important among them, which also appears in other religions. For example, Jesus is claimed to have died at the age of 33 - a number that symbolizes sacrifice and redemption for the followers of the Christian faith.

THE GLOBAL DECEPTION

Just about everyone seems to have heard at least a couple stories about people who had some kind of otherwordly experience at some point in their lives, even if it was outside of their control. Whether or not one believes in it, it remains a fact that witchcraft has been practiced for thousands of years, with many doing it even in these modern times. In fact, as unfortunate as it is, cults, especially the ones based on some form of Satanism, are gaining more and more followers every day. This can certainly raise a few questions for the uninitiated, such as: why practice it if there are never any visible results? Who started it all and how did he know what to do and how to do it? Was there someone or something supernatural that taught and guided him?

These questions can lead one down a seemingly bottomless rabbit hole, and even if he delves into its depths, there is no guarantee that he will find a satisfying answer. Fortunately, for all intents and purposes, it's enough to simply know that certain people do believe in it and many of them are among the most influential ones in the world.

Perhaps not too surprisingly, these were exactly the kinds of things that some of the biggest names in the building and propagation of the heliocentric globe-hoax (and, no doubt, other ones as well) liked to meddle with. Most notably, Jack Parsons – the Marxist founder of the Jet Propulsion Laboratory (JPL) which was later transformed into NASA - was a famous and productive member of the Ordo Templi Orientist (OTO) - a Satanic cult built upon the ancient Egyptian-based philosophy of Thelema - and was heavily influenced by one of its founders (all of whom were high-ranking Masons), Aleister Crowley, a British occultist and ceremonial magician who is often referred to as the "Wickedest Man in the World" and called himself the "Beast 666". In turn, Crowley was also connected to L. Ron Hubbard, the world-famous American science fiction writer and founder of the Church of Scientology – an incredibly lucrative cult that's surrounded with ongoing legal and social controversies. Hubbard and Parsons became close friends after Hubbard moved into Parsons' home where he and his fellow cultists practiced their Satanic rituals – an activity in which Hubbard showed great interest. In fact, Parsons was so amazed by his new friend's knowledge of the subject that he wrote a letter of praise about him to Crowley, referring to Hubbard as an exceptionally good fit for their cult with an extraordinary amount of experience and understanding in the fields of the esoteric and the occult. Hubbard and Parsons even attempted to perform an elaborate spell called the Babalon Working, with which they aimed to remotely impregnate a woman who would then give birth to the Thelemic goddess Babalon (essentially a female Antichrist) – an endeavor that Parsons believed was successful. However, Hubbard turned out to be a bad friend, as he eventually took off with a large portion of Parsons' savings, as well as his lover.

Regarding the OTO, it is important to know that it mainly draws from and is strongly connected to the traditions of the Freemasonic and Rosicrucian movements of the 18th and 19th centuries, the crusading Knights Templars of the middle ages, as well as pagan mystery schools. It even has some Illuminist connections, which is explained by the fact that one of the OTO's founders, Theodor Reuss, an Anglo-German occultist was also responsible for the revival of an old secret society called the Bavarian Order of Illuminati.

The OTO's main figure, Crowley was so enamored with the idea of becoming one with the devil that he changed his name to how it's known today so that it (his first and last name together) would add up in both the English, the Hebrew and the Greek Kabbalistic numerology, or gematria, to 666. He was convinced he's about to bring the world "The Aeon of Horus" and thus greatly favored ancient Egyptian rites which he either performed in an authentic Egyptian ceremonial garb or a black robe and a pyramid-shaped hat with the symbol of the Sun on it. The purpose of many such rituals was, of course, to summon Horus, or as he is often called today, Lucifer. Crowley was also the member of the Hermetic Order of the Golden Dawn, a Masonic organization derived from the Rosicrucians, and, due to his exceptional achievements in the realm of "magick" (as he called his dark practices to distinguish them from the higher grade of "magic"), many consider him the most highly honored Mason in the world. Needless to say, similar practices are also present in Masonic lodges among high-ranking members who hope to achieve immortality through performing "magick", although those at the lower ranks are not told much of this, lest the uninitiated – and unreliable – get scared away by the true darkness of the society and spread the word among outsiders.

As one would expect, Crowley and his teachings began to become especially popular after his death, with many famous artists and musicians - such as John Lennon, Jimmy Page, Ozzy Osbourne, David Bowie, Bruce Dickinson, etc. - reading and being inspired by his work, as well as countless more in the entertainment industry who later integrated his ideology into their own doings. Even the hippie movement's philosophy of "free love" was based on his writings, eventually further helping the spread of his simple and increasingly popular, hedonistic, Satanic "law" of *do what thou wilt*.

So this is the movement that Parsons, the "father of rocketry", was a very prominent member of. He eventually met his end when experimenting with what some say were mere explosives (with which he was almost as obsessed as with performing witchcraft), while others claim a summoning spell, resulting in a blast that killed him. Of course, sending rockets high up into the air – which was thought to be impossible before his work - was actually a form of occult ritual to him. The rising phallic object represented to him what obelisks used to represent to those who raised them in ancient Egypt: a petrified ray of the sun associated with the sun god Ra - while it had to do just as much with the Thelemic (phallic) "magick" that Crowley taught him. This idea of fusing technology and witchcraft seems to correlate with what's become known as "Clarke's Third Law"; a quote from Arthur C. Clarke that appeared in a footnote in his 1973 revision of his book *Profiles of the Future: An Inquiry into the Limits of the Possible,* which states: *"Any sufficiently advanced technology is indistinguishable from magic"*. Nonetheless, Parsons became known as the father of rocketry and his occult legacy, the JPL, became NASA a few years after his death.

Likely to the surprise of none, this particular institution made no significant changes when it comes to ideologies, keeping all that was inherited from its predecessor, sending lewd-looking rockets high up into the air (and crashing them into the sea) as part of their – taxpayer-funded - occult rituals. As a matter of fact, one of the most highly esteemed Masonic lodges, the *Supreme Council 33° Southern Jurisdiction* of the U.S. even has one of their own flags on display in their headquarter's museum, which they proudly claim was taken to the Moon during the Apollo missions by Buzz Aldrin – who, of course, happened to be a 33rd degree Mason. He allegedly also carried to the Moon a special deputization from Grand Master (Mason) J. Guy Smith, with which to claim Masonic territorial jurisdiction over the Moon on behalf of the Grand Lodge of Texas. Of course, Aldrin wasn't the only "astronaut" who happened to be a Mason, in fact, evidence shows that most if not all of those who had any significant part in the Apollo missions were members of the brotherhood. As one would expect, the deceivers of our time tend to be no different, nor is the practice of hiring a group of Masons unique to this particular deception. It makes keeping a hoax under wraps that much easier for its planners, since this way the perpetrators are not only (more often than not) obligated to keep it a secret by military law, but also the extremely fierce and stringent oath they have to take when joining Freemasonry; an oath that implies that they will pay with their lives if they dare to speak up.

Another famous Mason that was very interested in certain forms of magic – and thus the occult - was none other than Walt Disney, whose obsession with it becomes blatantly obvious even when just looking at how many of his productions have the word "magic" in their titles or names. Not only that, but those who know what to look for can find a plethora of occult symbolism and "explicit" imagery scattered throughout his cartoons, which, naturally, also very often revolve around the theme of magic. Moreover, it is interesting to note that the font he chose for his name in the Disney logo makes it look like the first letter is a mirrored number 6, the dot on the letter "I" is another 6, with the last letter also strongly resembling a 6 – thus forming the Satanic 666, the Biblical number of the Beast, or the devil. In 1967, he even founded his own – to be infamous - Masonic-themed private club by the name of Club 33, where it is claimed that some quite horrible acts have been taking place. Anyone could join the club as long as they were willing to pay the initiation fee of $25,000 and cover the annual membership fee of $10,000. Needless to say, a large number of influential businessmen and celebrities soon joined the club - presumably to engage in the questionable activities it had to offer.

An interesting connection between Freemasonry and the models of deception introduced here, with special regards to theoretical physics, is the letter "G" in the main symbol of Masonry, which is supposed to stand for either Gnosis or "God" (as in *their* god), but may as well just stand for "gravity", since that is essentially the "godly entity" that keeps the sun-worship-based religions – such as heliocentrism - together. This symbolic connection is further proven by the fact that the so-called "gravitational constant", also denoted by the letter "G", is claimed to be approximately 6.67430×10^{-11} $\text{m}^{3} \cdot \text{kg}^{-1} \text{s}^{-2}$, based on arbitrary and ambiguous measurements. The initial apparent "66" in that string of nonsense is an important number to Masons that is derived from the double 33s often used in Masonic symbolism – although the first three digits forming the number 667 can also be interpreted as a rounded up 666, which we often see with numbers that would have originally given away the game too easily.

Knowing this, it is perhaps not too surprising that many, if not all, concepts in theoretical physics stem from the Kabbalah – and therefore Masonry. One such concept is the multiverse theory, that actually originates from the Kabbalistic belief that there are many other universes beside our own visible one, which all have different outcomes for all events that occurred - accessible through spiritual enlightenment. It is, in fact, claimed that once a Mason reaches the 33rd degree, he is handed the truth about such parallel timelines, as well as guidance to traverse them in order to choose the path that aligns with his preferred version of events.

The Kabbalah also includes a book called the *Sefer Yetzirah*, which describes the creation of the world similarly to the Big Bang, while the famous story of the golem – a statue that's brought to life by a Jewish mystic – corresponds with the modern pseudoscientific notion that inanimate objects at the dawn of time could have somehow turned into living beings without the need of a god.

Elizabeth Clare Prophet, an American spiritual leader, author, orator, and writer's 1997 book titled *Kabbalah - Key to Your Inner Power* contains the following on the matter (p. 3, 9, 11.):

"Although the teachings of Kabbalah are highly mystical, they are also highly practical. Jewish mystics received revelations about the creation of the universe that are strikingly similar to modern science's big bang theory. (…) Like modern scientists, Jewish mystics of the thirteenth century said that in the beginning there was nothing (…). Just as science has confirmed the ideas behind Jewish and Hindu creation myths, so it has lent credibility to other statements Jewish mystics have made about the universe. Although scientists are still refining their calculations, they believe that the universe is somewhere between nine billion and sixteen billion years old. About seven hundred years ago, the mystic Rabbi Isaac of Acco reached the same conclusion. He said the universe was over fifteen billion years old, but he didn't base his conclusion on precise scientific measurement. In his book The Treasury of Life, he said he based it on the hidden oral tradition."

Of course, it is not the case in reality that *"science has confirmed"* such ancient religious beliefs, but rather just that those who hold these beliefs in modern times have become so powerful and influential that they managed to shape the whole of so-called "science" in a way that it ended up reflecting and seemingly reinforcing their worldview.

Another pseudoscientific concept that was clearly based on ancient Kabbalistic ideas is Darwinism. This is just about self-evident in light of the fact that the Darwin-bloodline consisted of multiple high-ranking Masons, including Charles' father and grandfather – with Charles himself also showing telltale signs of being one, such as the Masonic "hidden hand" and "keep quiet" hand signs that can be seen on some of his portraits.

Indeed, the notion of humans originating from apes is an integral part of the Kabbalah, which writes about the world having been destroyed and reformed multiple times until the perfect form – and the upright standing posture - of the human body was achieved. This is why the numerical value of the Kabbalistic God is 26, relating to the 26 vertebrae in the human spine from the neck down (while the whole spine contains 33 of them – another sacred number in the Kabbalah), and to the 26 bones in the human foot. The sacred name of the Kabbalah's God known as the Tetragrammaton is a four-letter name written in Hebrew, and its specific pronunciation is considered a closely guarded secret in Jewish tradition. The four letters are usually transliterated as YHWH - letters which have numeric values of 10, 5, 6, and 5, adding up to 26.

The creation of all things is explained in the Kabbalah by the concept of the "Ein Sof": an infinite, limitless, and formless essence from which everything emanates - underscoring the fundamental unity of all existence, just like the "infinitely dense point" of the Big Bang's concept.

Daniel C. Matt, an author, teacher and scholar of Kabbalah wrote about the relationship between the theory of evolution and the Kabbalah in his 1995 book *The Essential Kabbalah - The Heart of Jewish Mysticism* as follows (p. 31.):

"The theory of evolution accords with the secrets of Kabbalah better than any other theory. Evolution follows a path of ascent and thus provides the world with a basis for optimism. How can one despair, seeing that everything evolves and ascends? When we penetrate the inner nature of evolution, we find divinity illuminated in perfect clarity. Ein Sof generates, actualizes potential infinity."

Another proof of Darwinism's occult origins is the naming of one of the most important, purportedly 3.2 million years old (based on the usual, completely unreliable ways of dating), so-called "missing links" known as "Lucy". While this name is often used by Satanists as code for Lucifer, this fact is not the only telltale sign of something fishy being afoot about the naming. In fact, it is claimed that the idea of naming the supposedly "discovered" skeleton "Lucy" came to the paleontologist who "found it" as he was listening to *Lucy in the Sky with Diamonds* from the Beatles.

This song is from their album *Sgt. Pepper's Lonely Hearts Club Band* whose cover artwork depicts such "luminaries" as Aleister Crowley, Karl Marx, and even Einstein. The song was, of course, written primarily by John Lennon, who was already mentioned in this chapter as one of the biggest fans of Crowley's occult teachings. Soon after its release, the song – similarly to many others that the band produced - was widely critiqued for promoting the use of psychedelic drugs, and for the fact that the first letter of each of the nouns in its title seemed to intentionally spell "LSD", the initialism commonly used for the hallucinogenic drug lysergic acid diethylamide.

Although the band kept denying the allegations and insisted that it was all "just a big coincidence", refuting the claims was not made easy for them by the fact that at least one of the members admitted – on multiple occasions - to having been the user of LSD himself. It also became apparent to many that the use of psychedelic drugs, and especially LSD, has seen a surge around the time the band was starting to become famous, which many would attribute to the ethereal, seemingly drug-hazed lyrics and tones of many of their songs. Another red flag about them was the fact that Aldous Huxley's face also appeared on the Sgt. Pepper-album's cover due to his 1954 work *The Doors of Perception* having been a required reading for the so-called "countercultural elite" at the time, as it details Huxley's own experiences of taking mescaline - another hallucinogenic drug like LSD.

Not only that, but the Beatles is also known for utilizing Crowley's method of subliminal messaging called "backtracking" – the placing of hidden messages in their songs when played backwards - more than almost any other Satanic band in history. Because of all this controversy, many researchers today suspect that bands like the Beatles – as well as the entire so-called "counter culture" of the 60s – must have been created and used by intelligence agencies for the purpose of getting as much of the youth hooked on drugs and hedonistic ideologies such as Satanism as possible, so that the future generations are weakened and thus easier to control. Even the seemingly wholesome anti-war message of the "counter culture" turned out to have been detrimental to society in the end, as hearing all the drugged up hippies repeat the same talking points over and over in their hazy voices just made the more conservative half of the population side with the mainstream narrative – unfortunately including wars – that much more.

And thus, the song from the high-level proponents of a clearly drug-fueled subculture with a Satanic foundation became the inspiration for the naming of the integral part of the evolution-hoax known as "Lucy", a common code for the name of the Antichrist.

Unfortunately, the other major deceptions in our world are not free from the influence of occultism and Satanism either, but to understand how and why they are related so closely, a deeper dive into Kabbalism is necessary. A book of the Kabbalah, the *Zohar*, or "book of radiance", writes about an infinite god that has a feminine and a masculine side, which one could relate to the modern hermaphrodite Satanic idol, Baphomet. According to the teachings of the Zohar, no word in Judaism has just a single meaning and everything has to be questioned and reinterpreted in accordance with the coding of the language that's being used. The Zohar is also where the previously mentioned Kabbalistic Tree of Life was introduced, which is a central concept in Kabbalistic thought, consisting of ten interconnected emanations or sefirot, each representing a different aspect of the divine, as well as a ten dimensional universe. This is why the number 10 – along with the aforementioned number 26 - is significant and holds symbolic importance in Kabbalah. The Tree also includes a lightning strike-formation, which relates to the lightning strike symbolism that is today used by Luciferians as an expression of homage to their idol who fell from heaven as a "lightning bolt" following his banishment.

In 2011, Kabbalah expert Billy Phillips interviewed Michio Kaku, the famous theoretical physicist whose name already came up in earlier chapters, as well as a few other – unfortunately unnamed - experts on the relationship between modern "science" and the Kabbalah. Once they were familiarized with the Zohar, they were asked to comment on how they think it relates to their areas of expertise, which resulted in a short documentary that can be found on a YouTube channel bearing Phillips' own name. In this, they – in a somewhat astounded manner - ascertain that (theoretical) "science" is indeed intertwined with and essentially based on the Kabbalah. Kaku and the other supposed "scientists" tell us the following relevant – and rather shocking - words in their snippets of monologues:

- *"I'm not a philosopher, however, I'm rather dazzled by the fact that many of the basic mysteries that we find in string theory - and the theory of everything – seem to be mirrored in the Zohar, and in the Kabbalah."*

- *"As a scholar, the most amazing thing of all is the degree to which modern astrophysics sounds like a Kabbalistic text."*

- *"We do know that Isaac Newton had access to certain mystical texts – certain texts of the Kabbalah."*

- *"It is certainly true that in string theory the number 10 is the dimension of spacetime for supersymmetrical string theories and 26 for bosonic string theories – stand[ing] out as a requirement of the mathematics."*

- *"All the things that could destroy string theory, all the things that do destroy every rival theory to string theory, they're all eliminated in precisely 10 and 26 dimensions. These dimensions are magic. We physicists don't know where these dimensions come from."*

- *"They* [the ancient Kabbalists] *knew things about the universe that took us 'til now to discover."*

- *"The Zohar's notion that light is a realm of no time and no space is quite consistent with special relativity."*

- *"What's been stopping it* [a certain kind of research process] *so far are, number one, the lack of a good concept, and I think the Kabbalah is offering that now in the context of modern sience, and two, a reticence on the part of both scientists and people in religion to mix the two."*

- *"It's rather amazing, its uncanny reflection of some of the most advanced cosmology coming from our satellites, coming from our atom smashers, coming from our blackboards that are mirrored in the Zohar and ancient Kabbalistic texts."*

Whether these "scientists" are truly this oblivious to the fact that their area of expertise is essentially nothing more than modernized versions of ancient occult teachings is anyone's guess, but it's certainly good to see that at least they are now starting to notice the connections.

Other than what was already mentioned, it is worth noting that – according to Kabbalah experts - the Zohar also describes what would essentially be called "black holes" today, while the Kabbalah spoke of a "round earth" a millennium and a half before Columbus, as well as 7 continents with multiple "time zones". Furthermore, it also described a kind of "theory of relativity" two millennia before Einstein claimed this hotchpotch as his own invention.

The number 13 is also a big favorite and one of the most sacred numbers of the Kabbalists, which is why it appears so prominently in Mason-founded countries such as the U.S. For example, the Great Seal of the United States (which also appears on the back of the modern 1 dollar bill), adopted in 1782, shows the 13 initial states of the country - which are formed into a Star of David -, as well as an eagle, a symbol of peak predation and a reference to Horus' form, holding an olive branch with 13 leaves and 13 olives in one foot, and 13 arrows in the other. This eagle is also holding a ribbon in its beak which writes the 13 letter phrase "E pluribus unum" (Latin for *"Out of many, one"* – clearly a reference to the One World Order they've already started planning then), and is covered with a shield that has 13 stripes on it. The other side of the seal shows a Masonic pyramid with 13 layers, while in front of the pyramid 13 patches of grass can be seen, and above it floats the All-seeing Eye (of Lucifer) and the 13 letter phrase "Annuit Coeptis" (Latin for *"He* [their god] *has approved our undertakings"*).

Moreover, the Knights Templar, a medieval Masonic-Christian military order founded in the early 12th century, whose surviving members later became the first "modern" Masons, is said to have had 13 initial members and 13 rank levels. The Templar Order also happened to be the predecessor of DeMolay International, a Masonic fraternal organization for young men between the ages of 12 and 21, founded in Kansas City, Missouri, in 1919 by Frank S. Land. Its name is derived from Jacques de Molay, the last Grand Master of the Knights Templar, executed on friday the 13th in 1314

– and thus such days became known as unlucky among the followers of the Templars' teachings. This is the more mundane reason the number 13 brings up a certain feeling of unease in Kabbalists, while in gematria the number 12 is seen as a symbol of completeness (e.g. 12 months, 12 zodiac signs), and the addition of one disrupts this completeness, leading to a perceived imbalance - although it also symbolizes rebirth after death at the same time. This superstition is why (especially) in New York city, which many consider the capital of the world, and especially the capital of the Jewry, all buildings skip the 13th floor to avoid the feared number.

It is also worth exploring some of the details of the Apollo 13 mission, especially those of the supposed explosion that's claimed to have occurred on the "spacecraft", as it is just as riddled with this kind of numerology (starting with the number in the mission's name), as well as plenty of esoteric symbolism. The first thing that might catch one's eye is that they named the "lunar module" that the "astronauts" purportedly ended up escaping in "Aquarius", which is the name for a "new age" in astrology. The time of the supposed launch of the "spacecraft" is also cause for suspicion, as it's claimed to have happened at exactly 14:13 Eastern Standard Time (EST) on April 11, 1970. Furthermore, the alleged explosion of the oxygen tank on the "service module" is said to have occurred on April 13 and noticed and communicated to mission control at 10:55 EST (55 being an important number in astrology that signifies major positive changes), which was 55 hours and 55 minutes into the mission, which, in turn, would have been 1 hour and 13 minutes after the actual explosion.

As one might expect, the made up figures that the models of the "global" deceptions were based on are also filled to the brim with hidden – as well as not so hidden - occult numerology. Perhaps the most prominently occuring number is, of course, the number of the

Beast, 666 - sometimes written in a more cryptic way like 36, as in 3×6, meaning "three sixes". Other than that, the Masonic 33 and its counterpart, 66 are also often used - as well as plain sixes, which have great importance in the Hebrew gematria, as they're associated with harmony, balance, and earthly matters. There are also some less frequent, but still significant numbers, such as 11 and 22, which are known as master numbers in the Kabbalah (similarly to 33). The number 93 also appears more often than would be statistically likely, and is associated with Aleister Crowley's Thelema. The central tenet of Thelema, *"Do what thou wilt shall be the whole of the Law"*, has a gematria value of 93, just as the word "Thelema" itself does, while this number is also integrated into various rituals, writings, and symbolism within Crowley's teachings.

So let us now examine the plethora of so-called "scientific" data of the major deceptions, as well as some "historical" data that contain the aforementioned ominous numbers.

- One solar cycle involving variations in the Sun's magnetic activity and the number of sunspots is said to last approximately 11 years.

- Jupiter is claimed to have 11 asteroids called "Jupiter Trojans" nearby that share an "orbit" with it.

- The Moon landing hoax was perpetrated within the Apollo 11 mission.

- The "dwarf planet" Ceres is claimed to have an orbital speed of approximately 11.1 miles per second. Moreover, its synodic period (the time it takes for the object to return to the same position relative to the Sun and Earth as observed from Earth) is said to be 466.6 days, while it would make a full "orbit" in 4.6 years, which is 1679 days. 1679 divided by 466.6 roughly equals 3.6.

- Refraction, reflection, and dispersion of light in ice crystals in the Earth's "atmosphere" can cause a circular halo around the Sun or Moon, which is called a "22-degree halo".

- The geostationary (Clarke) "orbit" is described to be at an altitude of roughly 22,000 miles, which translates to about 36,000 kilometers.

- "Escape velocity", the minimum speed an object needs to escape Earth's "gravitational pull", is claimed to be is approximately 11.2 kilometers per second (or 132283464 feet per hour, or 2204724 feet per minute, or 36745 feet per second), which roughly equals 33 times the speed of sound.

- Earth's axial tilt is currently claimed to be 23.4 degrees, leaving an "orbital inclination" angle of 66.6 degrees, while the lowest value it's ever been is said to be 22.1 degrees.

- The diameter of the oxygen tank allegedly used on the Apollo missions is claimed to be 66 centimeters.

- The numeric value of NASA's full name, National Aeronautics and Space Administration, adds up to 365 in English and 666 in reverse English gematria.

- The "Moon rock" (which turned out to be mere petrified wood) that the NASA "astronauts" "brought back" was claimed to have been carbon dated at 3.6 million years old according to Bill Clinton, as mentioned by him in an interview with Neil deGrasse Tyson.

- Mercury's average distance to the Sun is claimed to be 36 million miles.

- In terms of diameter, Earth is claimed to be 3.666 times larger than the Moon.

- Elon Musk's project *Starlink* is claimed to have 3,660 active satellites as of 2023. Moreover, Musk seems to be obsessed with the letter *X*, which occultists often use as a symbol of the Antichrist. He also dresses up as "Devil's Champion" for a Halloween party in 2022 and changed his *X* (formerly known as *Twitter*) profile picture to the shot made of him in the ominous costume, which he then used for quite some time for no apparent reason.

- Peggy Whitson, the "first female commander" of the "International Space Station" is claimed to have set the U.S. record for spending the most total time living and working in "space" with 666 alleged days.

- The mass extinction event that would have led to the extinction of the "dinosaurs" is claimed to have occurred approximately 66 million years ago.

- The mean "orbital velocity" of Pluto (also known by the number *134340*) is claimed to be 4.666 kilometers per second. Moreover, the name Pluto was chosen after the Roman god with the same name, who is the equivalent of the Greek Hades, god of the Underworld, the realm of the dead.

- Mars' aphelion (its greatest distance from the Sun) is claimed to be roughly 154.8 million miles, which equals 1.666 astronomical units (AU).

- The comet Shoemaker-Levy 9 (SL9) is claimed to have collided with Jupiter in 1994 traveling at approximately 216,000 kilometers per hour, which is 6×6×6000.

- According to the globe model, the Earth's circumference is 24,900 (statute) miles, which equals approximately 21,600 nautical miles, which is 6×6×600.

- The diameter of the Moon is claimed to be 2160 miles, which is 6×6×60.

- Our average distance to the Moon is claimed to be about 239,000 miles, which is approximately 6×60×666.

- The Earth is claimed to be "orbiting" the Sun at 66,600 miles per hour.

- The mass of Earth is claimed to be approximately 6×10^{24} kilograms.

- The mass of the Sun is claimed to be approximately 333,000 times that of Earth.

- On the heliocentrists' globe-Earth model, the Arctic and Antarctic circles run about 66°33'39", or roughly 66.6°, north and south of the Equator respectively.

- The temperature on Venus is claimed to be about 464° celsius or 867° fahrenheit, whose rounded median would be 666. Moreover, the pressure near the surface is claimed to be 93 bar (1,350 psi).

- The "observable" universe is currently claimed to be approximately 93 billion light years across.

- The Earth's distance to the Sun is claimed to be 93 million miles.

- The average closest distance from Earth to Mars is claimed to be 33.93 million miles.

- The impact of the "asteroid" – which is claimed to have been about 6 miles in diameter - that supposedly killed the "dinosaurs" is said to have created the Chicxulub crater, which is allegedly about 93 miles in diameter.

- The division of the day into 24 hours, each hour into 60 minutes, and each minute into 60 seconds – resulting 3,600 seconds per hour - became established in ancient Babylon, which many consider the cradle of occultism itself.

- The European Organization for Nuclear Research, commonly known as CERN (Conseil Européen pour la Recherche Nucléaire), a major international research institution focused on particle physics that's also the home of the Large Hadron Collider, has a logo that consists of multiple sixes. The acronym of CERN also shows suspicious similarity to the name of the Celtic horned deity, Cernunnos, associated with fertility, the wilderness, and the cycles of life, death, and rebirth. This deity was also the inspiration for the way the Satanic idol Baphomet became depicted. It is also worthy of note that the main square of CERN's campus features a large sized idol of Nataraj, a form of the Hindu deity Shiva, who is associated with the destruction and rebirth of the world.

- Saturn's mean "orbital" distance to the Sun is said to be 9.5 AU, which is 1,426,666,000 kilometers. It's also claimed to have a hexagonal cloud pattern (whose supposed "photo" looks like a giant eye) around its "north pole"; a 6 sided, 6 pointed polygon representing a two dimensional cube containing 6 triangles with 60° angles - while it's also said that Saturn is the 6th "planet" from the Sun. Cubes – as well as hexagons - play an important role in the Kabbalah's so-called "sacred geometry", containing all the right numbers and representing the cubic nature of Solomon's Temple. Moreover, this luminary is often identified with the Sun by occultists, as it is considered the most conspicuous star on the sky. In ancient Rome, their god Saturn, the god of time, was celebrated during a holiday of utter debauchery called Saturnalia, which started on December 17th, lasting until two days before the winter solstice, which marked the day of the celebration of the Unconquered Sun (Sol Invictus) - today known as Christmas. Saturn is also often represented by the occult ouroboros symbol which depicts a snake swallowing its own tail, just as the Roman god Saturn ate his own children and joined together the first and last months of the year. This god of the Romans is also referred to as Marduk, whose name means "the horned one", or Kronos, meaning "time", to whom certain cultures used to sacrifice children, just like to the also bull-horned (although sometimes shown as owl-headed) – Canaanite – fire god called Moloch, "devourer of children", also known as Baal – all depictions of Saturn. He was later also named the Grim Reaper, due to his influence and control of time; thus contributing to aging and the death of all living organisms in the world. Because of this, Saturn, or the Grim Reaper, is presented with a scythe in his hand to this day, symbolizing death and decay. Needless to say, the name of Satan, as well as Santa (Claus), also originate from the word *Saturn*, with the former inheriting its horns from its more wicked depiction, and the latter inheriting his white beard from the way Saturn (or "Kronos", or "Father Time") and other ancient deities such as the Greek Zeus or the Norse Odin are depicted.

Knowing all of the above, it is perhaps not hard to see why many suspect that the final goal of such cults and secret societies as mentioned is to usher in the Antichrist and begin a new occult age of the "One World Order", where they reign supreme and none can ever take their power away again. Such ambitions would certainly explain why they hold secrecy so crucially important, as well as all the "charitable" efforts that they often like to hold up high as a front for their otherwise very much sinister deeds and dark intents.

One of the most prominent of such agendas that they're pushing is that of "oneness": the notion that all humans are essentially the same and "we're all brothers and sisters". This ties in with what the One World Order is all about: creating a world where the entire human population is just a big, rootless lump of biomass with no real identity, traditions or cultural heritage, sharing the same religion. Therefore, it should be obvious that the reason for inventing the idea of "prehistoric times" or "cavemen" was not only to reinforce humanity's belief in an extremely old world and the theory of Darwinian evolution, but also to have us believe that once upon a time we were all one very primitive race, and thus have the same ancestors. A teaching, which, in its modern form, could be summerized quite well as the essence of cultural Marxism. An extension of this ideology are claims such as that *all life came from a single cell in the sea*, and, as a support for this, that *we have better maps of Mars than the seas*.

The term "prehistoric" refers to the period of time before the development of written records. In the context of human history, "prehistoric times" cover the vast span of time before written language was used to record events. This is extremely convenient for the powers that wish to deceive us, as it provides them with a blank check to tell us about "those times" whatever best fits the narrative of their agenda - then they just have to hope we are gullible enough to believe every word they say without question. The historical timeline that they present to us, with "dinosaur" coming before humans, suggests an imperfect creator of the world, who came up with the idea of man as an afterthought, thus demoting us in the ranks of all living beings, as well as undermining the biblical idea that God could have created man in His own image.

Although the powers that be would love nothing more than being absolved of all their sins and getting away with the horrible things they're doing to humanity, it is true that we cannot simply put all the blame on them for deceiving us, since the information needed to reveal all their lies is, in fact, available to everyone – even if it can be somewhat difficult to find. It's clear that everyone with a functioning brain knows well that the ruling elite lie to their subjects on a regular basis - only the exact size and frequency of their lies may be debated.

Therefore, it should also be obvious that it is useless to turn to governments for solutions to our problems, because the governments *are* the problem. In other words, the *system* works without any issues, but the *system* itself is the issue. This means that the only way we can ever hope to defeat these evil forces is by weakening this system that they've built to enslave us. However, as long us the people feed it by obeying its rules and paying taxes to it, it will keep growing more and more powerful, continuallly making all of our lives harder and our future more grim. This is why becoming as independent, self-sufficient and disconnected from the system as possible, as well as using decentralized currencies instead of the banker-class' infinitely deflatable scam-currencies should be the number one priority of all those who wish to live as free people. They shall also never forget: the state and its law enforcement do not stand for law and order, but for the law of the One World Order.